D1084967

This book analyses the widely-held view of the merits of the 'bank-based' German system of finance for investment, and shows that this view is not supported by evidence from the post-war period. The institutional features of the German system are such that universal banks have control of voting rights at shareholders' meetings due to proxy votes, and they also have representation on companies' supervisory boards. These features are claimed to have two main benefits. One is that the German system reduces asymmetric information problems, enabling banks to supply more external finance to firms at a lower cost, and thus increasing investment. The other is that German banks are able to monitor and control managements of firms on behalf of shareholders, and thus ensure that firms are run efficiently. This book assesses whether empirical evidence backs up these claims, and shows that the merits of the German system are largely created.

Banks, finance and investment in Germany

Centre for Economic Policy Research

The Centre for Economic Policy Research is a network of more than 180 Research Fellows, based primarily in European universities. The Centre coordinates its Fellows' research activities and communicates their results to the public and private sectors. CEPR is an entrepreneur, developing research initiatives with the producers, consumers and sponsors of research. Established in 1983, CEPR is already a European economics research organisation with uniquely wide-ranging scope and activities.

CEPR is a registered educational charity. Grants from the Leverhulme Trust, the Esmée Fairbairn Charitable Trust, the Baring Foundation, the Bank of England and Citibank provide institutional finance. The ESCR supports the Centre's dissemination programme and, with the Nuffield Foundation, its programme of research workshops. None of these organisations gives prior review to the Centre's publications nor necessarily endorses the views expressed therein.

The Centre is pluralist and non-partisan, bringing economic research to bear on the analysis of medium- and long-run policy questions. CEPR research may include views on policy, but the Executive Committee of the Centre does not give prior review to its publications and the Centre takes no institutional policy positions. The opinions expressed in this volume are those of the authors and not those of the Centre for Economic Policy Research.

Banks, finance and investment in Germany

JEREMY EDWARDS

and

KLAUS FISCHER

CAMBRIDGE
UNIVERSITY PRESS

Published by the Press Syndicate of the University of Cambridge
The Pitt Building, Trumpington Street, Cambridge CB2 1RP
40 West 20th Street, New York, NY 10011–4211, USA
10 Stamford Road, Oakleigh, Melbourne 3166, Australia

© Cambridge University Press 1994

First published 1994

Printed in Great Britain at the University Press, Cambridge

A catalogue record for this book is available from the British Library

Library of Congress cataloguing in publication data
Edwards, J. S. S. (Jeremy S. S.)
Banks, finance and investments in Germany / Jeremy Edwards and Klaus Fischer.
    p.   cm.
ISBN 0 521 45348 8
1. Banks and banking – Germany.   2. Business enterprises – Germany – Finance.
3. Investments – Germany.
I. Fischer, Klaus. II. Title.
HG3048.E38 1994
332'.0943 – dc20   93-25115   CIP

ISBN 0 521 45348 8 hardback

Contents

Figures

Tables

Preface

The research on which this book is based forms part of the Centre for Economic Policy Research (CEPR) project *An International Study of the Financing of Industry*. The work which is reported in this book was financed by the Anglo-German Foundation for the Study of Industrial Society. The CEPR project as a whole was also financed by the Bank of England, the Commission of the European Communities, the Economic and Social Research Council, the Esmée Fairbairn Charitable Trust, the Japan Foundation, and the Nuffield Foundation. We are very grateful to all these organisations for their support.

We have incurred many debts to individuals while writing this book. Our colleagues on the CEPR project have made a great contribution to the book, both by commenting on the ideas in it, and by providing the intellectual framework within which it developed. We are, therefore, extremely grateful to Ian Alexander, Elisabetta Bertero, Jenny Corbett, Tim Jenkinson, Colin Mayer, and Masako Nagamitsu. We received help and advice from a number of people in the course of undertaking the research on which this book is based, and it is a pleasure to thank them: Luca Anderlini, Margaret Bray, Martin Hellwig, Alan Hughes, Jane Humphries, Christel Lane, Bruce Lyons, Geoffrey Meeks, Manfred J.M. Neumann, Marcus Nibler, Bernd Rudolph, and Martin Weale. For reasons of confidentiality, we cannot thank by name the various individuals at German banks and firms who generously gave time to participate in interviews, but we are very grateful to all of them. We are also grateful to a number of members of the staff of the Deutsche Bundesbank, who answered many questions for us and provided us with unpublished data. In particular, we would like to thank Dr P.W. Schlüter for his help in organising a visit by us to the Bundesbank. Drafts of several of the chapters have been read by Wendy Carlin, Robin Nuttall, Paul Seabright, and Geoffrey Whittington, and their comments have materially improved the book. A complete draft of the manuscript was read very closely by Sheilagh Ogilvie, and her detailed comments and criticisms have made a major contribution to the argument of the book.

Finally, we would like to thank Nacirah Lutton for typing and retyping successive drafts of the manuscript, with enormous efficiency and great good humour.

1 Introduction

Conventional wisdom about German banks and investment finance

Banks play a major role in the German system of finance for investment, so much so that it is often characterised as being a 'bank-based' system. This is a reflection of the fact that German banks are typically universal ones. The term 'universal bank' is normally taken to refer to a bank providing a complete range of commercial and investment banking services (see Schneider, Hellwig and Kingsman, 1978), but is sometimes extended to mean a bank which also has close links with, and influence over, non-banks (see Krummel, 1980; World Bank, 1989, p. 50). The 'bank-based' German system of finance for investment is widely regarded as having made an important contribution to the successful performance of the German economy during the 'economic miracle' following the Second World War. A representative view of the role played by German banks in the German economy in this period is the following statement by Hallett (1990, p. 83):

> The banks helped to rebuild German industry ... after 1948. Firms rely extensively on loan, as against equity, finance, and the banks exercise an important monitoring role through their representatives on the Supervisory Board ... the role of the banks tends to counter 'short-termism', and provides a mechanism for reorganising management in good time, when a company starts running into trouble.

As this quotation illustrates, the German system of finance for investment is commonly perceived to be one which has two main distinguishing features. The first is that a large part of the funds for investment are provided in the form of bank loans, while the second is that banks monitor the performance of firms closely, and restructure firms and their management where necessary. The close involvement of German banks with firms is seen as having the consequence that German banks are more willing to provide finance for long-term investment than is the case in most other economies.

1

The conventional wisdom that Germany's 'bank-based' system of investment finance has been an important factor in German economic success underlies much criticism of the 'market-based' system in the UK. Carrington and Edwards (1979, p. 191) argue that the German system of finance for investment, along with that of Japan, constitutes an

> alternative western capitalist tradition ... [with] a high debt and low equity capital structure, where a major source of the new long-term company investment is bank loans ... It can hardly be doubted that the sources of industrial investment capital ... are more adequate [in Germany and Japan] than they are in the USA or the UK. It is also difficult to deny the observation that those nations with high debt ratios in the capital structure of their companies have been most successful in the economic growth league tables.

This quotation illustrates another feature of the common perception of the German system of investment finance, which is that it is essentially the same as the Japanese one. The financial systems of these two economies are taken to epitomise the 'bank-based' system which is regarded as being superior to the alternative 'market-based' system.

A more recent critical analysis of the UK system of finance for investment, which reflects the growing concern during the 1980s in both the UK and USA that hostile takeovers were harmful to economic performance in those two countries, is that of Charkham (1989). Charkham argues that comparisons with Germany and Japan provide important insights into weaknesses of the UK system of corporate governance and its relation to the stock market. As far as the supply of external finance by banks is concerned, Charkham (pp. 8–9) contrasts

> two distinctly different ways of approaching lending ... In Japan and Germany the banks take a long view *ad initio*. If it is worth lending it is worth lending long: if it is worth lending long it probably means lending more later. Taking this view the banks have set about getting to know companies and the people who run them really well, in order to assess, help and guide them. This in turn has often led to the banks having good internal information systems on which to base advice: and to extensive training so that bank staff are qualified to advise ... In the United Kingdom the banks have been most anxious not to get so involved.

However Charkham (p. 8) argues that 'it is not just the banks' role as providers of finance that is important ... but also their direct help to, and influence on, company management'. Charkham (p. 13) sees the influence of German banks on management as deriving partly from the degree of knowledge the banks have about German firms, and partly from the banks' role as monitors of management acting on behalf of shareholders: 'In West Germany ... the banks ... are often substantial shareholders in their own right, but even more important act for those who deposit shares with them.'

The perceived superiority of the 'bank-based' system of business finance in Germany by comparison with the 'market-based' system in the UK has naturally resulted in policy recommendations which are based on the view that economic performance in the UK would be improved if the UK system of investment finance were altered to be more like the German one. Carrington and Edwards (1979, p. 220) say that

> there are three main choices for the future funding of industrial investment. First, nothing or very little may change; second, there could be a higher state involvement in banking; and third, banks could provide long-term funds for industrial investment on the German or Japanese pattern.

In their view, the third choice is clearly the appropriate one for the UK to make. At the conclusion of their discussion of takeovers and short-termism in the UK, Cosh, Hughes and Singh (1990, pp. 19–20) argue, following Charkham, that

> the institutional shareholder [in the UK] should take a much more active and vigorous part in the internal governance of corporations ... in order for such a proposal to be effective both in disciplining inefficient managements and promoting long-term investments, far reaching changes in the internal workings and behaviour of the financial institutions would be required. The financial institutions would need to pool their resources together, set up specialised departments for promoting investment and innovations – in other words behave like German banks.

It is not simply in the post-Second World War period, however, that German banks have been seen as making a major contribution to good German economic performance. German banks have also been argued to have had an important influence on the rapid industrial development of the German economy in the latter part of the nineteenth century. Gerschenkron (1968, p. 137) is only one of several authors to assign a major role to German banks in German industrialisation:

> In Germany, the various incompetencies of the individual entrepreneurs were offset by the device of splitting the entrepreneurial function: the German investment banks – a powerful invention, comparable in economic effect to that of the steam engine – were in their capital-supplying functions a substitute for the insufficiency of the previously created wealth willingly placed at the disposal of entrepreneurs. But they were also a substitute for entrepreneurial deficiencies. From their central vantage points of control, the banks participated actively in shaping the major – and sometimes even not so major – decisions of the individual enterprises. It was they who very often mapped out a firm's paths of growth, conceived far-sighted plans, decided on major technological and locational innovations, and arranged for mergers and capital increases.

Kennedy (1987, p. 130) contrasts the operation of German banks in the late nineteenth century with that of the UK banks, and argues that the failure of UK financial intermediaries to behave in the same way as German banks hampered UK economic performance in this period:

> In Germany ... banks acted to evaluate managerial performance by rewarding good results and punishing bad ones, in short acting as a very large shareholders' protection agency ... In addition the extensive commercial intelligence of large banks provided the management of client firms with information both of relevant production and investment decisions taken elsewhere and of possible investment or marketing opportunities while providing the banks with a ready measure of their clients' successes and failures ... Intermediaries did not play such a role in Britain however.

The view that useful lessons for the UK system of finance for investment could be learned from the operation of the German one was sufficiently influential in UK policy circles for the Committee on Finance and Industry (1931, p. 163) to state that

> in Germany ... the banks were driven to assist industry to obtain permanent as well as short-dated capital. Accepting these heavy responsibilities, they were obliged to keep in more intimate touch with and maintain a more continuous watch over the industries with which they had allied themselves than were the English banks

and (p. 171) to say in relation to

> the more general question of the relations between finance and industry, and in particular to the provision of long-dated capital, we believe that there is substance in the view that the British financial organisation concentrated in the City of London might with advantage be more closely co-ordinated with British industry, particularly large-scale industry, than is now the case.

To achieve this the Committee recommended (p. 172) that an industrial financing concern should be established, to perform the functions of 'Acting as financial advisers to existing industrial companies ... assisting in ... founding companies for entirely new enterprises ... and generally being free to carry out all types of financing business.'

A particularly clear summary of the view that German arrangements are superior to UK ones was made by Crafts (1992):

> there are good reasons to choose the German rather than British style of capital markets: substantial bank involvement both in long-term lending and management of industrial companies, discouragement of hostile takeovers. In practice, the effectiveness of German banks as monitors of company performance (Cable, (1985)) and the apparent ineffectiveness of the British takeover mechanism in eliminating poor performance and creating post-merger efficiency gains (Cowling et al. (1980); Meeks,

(1977); Singh, (1975)) makes the German system unambiguously superior.

Although the view that the German system of finance for investment is better than the UK one is thus widely-held, there is only rather limited evidence available to support it. Crafts, for example, refers to one empirical study, by Cable, which attempts to link the performance of German firms directly to the role played by German banks, and three empirical studies which show that firms which have been taken over in the UK are not especially unprofitable, and that profitability after takeover does not improve. On its own terms, this evidence is limited, at best. Cable's study is the only one available which provides any evidence of a relationship between firm performance and bank involvement in Germany, and even Cable's work does not definitely establish that such a link exists.[1] There are many studies other than the three referred to by Crafts which provide evidence of the relative ineffectiveness of the takeover mechanism in improving firm performance in the UK, but all of these studies, including the three mentioned by Crafts, suffer from not distinguishing between hostile and friendly takeovers. Since the theoretical arguments that suggest takeovers are a mechanism for improving firm performance apply only to hostile takeovers, and since there are reasons to expect friendly takeovers to be motivated by very different considerations – for example, the desire of the owner-manager of a profitable and successful small firm to sell his or her controlling interest – it is important to make this distinction when undertaking empirical analyses of takeovers. There are some empirical studies of takeovers in the USA which do differentiate between hostile and friendly takeovers (Mørck, Shleifer and Vishny, 1988; Ravenscraft and Scherer, 1987). These studies suggest that it is potentially misleading to draw conclusions about the effects of hostile takeovers from empirical work which does not distinguish between hostile and friendly takeovers. In particular they find some evidence that firms which are the subject of hostile takeovers have been performing poorly, in contrast to the findings of studies which do not distinguish between the two types of takeovers, although their results do not provide any evidence that performance improves after a hostile takeover. Nevertheless, in order to argue that hostile takeovers are ineffective in the UK, it is necessary to have evidence which specifically relates to hostile takeovers, and at present such evidence does not exist.

Even if the evidence provided by Cable, and by studies of takeovers in the UK, were not subject to any qualifications, such evidence would not be sufficient to establish that the German system of investment finance

---

[1] Cable's study is discussed in detail in Chapter 9.

was unambiguously superior. It is to some extent inevitable that only very limited evidence is available to support the widely-held view of the merits of the German system, because the question which is being addressed is a very difficult one to answer. The evidence that would be required to answer this question satisfactorily would involve a comparison of investment and growth by German firms under the actual German system of financing investment, and under a hypothetical alternative, such as the UK system. A similar comparison of investment and growth by UK firms under the actual UK system, and under a hypothetical alternative, such as the German system, would also be needed. It is clearly very difficult to assess the alternatives involved. Ideally an empirical model of economic growth in which the significance of all possible influences on relative growth performance were identified and quantified would be used. But a model of this sort does not exist, and is unlikely to do so for some time given the present state of knowledge concerning the explanation of relative growth performance. This being the case, it must be recognised that the question, say, of the contribution made by the German system of business finance to German industrialisation in the nineteenth century is one to which it would be very difficult to give an unambiguous answer, even if there were not data deficiencies. As such deficiencies do exist, it is not surprising that Lee (1991, p. 14) should write that 'the precise role of ... the banking mechanism in general on German industrial growth [during German industrialisation] must remain open'. It is also not surprising that, in general, the empirical basis for the claims made about the significant contribution of the German system of investment finance to German economic success in the post-1945 period takes the form of simple correlations – German economic performance has been superior to that of the UK, German investment as a proportion of GDP has been higher than in the UK, and the German system of finance for investment is different from that of the UK. The temptation to use such simple correlations is understandable, given the difficulty of the question that is being addressed. But since there are many other respects in which Germany differs from the UK that may be relevant for relative economic performance since 1945 – for example, in its system of education and training, or in its macroeconomic policy – it is impossible to conclude anything about the contribution of the German financial system to German economic performance on the basis of simple correlations which do not take account of other possible influences.

Because we think that it is not possible to assess how far good German economic performance in the post-1945 period was due to the German system of investment finance as compared to, say, education and training in Germany, the approach taken in this book is more modest, but as a result, we believe, more informative. We attempt to establish the extent to which the various components of the commonly-held view about the contribution of the German system of business finance to German economic success are supported by evidence for the post-1945 period. In contrast to many previous studies of the German financial system we use an analytical framework derived from modern theories of business finance and financial intermediation as the basis for our empirical work. This has the advantage of focusing attention more sharply on the issues for which it is important to have empirical evidence in order to assess the plausibility of the widely-held view of the benefits the German economy has derived from its system of investment finance.

Before proceeding with the analysis, it is useful to set out in some detail the various components of the view that the German system of finance for investment has contributed to good German economic performance. As is apparent from our discussion above, there are several different ways in which the important position of banks in the German system of business finance is seen as producing favourable outcomes for the quantity and quality of investment in the German economy. For analytical purposes, it is helpful to enumerate them systematically.

The merits of the German system of finance for investment: elements of a widely-held view

What we have called the 'widely-held view' has a number of different components, and in this section these various elements are set out. In assembling these various components, we have drawn indiscriminately on arguments expressed with reference to the pre-1914 and post-1945 period, because although we recognise that there are significant differences between the German economy in these two periods, the ways in which the German system of investment finance has been argued to benefit the economy in the two periods are very similar.[2]

A central feature of the widely-held view is that German banks are supposed to be much more closely involved with the firms to which they supply funds than are UK banks. This close relationship between banks and firms in Germany is seen as being partly the consequence of some German institutional features which are not present in the UK. One is the

---

[2] For example, Carrington and Edwards (1979, p. 120) in their discussion of the contribution made by banks to the economic success of West Germany since 1945 say that 'this industry-assisting role of German banks goes back to the mid-19th century', while Eatwell (1982, p. 79), another proponent of the view that German banks are an important factor in German economic success, states that 'the close relationship which exists today between industry . . . and the banks in Germany derives from institutional arrangements developed in the nineteenth century'.

convention that in Germany 'every borrowing company has a house bank [which] acts as continuous financial adviser and confidant to the company in question' (Bayliss and Butt Philip, 1980, p. 188). Another is the extensive representation of banks on the supervisory boards of German companies as a result of both their own shareholdings and the proxy votes they exercise on behalf of other shareholders who have deposited their shares with the banks for safekeeping.

The closer involvement of German banks with the firms to which they supply funds leads to the view that German banks are superior to UK banks in terms of overcoming the information asymmetries which are inherent in the supply of resources by savers to investors. There are a number of strands to this general argument. One is that German banks have the technical expertise and information to assess the risks involved in supplying finance to firms more accurately than UK banks do. Marshall (1919, p. 347) argued that finance for new inventions was not easily available in the UK and, quoting from a pamphlet by a Mr William Olsson, stated that

> In Germany, on the other hand, 'the pioneer would take his proposal to one of the great banks with an industrial department; and the proposal would immediately be put before experts, scientific and technical, well known to the banks and thoroughly trusted who (on the assumption that the proposed business was really good) would report well on it, *and would be believed.*'

Lavington (1921, p. 210), describing the Deutsche Bank in 1914, says that 'it has a distinct staff of some eight or nine industrial experts usually drawn from industry itself, and a highly developed department of information.' This view is reiterated by Prais (1981, p. 51), who writes that 'it is arguable that the success of German banks in providing industrial finance depended on their ample staffs of technical advisers, capable of assessing industrial prospects and risks.'

A second strand of the general argument that German banks are better than UK banks in dealing with asymmetric information problems concerns bank representation on the supervisory boards of German companies. This is seen as improving banks' information about the firms they lend to, thus permitting German banks to lend on more favourable terms than would be possible in the UK. Cable and Turner (1983, pp. 19–22) argue that

> the banks are extensively represented on the supervisory boards of German companies ... [which hold] regular meetings to monitor and approve corporate strategy, and [have] legally backed rights to internal information that are specified in detail in German company law ... Thus

... there is a widespread absence of the informational asymmetry which ... can cause credit-rationing and strong loan-collateral requirements.

The informational advantages that German banks are supposed to enjoy in comparison with UK banks are partly a consequence of the house bank relationships between particular firms and particular banks, which are by their nature long-term. A long-term relationship between a bank and a firm is held to enable the bank to understand the business and personnel of the firm to which it is lending, thereby improving the bank's ability to assess the risk of its loans. At least for the late nineteenth and early twentieth centuries there is some justification for interpreting the house bank relationship in Germany as a relationship in which a particular firm conducted its banking business exclusively with its house bank: Kocka (1980, p. 90) describes the objectives of the large German corporate banks in this period as being 'to monopolize the financial arrangements of industrial concerns and to serve them with comprehensive policies "from the cradle to the grave"'. If a house bank relationship meant that the house bank was the sole lender to a firm, this further reduced the risk to the bank since it was easier for the bank to monitor the firm's total outstanding debt and hence its likelihood of insolvency.[3] It has been argued by Mayer (1988, p. 1179) that in return for the restriction of competition implied by a house bank exclusively financing a firm, the bank will commit itself to taking a long-term view and supporting the firm in situations of temporary financial distress. This situation is contrasted to the one which is claimed to be typical of the UK, where banks' horizons are perceived as being short-term, and banks are claimed to be insufficiently willing to support firms with finance when they get into difficulties.

A final strand of the general argument that German banks do better in overcoming information problems in the capital market relates to the role of financial intermediaries in bringing firms to the stock market for the first time. Kennedy (1987, pp. 144–145) regards the failure of UK banks to perform a screening role in this regard as a significant impediment to economic performance in the UK in the late nineteenth century because, combined with the banks' refusal to provide long-term loans, it deprived UK firms of access to long-term external finance:

> Had [UK] banks been thoroughly committed to underwriting, and had they been responsibly involved subsequently in the management of the firms they launched, their financial and informational resources would have offered much greater reassurance to outside investors than the

[3] Jeidels (1905, p. 63) argues that 'it is in the interest of the security, profitability and permanence of a bank ... to do all the credit business of an industrial company from its foundation up to its liquidation' (quotation has been translated).

> words of loose, uneasy coalitions of undercapitalized promoters and
> stock brokers. But such involvement was foreclosed in the course of
> [UK] bank evolution in the nineteenth century ... As a consequence of
> these institutional developments, an important bias operated in British
> capital markets ... towards safe, well-known securities in general, a
> great number of which were foreign, and away from riskier, smaller, but
> ultimately from an economy-wide viewpoint, much more profitable
> ones.

In contrast, the close involvement of German banks with German firms
during this period is seen as enabling the banks to 'investigate the earning
capacity of ventures in need of capital, select the most promising, and sell
their securities to the investing public with an implicit assurance that the
venture had a reasonable prospect of success' (Lavington, 1921, p. 209).
The supply of finance to firms in the UK through the purchase of shares
is thus also seen as being limited by the absence of close bank-firm
relationships.

So far our discussion has concentrated on the way in which the role of
banks in the German system of investment finance has been argued to
result in funds for investment being supplied more efficiently than in the
UK system. We turn now to the second main component of the widely-
held view, which concerns German banks' role in monitoring and
replacing managements of firms.

It is argued that German banks have significant control of the equity
voting rights in German companies, largely through the proxy votes they
exercise on behalf of individual shareholders who deposit their shares
with banks. Such control of voting rights is held to give banks the ability
to exert a major influence on supervisory board membership, not only by
placing bank representatives on supervisory boards but also by influencing the composition of the other shareholder representatives on supervisory boards. This institutional arrangement is seen as having the
potential to reduce the agency costs involved in the owner-manager
relationship for large firms. Cable (1985, p. 121) suggests that

> the combination of bank representation and control of voting rights
> could reduce the transactions costs of constraining managerial decision-
> making in accordance with shareholders' preferences, and therefore
> produce greater conformity to cost-minimising, profit-oriented goals.

The absence of this institutional arrangement in the UK is seen as
leading to short-termism – the excessive concentration by firms on investments which yield short-term returns at the cost of long-term investment
which is actually more profitable – because the UK has to rely on hostile
takeovers as a mechanism for imposing discipline on the managers of
large firms. Briefly put, the argument here is that stock market prices do

not accurately reflect the true long-term expected profits of firms and instead place too much weight on short-term returns.[4] A firm that undertakes a profitable long-term investment may therefore find that its stock market valuation falls, leaving it vulnerable to a takeover bid. Such bids are likely to be successful even if the firm's existing management is efficient, it is argued, because the managers of the share portfolios of the large institutions which dominate the UK stock market are subject to frequent short-term performance assessments and in any case are not well informed about the firms whose shares they hold. Hence undertaking a profitable long-term investment may lead to the managers of a firm losing their jobs as the result of a takeover, and so, it is argued, there is a tendency to short-termism in the UK. The argument that hostile takeovers promote short-termism has been the subject of a critical examination by Marsh (1990), and it remains controversial – see Cosh, Hughes and Singh (1990) for a statement of the case in favour of this argument. However, the view that, as a mechanism for monitoring managements and replacing inefficient ones, hostile takeovers are inferior to the German mechanism, which operates via the banks through their control of equity voting rights and positions on supervisory boards, is a central element of the perceived merits of the German system of investment finance.

To summarise, there are two main components of the widely-held view that the role of banks in the German system of finance for investment benefits the German economy. One, which has several different strands, is that investment funds are supplied more efficiently as a consequence of the banks' ability to overcome problems created by information asymmetries between savers and investors. The second is that the banks provide an efficient system of monitoring and replacing the managers of firms. The aim of this book is to assess whether evidence for the post-war period until 1989 supports these claims. Before describing the contents of the book, however, we compare the investment and growth records of the German and UK economies in the period 1950–1989.

Investment and growth in Germany and the UK, 1950–1989

According to the widely-held view of the merits of the German system of finance for investment, the way in which the German economy benefits from its system of investment finance is that investment, and hence

---

[4] This claim is, of course, subject to the criticism that it presumes that stock market prices are not efficient in the sense of fully reflecting all available information, a presumption that is contradicted by much empirical evidence. The proponents of the short-termism argument, however, question the strength of the evidence that stock market pricing is

economic growth, is promoted. By comparison with other economies, particularly that of the UK, the institutional features of German system of finance for investment are seen as enabling funds for investment to be supplied at a lower cost, so that, *ceteris paribus*, German firms can undertake more investment than, say, UK firms. In addition, the performance of managers of firms is seen as being more effectively monitored in Germany than in the UK as a result of the reliance on banks rather than hostile takeovers, so that the returns from investment in Germany are higher. Together the lower cost of investment finance and greater returns from investment in Germany are seen as creating a virtuous circle which permits high levels of investment to be undertaken. The precise way in which high investment leads to rapid economic growth is not made clear in the widely-held view, but it is possible to justify such a causal relationship in terms of modern theories of endogenous growth (Romer, 1986; Scott, 1989).

It is therefore important to investigate the extent to which German economic growth has been superior to that in the UK, and whether investment has been higher in Germany than in the UK. This section examines the statistical record on investment and growth in Germany over the period 1950–1989, in order to provide a background to the detailed analysis of the German system of finance for investment which is carried out in this book.

Figures 1.1 and 1.2 plot the annual levels and rates of growth respectively of real per capita GDP in Germany and the UK over the period 1951–1988. The source of this data is the Penn World Table (Mark 5), which gives internationally comparable estimates of real product (see Summers and Heston, 1984, 1988 for a description of the basis of these estimates). The particular series for real *per capita* GDP which is shown in Figures 1.1 and 1.2 is a chain index of real *per capita* GDP in US dollars in which 1985 is taken as the base year, and the series is defined in terms of a chain of ratios of consecutive years' *per capita* GDP. Each element of the chain is the ratio of per capita GDP in year $t+1$ to *per capita* GDP in year t, where both numerator and denominator are valued in international prices of year t. The reason for using this chain index of real *per capita* GDP is that a real *per capita* GDP series computed using 1985 base year price weights would result in intertemporal comparisons involving years far from 1985 being made in terms of price weights that were rather remote. The chain index has the advantage that intertemporal com-

---

efficient, reflecting a more widespread doubt that has emerged in recent years about the quality of the evidence in favour of stock market efficiency (see, for example, LeRoy, 1989).

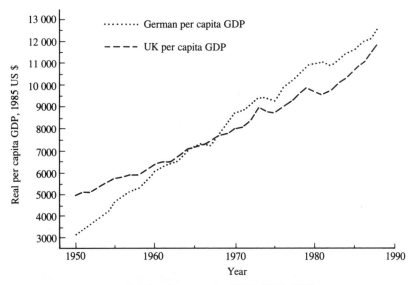

Figure 1.1   German and UK real per capita GDP, 1950–1988

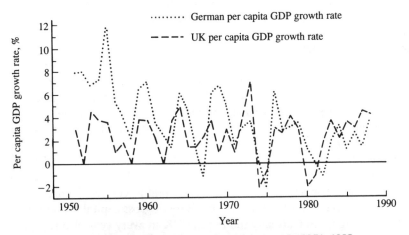

Figure 1.2   German and UK real per capita GDP growth, 1951–1988

parisons can be based on much more current price weights (Summers and Heston, 1988, p. 13).

Figures 1.1 and 1.2 show that, in terms of real *per capita* GDP, Germany's growth performance was generally superior to that of the UK in the period 1950–1981, but that the difference between German and UK growth rates was narrowing over these three decades. From 1982 to 1988

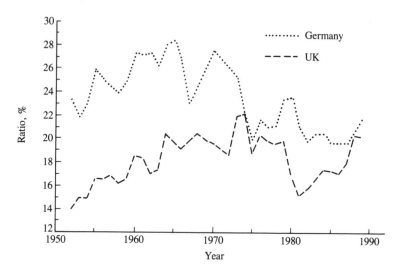

Figure 1.3   Ratio of total investment to GDP, Germany and UK, 1952–1989

Germany's growth performance was generally inferior to that of the UK. In 1950 German real per capita GDP was only 62.9% of the UK level, but by 1985 German real *per capita* GDP had overtaken that of the UK, and was 101% of the UK level. Throughout most of the 1970s there was little change in the relationship between German and UK real *per capita* GDP, the former being usually about 109% of the latter. By 1981, however, German real *per capita* GDP was 115.3% of the UK level. The generally superior UK growth performance over the rest of the 1980s meant that in 1988 German real *per capita* GDP had fallen relative to that of the UK, to 105.2% of the UK level.

Figure 1.3 plots the ratio of gross capital formation (the sum of gross fixed capital formation and the value of the physical increase in stocks) to GDP at market prices, both measured in current prices, for Germany and the UK over the years 1952–1989. The share of gross capital formation in GDP was higher in Germany than in the UK in every year of this period except 1974. The difference was greatest in the 1950s and 1960s: in 1952–1959 the gross capital formation to GDP ratio averaged 24.1% in Germany and 15.8% in the UK, while in 1960–1969 it averaged 26.5% in Germany and 19.1% in the UK. The corresponding German and UK figures for 1970–1979 were 23.5% and 20.0% respectively, while in 1980–1989 they were 20.7% and 17.4%.

For the purpose of providing a background for the analysis of the German system of finance for investment, however, it is more appropriate to compare investment by non-financial enterprises in the two economies, rather than their rates of total investment. The supposed merits of the German system of investment finance are seen as leading to greater investment specifically by firms. Unfortunately the definitions of the non-financial enterprise sector in the German and UK national accounts are not precisely comparable. As is discussed in greater detail in chapters 3 and 4, the non-financial enterprise sector in Germany comprises all private and public enterprises which produce goods and non-financial services for sale, other than those whose activities are concerned with housing.[5] It includes unincorporated enterprises, and in this respect differs from the non-financial enterprise sector as defined in the UK national accounts: in the UK, unincorporated enterprises are classified as part of the personal sector. The measure from the UK national accounts which is most closely comparable to the non-financial enterprise sector as defined in the German national accounts is the sum of industrial and commercial companies and public corporations. Like the German category, this excludes housing and the activities of financial companies; the only difference from the German definition is that it excludes unincorporated enterprises. As chapter 4 shows, unincorporated enterprises play a more important role in the German than in the UK economy. The limited data available on the importance of unincorporated enterprises (partnerships and sole proprietorships) relative to companies in the UK suggests that they account for about 20% of total enterprise turnover in the UK. It follows that the national accounts data for investment by non-financial enterprises in the UK will underestimate the share of such investment in GDP by comparison with the German national accounts data, although the size of this downward bias is unknown. Since unincorporated enterprises are typically engaged in activities with relatively low capital requirements, it is likely that grossing up the UK data on industrial and commercial companies plus public corporations by 25%, as would be implied by the turnover-based estimate of the relative importance of unincorporated enterprises in the UK, would considerably overestimate the size of UK non-financial enterprise investment relative to that in Germany.

One other problem which arises in comparing investment by non-financial enterprises in Germany and the UK is that separate data for UK industrial and commercial companies is available only from 1959. Before 1959, industrial and commercial companies were not distinguished from financial companies. The series for investment by non-financial enterprises in the UK used below was obtained by using the relationship

[5] This is described as the producing enterprises sector in the German national accounts.

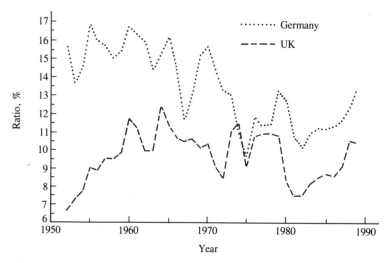

Figure 1.4 **Ratio of non-financial enterprise investment to GDP, Germany and UK, 1952–1989**

between investment by all private companies and investment by industrial and commercial companies in 1959 to estimate the 1952–1958 figures for investment by industrial and commercial companies from the data for all private companies.

Figure 1.4 plots the ratio of gross capital formation to GDP at market prices for producing enterprises in Germany and industrial and commercial companies and public corporations in the UK from 1952 to 1989. Taking no account of the difference in the German and UK definitions of the non-financial enterprise sector, the share of non-financial enterprise gross capital formation in GDP was higher in Germany than in the UK in every year of the period except 1974. The German ratio fell steadily over the period 1952–1989: in 1952–59 it averaged 15.4%, in 1960–69 14.9%, in 1970–79 12.5%, and in 1980–89 11.7%. In the UK the ratio was higher in the 1960s and 1970s than in the earlier or later decades: it averaged 8.5% in 1952–59, 10.9% in 1960–69, 10.3% in 1970–79, and 8.7% in 1980–89. The difference in this ratio between Germany and the UK was most marked in the 1950s. The average value of this ratio in Germany over the period 1952–1959 was 81.2% larger than the average value of the ratio in the UK, 36.7% larger in 1960–69, 21.4% larger in 1970–79, and 34.5% larger in 1980–89. It was argued above that increasing the UK figures for the share of non-financial enterprise investment in GDP by 25% would more than compensate for the difference in the German and UK definitions of the non-financial enterprise sector. The average figures for the various decades show that, even allowing for the difference in sectoral definitions, German non-financial enterprise investment was clearly higher, as a proportion of GDP, than UK non-financial enterprise investment in the 1950s, 1960s, and 1980s. It is also likely that, when account is taken of the difference in sectoral definitions, non-financial enterprise investment in Germany was higher than in the UK in the 1970s, although since the average value of the measured German share was only 21.4% larger than the average value of the measured UK share the difference in this decade was probably quite small once allowance is made for the exclusion of unincorporated enterprises in the UK.

We can therefore conclude that, on average, investment by non-financial enterprises has been a higher proportion of GDP in Germany than in the UK in all four decades of the period 1950–1989. The difference was especially pronounced in the 1950s, and least pronounced in the 1970s. The growth of real *per capita* GDP was, on average, more rapid in Germany than in the UK in the 1950s, 1960s, and 1970s, with the difference being especially marked in the 1950s, but in the 1980s UK real *per capita* GDP growth exceeded that in Germany. The investment figures which have been presented confirm the view that investment by firms in Germany has generally been higher than in the UK throughout the period 1950–1989, while the growth figures show that German growth performance has generally been superior to that in the UK between 1950 and 1981. The fact that the ratio of non-financial enterprise investment to GDP in Germany was a larger proportion of the corresponding UK ratio in the 1980s than in the 1970s, while the UK's growth performance relative to Germany's was better in the 1980s than in the 1970s, shows that the relationship between relative investment and growth performance is not entirely straightforward. Nevertheless, investment by firms in Germany has been higher than in the UK in the period 1950–1989.

Outline of the volume

The plan of this volume is as follows. Chapter 2 surveys modern theories of business finance and financial intermediation, in order to provide a theoretical basis for evaluating the widely-held view of the merits of the German system of finance for investment. This chapter shows that it is possible to provide a solid analytical basis for the commonly-held view, and that, at least in theory, the German system of universal banks with proxy voting rights and representation on supervisory boards is well suited to exploiting economies of scale and scope that may exist in information-collection and the exercise of the control rights attached to debt and equity finance. The theoretical framework developed in chapter

2 forms the basis of the empirical work reported in subsequent chapters of the book. These assess the extent to which evidence on the operation of the German system of investment finance during the post-war period until 1989 supports the theoretical arguments which underlie the widely-held view of the merits of this system.

Chapter 3 analyses the finance of investment by the German non-financial enterprise sector from 1950 to 1989, in order to assess the importance of bank loans as a source of finance in Germany. International comparisons of the finance of investment have to be made with great care, but chapter 3 argues that an approach based on national accounts flow of funds data allows meaningful comparisons to be made. Using this approach, the finance of investment by non-financial enterprises in Germany is compared with that for the UK during the 1970s and 1980s. This evidence casts doubt on one of the most basic components of the conventional view of the German system of investment finance.

In order to assess the merits which the German financial system is claimed to possess, however, it is necessary to go beyond aggregate evidence of the type presented in chapter 3. Chapter 4 begins a more detailed analysis by describing the various legal forms that enterprises can take in Germany, and their relative importance within the economy. It examines what proportion of German firms possess supervisory boards, and the proportion of total turnover they account for within the German economy. It also examines the significance within the German economy of firms in which there is scope for divergences between ownership and control to arise, and compares these findings with the UK. Finally, chapter 4 provides an analysis of the relative importance of sources of investment finance according to different legal forms of enterprise.

Chapter 5 investigates the structure of the German banking system. It examines the main categories of universal and specialised banks, and analyses their relative importance within the banking system. It then examines whether there is evidence of concentration within the German banking system, using data on the total volume of banking business, bank lending to domestic firms, bank control of proxy voting rights, bank supervisory board representation, and bank membership of new share issue syndicates. Chapter 5 also examines whether there is any evidence of a greater supply of new equity finance having been made available to listed German companies as a result of the banks which lead issuing syndicates having a corporate governance role within these companies. The results of the analysis in chapter 5 raise doubts about the hypothesis that economies of scope exist between the monitoring of firm performance via supervisory board representation, and the efficient supply of bank loan finance.

Chapter 6 provides a detailed analysis of a number of aspects of German bank lending to firms. It examines whether there is any evidence to support the view that representation on the supervisory boards of firms enables banks to supply a greater volume of loan finance to these firms. It also investigates whether representation on a firm's supervisory board gives a bank any competitive advantage in making loans to that firm, an important indication of whether in fact there exist any economies of scope between lending and supervisory board representation. These findings are also important for establishing whether there is in fact much scope for long-term commitments between banks and firms to arise as a result of the restrictions on competition involved in exclusive house bank relationships. Chapter 6 also investigates whether there is reliable evidence of more long-term lending in Germany than in the UK, and whether there is a clear theoretical basis for thinking that it is more efficient for a higher proportion of investment to be financed by long-term loans. Finally, chapter 6 examines German banks' loan decision-making, to see whether there is evidence of banks having special technical expertise with which to evaluate loan applications, or of reduced asymmetries of information between banks and firms being reflected in lower collateral requirements for loans.

Chapter 7 turns to the issue of whether German banks can reduce the costs of financial distress and bankruptcy. It examines whether there is any evidence that bank representation on supervisory boards enables banks to identify financial distress at an early stage or to control managers' actions before bankruptcy actually occurred. It analyses the variation among banks both in their ability to detect problem loans and in their ability to reorganise firms in financial difficulty, and the extent to which German banks become directly involved with managing firms that are attempting to reorganise. Chapter 7 also investigates the incentives for banks to reorganise rather than to liquidate a bankrupt firm. These incentives depend on the extent to which banks' loans are secured by collateral, and on the extent to which banks have an equity as well as a debt stake in a financially-troubled firm, and evidence on both considerations is presented in the chapter.

In chapter 8 the focus of the analysis moves from the supply of external finance by German banks to their role as monitors of the managers of firms on behalf of shareholders. The degree to which German banks are direct owners of shares in public companies is examined, relative to the size of other shareholder groups in Germany. A more detailed examination of share ownership in individual German companies is then undertaken, in order to find out what proportion of large companies in Germany, compared to the UK, have an ownership structure in which a single shareholder has an equity stake of sufficient size to permit effective control of the firm. The typical structure of share ownership in large companies is an important indication of the probability that problems arising from a lack of monitoring and control of managers by shareholders will be serious. The chapter links this evidence to the absence of hostile takeovers in Germany. Chapter 8 also examines the extent to which German companies with a dispersed share ownership have shareholdings in other German firms. If German banks were able to ensure that the managers of this small number of large, widely-held German companies acted in shareholders' interests, the effect of this behaviour by the banks might be important for the whole economy, since it would spread widely via the shareholdings of this small group of companies.

Chapter 9 therefore provides a detailed analysis of the view that German banks use their control of proxy votes and supervisory board representation to monitor the managers of large German companies on behalf of shareholders. It examines the extent to which proxy voting rights give German banks the ability to influence the outcome of votes at shareholders' meetings. It analyses the evidence for whether there is any association between the number of bank representatives on a company's supervisory board and the degree of bank proxy voting power in that company. This sheds light on the basic hypothesis that banks control managers on behalf of shareholders by using proxy voting power to put bank representatives on supervisory boards. The chapter investigates whether the number of bank representatives on companies' supervisory boards is large enough for banks to be able to determine supervisory board decisions. It also examines the incentives for the managements of banks to act as monitors of the managers of other large companies, in light of the fact that the three big banks are all part of the small group of large, widely-held German companies. The results of this analysis suggest that German banks do not act as monitors and controllers of managers on behalf of shareholders, but in the end empirical evidence of the relationship between bank control of voting rights and firm perform-ance is required to evaluate this view. Chapter 9 therefore concludes with a discussion of the influential empirical study by Cable (1985), which is widely cited in support of the claim that German banks improve the performance of German companies via their control of voting rights and representation on supervisory boards. It is shown that the wide-spread interpretation given to Cable's results is misleading in several important respects. The conclusions of the book are set out in chapter 10.

One last point that we wish to make before beginning our analysis concerns terminology. The empirical evidence used in this book relates to the economy of West Germany in the period from the end of the Second World War to the reunification of Germany in 1990. Throughout the book we use the term 'Germany' rather than 'West Germany'; we hope that our use of the simpler term will not cause any confusion.

2 A theoretical framework for analysing the effects of the financial system on economic performance

Introduction

This chapter reviews existing theories of business finance and financial intermediation in order to provide a theoretical basis for analysing the effects of the system of finance for investment on economic performance. It is essential to have a general theoretical framework as a starting point for the assessment of the various claims that have been made about the extent to which the German economy benefits from the distinctive characteristics of the German system of investment finance. Without some idea of the functions that an economy's system of finance for investment performs, and the different circumstances in which one set of institutional arrangements within the financial system is likely to be more efficient than another, an adequate assessment of the evidence in support of these claims is not possible. The second section provides a survey of theoretical analyses of firms' financing decisions. The third section considers the role which theory suggests financial intermediaries may play in the provision of finance for investment. The fourth section examines the general implications of the theoretical discussion in the second and third sections for claims about the superiority of the German system of investment finance compared to that of the UK. The final section draws a brief conclusion.

Theoretical analysis of the financing decisions of firms

The financial system acts as a mechanism for savers to provide resources to investors who have more productive uses for them: the improvement in the allocation of resources, by comparison with the situation in which investment is entirely self-financed, can in principle make both savers and investors better off. The investors to which savers provide resources via the financial system are typically firms. The firm has usually been treated in economic theory simply as a production function which transforms inputs into outputs in such a way as to maximise profits. This standard approach, however, ignores some central issues arising from the fact that firms are institutions within which trade between individuals takes place in non-market or administrative ways, even though it would be possible for this trade to occur via market exchanges. The view of a firm as an alternative mechanism to the market as a means of organising trade originates with Coase (1937), who argued that 'the distinguishing mark of the firm is the supersession of the price mechanism'. However, the profound implications of this view for economic theory – namely, that if the firm is an alternative to the market as a means of organising trade, then it is inappropriate to treat the firm as a single agent which mechanically transforms inputs into outputs in a profit-maximising way – have received close attention only recently. The analysis of the firm as an institution within which the different interests of managers, workers, suppliers of finance and so on impinge and are resolved is now a very active field of research (see Holmstrom and Tirole, 1989, for a survey), and the recognition of the need to apply economic analysis to the internal organisation of firms has stimulated theoretical work on a number of questions, such as the role of management and the role of internal hierarchies. For the purposes of this chapter, however, it is the theoretical developments concerning the finance of the firm – in particular, the combination of debt and equity in it – which are of greatest interest.

If firms are taken to be simply profit-maximising production functions, then the Modigliani–Miller theorem (Modigliani and Miller, 1958; Stiglitz, 1974) seems to be the inevitable implication, so far as firm financing is concerned. According to this theorem, if firms and individuals have the same financial opportunities then under conditions of perfectly competitive capital markets, no asymmetries of information between different agents, and no variations in the tax treatment of different forms of firm finance, the firm's financing is a matter of complete irrelevance. The basic argument underlying the theorem is a simple arbitrage one. If the firm's return stream is given, as is the case when firms are taken to behave simply as profit-maximising production functions, then if the firm's value could be altered by changing its financial mix there would be a pure arbitrage opportunity. In equilibrium, therefore, the firm's financial policy is irrelevant, as debt and equity are simply different ways of packaging a given return stream determined by the profit-maximising decision of the production function which is the firm.

The stark contrast between the Modigliani–Miller theorem on the one hand and empirical observations of the importance attached to firm financing decisions by both firms and suppliers of finance on the other is troubling. Efforts have been made to provide a theoretical explanation of the importance attached to firm financial policy in practice by relaxing various assumptions of the Modigliani–Miller theorem. The differential taxation of alternative forms of finance has been introduced into the Modigliani–Miller framework, but this does not seem able to explain many features of firm financial policy in practice (see Edwards, 1987). It has also been suggested that, because of the limited liability provision in corporate bankruptcy, borrowing by companies increases their value by introducing a security that was previously unavailable, but this argument is not unambiguously correct (see Hellwig, 1981). However if the firm is viewed not as a profit-maximising production function but as an organisation comprising a number of constituent agents whose aggregate behaviour depends on many different incentive mechanisms, then it is possible that the finance of the firm influences its return stream by its effect on the firm's behavioural incentives. A number of recent attempts to explain firm financing have been based on this idea.

When making decisions about the provision of resources to firms via the financial system savers will be concerned with firms' incentives to use these resources in savers' best interests. A number of complicated issues arise here. For one thing, it is not clear what acting in 'savers' best interests' means. The standard assumption is that savers will all agree that firms should maximise profits, or more generally their market value,[1] but this can be rigorously justified only if firms are price takers in all the markets (including the capital market) in which they operate (see Kreps, 1990, ch.19.1 for a clear exposition). Although the problem of defining what are savers' best interests is a serious one theoretically, it is not clear that it is important in practice. The price-taking assumption is required in this context because without it firms can influence savers' welfare by affecting both the prices of goods consumed by savers and, through profits, savers' budget constraints. Tirole (1988, p. 35) argues that in practice the savers who have supplied funds to a particular firm will consume only a very small amount of the goods produced by that firm, and hence the price effects will be small relative to the income effects generated by the firm's profit levels. In what follows, savers will be assumed to agree that firms should act in order to maximise the returns on the funds that savers have provided, on the grounds that this seems to be a reasonable description of savers' behaviour in practice.

Savers, therefore, would like firms to act so that the return on the finance they have supplied is maximised. But it is not clear how savers can ensure that this is how firms do behave. The returns the firm generates from investments depend partly on the behaviour of the various members of the

---

[1] The market value of the firm is the present value of its profit stream.

firm, which savers will have difficulty in observing, and there is no reason to take as axiomatic the view that the interests of the members of the firm will coincide with those of savers. Recent theoretical models of firm finance have formalised this issue by assuming that the firm's production decisions are determined by managers who have interests which conflict with those of savers – for example the firm's returns may depend on managerial effort which is costly to managers, or the managers may wish to divert some of the funds provided by savers to private benefits enjoyed only by themselves.[2] Savers are assumed not to be able to observe the occurrence of managerial behaviour which runs counter to their interests, so that there is an asymmetry of information, and given that the returns from investment are intrinsically uncertain savers cannot infer such managerial behaviour from observing these returns. However, savers will be aware of the incentives for managers of firms to use the finance provided in ways which differ from savers' interests. In making and following up arrangements for providing finance to firms savers will therefore be concerned to provide incentives for managers to act in ways which are more closely aligned with their interests.

The theoretical discussion usually considers two forms in which external finance can be supplied: debt and equity. Debt finance yields a fixed return to its suppliers in states when the firm is not bankrupt (that is, the firm has sufficient funds to make the fixed payment), while in states when the firm is bankrupt the suppliers of debt finance receive such funds as are available to the firm and also the right to make decisions about the firm's subsequent operation. Equity finance gives its suppliers the right to the firm's residual returns after payments to the suppliers of debt finance, and in addition the right to vote on decisions concerning the firm's operation in states when the firm is not bankrupt. In states when the firm goes bankrupt, limited liability provisions mean that suppliers of equity receive nothing. They also lose the right to make decisions about the firm's operations in such states. Although suppliers of equity finance have the right to the firm's residual returns in non-bankruptcy states, they do not have a right to receive a fixed payment in every period: those of the firm's returns which belong to the suppliers of equity may be retained by the firm's managers to finance further investment in it.

The first attempt to explain the mixture of debt and equity in a firm's financing in terms of the incentives thereby created for managers of firms to act in savers' interests was made by Jensen and Meckling (1976). Their argument was as follows: suppose that a firm's profits depend on both the level of effort chosen by a risk-neutral manager, which is assumed to be

---

[2] These are interpreted as managerial perks of various kinds.

costly for the manager, and the riskiness of the investment strategy chosen by the manager. Neither of these choices can be observed by the suppliers of outside finance. The realised value of the firm's profits can, however, be observed by savers. Given this information structure, how does the form in which external finance is supplied affect managerial incentives to act in savers' interests?

If savers supply funds to the firm in the form of equity, then some fraction of the firm's profits accrue to them rather than to the manager. The manager will therefore choose an effort level at which the marginal cost of effort equals the marginal benefit to the manager of the extra profits resulting from additional effort. Since some of the extra profits resulting from more effort go to the suppliers of equity finance rather than to the manager, the manager will not take these into account and hence will choose an inefficiently low level of effort. But if savers supply funds to the firm entirely in the form of debt, the manager becomes the residual claimant in the firm and so receives all the extra profits resulting from additional effort. In these circumstances, the manager will choose an efficient level of effort. External finance should therefore take the form of debt, in order to induce risk-neutral managers to choose the efficient level of effort. However, if all external finance is debt, then a risk-neutral manager will not in general have the right incentives to make an efficient choice of the riskiness of the firm's investment strategy. The manager, owning all the equity in the firm, will not receive any returns in states when the firm goes bankrupt, and therefore, in choosing an investment strategy, will take no account of returns in such states, which will result in an inefficient choice of the riskiness of the firm's investment. But if the external finance is entirely in the form of equity the firm will never go bankrupt and the manager will receive a proportional share of returns in all states, and so will make an efficient choice of the riskiness of the firm's investment. External finance entirely in the form of equity thus provides the correct incentives for the manager's choice of riskiness of investment but not for effort; external finance entirely in the form of debt provides the converse incentives to managers. If savers are concerned about both aspects of managerial choice then they will supply external finance to the firm in the form of both debt and equity, with the relative importance of the two forms depending on the relative importance of providing appropriate managerial incentives for effort and riskiness (see Bester and Hellwig, 1987).

This account is a very simple one which leaves out a number of considerations. Suppose, for example, that the manager of a firm is risk-averse, because a large part of his or her consumption depends on the firm's uncertain returns and the associated risk cost cannot be diversified, while savers are risk-neutral because diversification of their portfolios has eliminated all risk. Then an efficient incentive arrangement for the manager will involve some sharing of risk with the savers, which provides an additional reason for external finance to be provided in the form of equity, as risk-sharing is achieved by sharing the realised returns between manager and savers. However the general point remains valid: the forms in which external finance is provided to firms can in principle be explained in terms of the theory of efficient incentive contracts in situations where agents (managers of firms in this context) take some unobserved actions.[3] The fact that firms finance themselves by both debt and equity is explained as being a Pareto-efficient incentive contract between managers and savers subject to the informational constraints.

There are several problems with this approach to understanding the forms in which external finance is provided to firms. One difficulty is that it is not clear that a combination of debt and equity finance does result in an efficient incentive contract subject to the informational constraints. The theory of efficient contracts between principals and agents suggests that in the particular framework analysed, where managers take actions that savers cannot observe, an efficient incentive contract does not need to be based on a mixture of debt and equity finance but can be implemented directly via the manager's compensation contract.[4] Even if it is assumed that the only way to influence managerial incentives is through the forms in which external finance is provided, it is not clear why debt and equity should be the only sources of external finance. Debt and equity influence managerial behaviour through the relationship these two forms of finance yield between the share of the firm's returns received by the manager and the firm's profit before payments to suppliers of debt. If any form of finance can be used to provide appropriate managerial incentives via the relationship it implies between the manager's share of the firm's returns and the firm's profit, then there is no reason why a combination of debt and equity should generally emerge as the efficient incentive contract. Hellwig (1989) argues that it is possible that efficient incentives for a manager will involve rewards for intermediate profit realisations and

---

[3] Sappington (1991) gives a clear non-technical account of the theory.
[4] For example, in the case discussed in the text of the risk-neutral manager choosing effort and riskiness, the incentive contract resulting from the optimal mixture of debt and equity is dominated by a franchise contract in which the manager becomes the residual claimant by paying savers a fixed fee equal to the expected returns from operating the firm efficiently. This arrangement differs from debt finance because the amount paid to savers does not depend on the firm's realised returns. Risk-neutrality of the manager is clearly crucial to the efficiency of this contract. In more complex cases the efficient contract would involve some sharing between manager and savers, but the general point is that in any particular case the incentive contract resulting from the optimal debt-equity combination will be dominated by one which can be implemented via managerial compensation.

penalties for both very low profit realisations (to discourage shirking) *and* very high ones (to discourage excessive risk-taking). Such incentives require that the manager's share of the firm's returns be first increasing and then decreasing in the firm's profit before payments to suppliers of debt, and cannot be achieved with any combination of debt and equity, under which financial mixture the manager's share of firm returns is always non-decreasing in the firm's profit before payments to suppliers of debt.

The fact that a mixture of debt and equity finance does not result in the efficient incentive contract between managers and savers subject to the informational constraints suggests that a degree of caution is required in adopting an explanation of the importance attached to debt and equity financing decisions purely in terms of their incentive effects on management, but it does not vitiate the whole approach. The view that actual behaviour is always to be understood as an efficient solution to a particular incentive problem assumes a very high order of rationality, and says nothing about the process by which an efficient arrangement is actually reached. Consequently, although it is possible to argue that more efficient incentive contracts between savers and managers exist than those involving simply some combination of debt and equity finance, it does not seem reasonable to argue on these lines that incentive considerations of this type have no part to play in the explanation of the importance attached in practice to the mixture of debt and equity in a firm's finance.

A more significant problem with the explanation of debt and equity finance in terms of their effects on managerial incentives is that the analysis of the incentive effects of these two forms of finance has almost always been conducted in single-period models, so that a number of important issues do not arise. One such issue is the possibility of using repeated observations by savers of firm profit realisations to design an incentive scheme which aligns managerial interests more closely with those of savers than is possible when only a single profit realisation is observed. This issue can be seen as another variant of the objection that debt and equity finance do not result in an efficient incentive contract between savers and managers.

A second issue which does not occur in single-period models is the difference between debt and equity arising from the firm's commitment under debt finance to make a fixed payment to the suppliers of debt or transfer the right to make decisions about the firm's operations to them. By contrast, the suppliers of equity finance, although they have a claim to a share of the firm's residual returns and the right to vote on decisions about the firm's operations in non-bankruptcy states, do not have a right to receive fixed payments in any particular period. This distinction is obscured in single-period models, because external suppliers of equity finance automatically receive a payment from the firm's profit realisation in non-bankruptcy states at the end of the period as there is no other possible use for their share of the firm's profits. But in a many-period model the managers of the firm can choose, subject to various constraints, to retain profits to finance further investment rather than pay profits to the external suppliers of equity finance. In a many-period model, therefore, the managers of a firm which raises external finance in the form of debt are committing themselves to make payments to the suppliers of external finance in a way which does not apply if external finance is raised in the form of equity, and this difference may mean that debt finance has incentive effects on managers which are desirable from the savers' point of view.

One example of favourable incentive effects resulting from the managerial commitment to make payments under debt finance is contained in Jensen's free cash flow theory (1986). Free cash flow is cash flow in excess of that required to fund all projects with positive net present values at the relevant cost of capital. Jensen argues that many firms will generate substantial free cash flow, and that managers may wish (because so doing benefits them personally) to invest it in projects which yield less than the cost of capital rather than pay it out to the suppliers of finance. If the firm finances itself with debt rather than equity then the managers are committed to paying out some free cash flow to suppliers of finance, and the consequent reduction in managerial ability to misallocate funds has favourable effects from the savers' point of view.

A fully worked out model which also analyses the effects of debt on managerial incentives arising from the commitment to make payments under debt finance is that of Grossman and Hart (1982). In this model managers wish to raise external finance to fund an investment the cost of which cannot be observed by the suppliers of finance. The managers wish to raise as much external finance as possible, because the surplus over the cost of the investment can be diverted to their private consumption. These consumption benefits are enjoyed by managers only if the firm does not go bankrupt, so it would seem not to be in managers' interests to issue debt because bankruptcy occurs only if the fixed payments to suppliers of debt are not made. But as bankruptcy is costly to managers (since they lose their private consumption benefits from the firm) suppliers of external finance recognise that issuing debt increases managers' incentives to adopt profit-maximising policies, because adopting such policies reduces the probability of bankruptcy occurring. Hence the higher is the level of debt the more funds are these suppliers of finance willing to supply to the firm. In deciding how much external finance to raise in the form of debt, therefore, managers must consider two effects that the level of debt has on their expected private consumption benefits from the firm. Higher debt reduces these expected private benefits by increasing the probability of bankruptcy. But higher debt also increases these expected benefits by raising the overall amount of finance that can be raised, because it improves managerial incentives to adopt profit-maximising policies. In general, managers will choose to finance the investment with a combination of debt and equity. Grossman and Hart's formal model is only a single-period one, and thus requires the somewhat artificial assumption that if bankruptcy occurs at the end of the period managers lose their private consumption benefits from the firm. However costs of bankruptcy to managers in the form of lost private consumption seem to arise more naturally in a many-period model, in which bankruptcy in a particular period removes managers from the firm in subsequent periods.

In a many-period framework, therefore, debt finance may have additional incentive effects on managers as a result of the commitment to make payments to suppliers of debt finance or go bankrupt. Explanations of the importance of debt in a firm's financing along these incentive lines are, of course, subject to the same objections that were mentioned above to the efficient incentive contract approach to firm financing in the single-period framework: first, more direct managerial compensation schemes appear to dominate those resulting from debt-equity combinations; and second, even if managerial incentives can only be affected via financial arrangements, financial instruments other than debt and equity might be part of the efficient incentive scheme. In turn, the same defence as before can be made, namely that these objections take no account of problems of bounded rationality or of the process by which an efficient outcome is actually reached. There do seem to be potentially important incentive effects which result from the commitment to make payments under debt finance that do not arise in a single-period analysis.

Perhaps the most important omission from single-period analyses of the ways in which savers will seek to ensure that the funds they provide to firms will be used in their interests is one that was touched on above in the discussion of the Grossman and Hart model. In a single-period model, control of the firm cannot be removed from the existing management, but in a many-period setting, where decisions about the firm's operations are made repeatedly over time, the incumbent management can be replaced, and control of the firm can be given to a new group of managers. Debt and equity finance have different rights attached to them which enable the suppliers of these forms of finance to remove control of the firm from the incumbent managers in different circumstances. If the firm cannot make its promised payments to the suppliers of debt it goes bankrupt and the existing managers of the firm lose control: the suppliers of debt then decide whether the firm should be liquidated or reorganised under a new management. Suppliers of equity finance are the ultimate owners of the firm and have voting rights in proportion to their share of the firm's total equity. It is therefore possible for a majority of the suppliers of equity to dismiss the incumbent management, either at the firm's annual meeting or following a takeover in which a single large holder of equity has emerged after acquiring the holdings of other suppliers of equity. Debt and equity finance thus offer savers different rights to remove control of a firm from a management which is not acting in their interests (in what follows these will be referred to respectively as debt and equity's control rights), and the possibility of losing control of the firm is likely to be a significant factor inducing managers to act in the interests of savers.[5]

How effective are the incentives for managers resulting from debt and equity's control rights likely to be? The extent to which managers will be constrained to act in the interests of suppliers of equity finance by the fear of being dismissed at the annual meeting of the firm's equity-holders depends on the degree of dispersion of equity ownership. If equity ownership is widely dispersed then no single supplier of equity finance has any incentive to devote resources to the monitoring and evaluation of the existing management, for there is a cost to obtaining the relevant information and essentially no benefit, since any small equity holder has a negligible effect on the outcome of a vote to dismiss the incumbent managers. In such circumstances suppliers of equity finance as a whole will devote too few resources to the evaluation of the incumbent management's performance, as each individual equity owner neglects the external benefits conferred on others by his or her decision to monitor management; the existing managers are therefore more likely to enjoy considerable discretion to follow policies which do not maximise profits without being dismissed by the equity owners' meeting. However, if equity ownership is not widely dispersed and large equity owners exist, the benefits of monitoring managers are internalised to a considerable extent, giving large equity owners stronger incentives to evaluate management performance carefully. The threat of dismissal by the annual meeting of the suppliers of equity finance if the firm does not act in their interests is likely to be a stronger constraining influence on managers if equity ownership is concentrated.

If equity ownership is widely dispersed, but the equity of the firm is in the form of shares which are freely traded on a stock market, another mechanism exists by which a management that fails to adopt profit-

---

[5] See Aghion and Bolton (1992) and Hart and Moore (1989) for formal analyses of the financial structure of the firm based on the control rights attached to debt and equity.

maximising policies will be subject to the threat of dismissal – the hostile takeover. If a firm's management is not pursuing profit-maximising policies, and this fact is reflected in the market price of the firm's shares, then an individual or another firm can seek to purchase all of the firm's shares by making a takeover bid for the firm. If successful, the takeover bid will concentrate equity ownership, replace (or more closely monitor) the existing management, and lead to the implementation of profit-maximising policies. The takeover raider will gain from the takeover so long as the difference between the present value of the firm's profits under profit-maximising policies and the amount paid to purchase the firm's shares exceeds the transaction costs of the takeover. If the firm's share price accurately reflects its performance under existing management, and a takeover raider can purchase shares at a price not too much higher than the price when existing management remains in control, the threat of hostile takeover thus acts as an incentive mechanism constraining incumbent managers to adopt policies which do not differ much from the interests of suppliers of equity finance.

The effectiveness of the hostile takeover threat has been questioned on a number of grounds. If equity ownership is widely dispersed among a large number of small shareholders, each individual shareholder will believe that his or her decision to sell shares to the takeover raider will have no effect on the success or failure of the bid. If the raid is expected to succeed then each individual shareholder will expect the price of a share after the raider takes over the firm to be higher than the price the raider is offering to pay, and so will not sell (Grossman and Hart, 1980). To overcome the problem posed for the existence of successful value-increasing takeovers by the free riding of individual small shareholders on the raider's bid to gain control, it is necessary that such free-riders are excluded to some extent from sharing in the improvements brought about by the raider. Grossman and Hart show that value-increasing takeovers can exist if a raider is able to transfer wealth from minority shareholders to itself. However a second problem is that it is costly for takeover raiders to identify firms which are not adopting profit-maximising policies: if such a firm is identified and a bid is announced this acts as a signal to other raiders that the target firm is undervalued relative to its profit-maximising potential. Each raider may therefore attempt to free ride on the information-gathering costs, by conducting an evaluation only of firms subject to a takeover bid, and so in aggregate raiders may devote too few resources to the evaluation of the performance of firms. Another difficulty with the view that the desire to avoid takeover induces managers to adopt profit-maximising policies is that takeover raiders are themselves often firms controlled by managers who are in a position to pursue their own objectives at the expense of savers' interests. A takeover may be an attractive project for managers, enabling them to move into a new industry or increase the size of their firm and thus reap personal benefits, even though it is not in the interests of the suppliers of finance to the firm. Indeed, Jensen's free cash flow theory argues that expenditures on take-overs are one of the possible misallocations of funds that managers can make as a result of their discretionary ability to use free cash flow in ways that suppliers of finance do not like. A final reason why takeovers may not induce managers of firms to act in the interests of savers is that the threat of takeover may lead managers to take actions which deter takeovers, such as poison pills,[6] rather than to maximise profits.

Ultimately, whether the threat of hostile takeover acts as a mechanism constraining managers to follow profit-maximising policies is an empiri-cal question, and a great deal of work has been carried out in an attempt to answer it. No attempt to survey this work will be made here – see *Journal of Economic Perspectives* (1988), Hughes (1991), and Scherer and Ross (1990) for an account of the extensive empirical literature. A reason-able summary of the results of this empirical work would be to say that the case for the takeover threat constituting a strong disciplining force on managers inducing them to act in the interests of shareholders is not proven. It is difficult, therefore, to argue that the takeover threat is a powerful mechanism inducing the managers of a firm with a widely dispersed equity ownership to act in the interests of the suppliers of equity finance. In any case, the takeover threat can only operate when the equity is in the form of shares traded on a stock market, so that when equity does not take such a form there is no obvious way in which the managers of a firm with a widely dispersed equity ownership will be subject to the threat of dismissal if they fail to follow profit-maximising policies.

It appears, therefore, that when the suppliers of external finance to a firm are a widely dispersed group equity's control rights may not constitute a very strong incentive for managers to act in savers' interests. In such circumstances is it possible that debt's control rights, which take effect in cases when the firm cannot make its promised payments to the suppliers of debt, and hence goes bankrupt, provide a more effective managerial incentive mechanism than those attached to equity? The obligation to make payments under debt finance, and the costs to managers if the firm does not do so and goes bankrupt, seem to provide a significant incentive for managers to act in savers' interests, as Grossman and Hart's analysis (1982) shows. When a firm raises external finance from a large number of

[6] Poison pills impose costs on a takeover raider when a bid is announced. The costs may take various forms, for example a dilution of the raider's equity holding or revoking the raider's voting rights.

individual suppliers, perhaps the most efficient financing arrangement from the suppliers' point of view is for the firm to have a very high proportion of debt in its total finance, so that the threat of bankruptcy is a powerful disciplining effect on managers.

There are, however, some reasons why a very high fraction of debt financing is not the most efficient arrangement. The higher the fraction of debt in a firm's overall finance, other things equal, the more often bankruptcy will occur. Although an increased threat of bankruptcy will induce managers to act more in savers' interests, by adopting policies closer to profit-maximisation, if they have no choice about which firm they manage, the private costs that managers incur when a firm they manage goes bankrupt will mean that if the risk of bankruptcy in a particular firm is high it may not be able to attract any managers, or can do so only by paying a salary which is so high as to be uneconomic. Even if this managerial participation constraint does not bind, a high probability of bankruptcy may be costly for suppliers of finance because it induces managers to act in ways which are contrary to savers' interests. The higher the fraction of debt in a firm's financing the more frequently the firm will be in a situation of financial distress, in which bankruptcy is imminent but has not actually occurred. In situations of financial distress managers, for whom bankruptcy is privately costly, may take actions to try and avoid bankruptcy which are harmful to the suppliers of external finance. For example, if the probability that the firm will go bankrupt is very high then managers may have incentives to undertake excessively risky investment projects and not to carry out worthwhile safe projects, because they will only be concerned with that part of a project's return which is large enough to enable the firm to avoid bankruptcy (see Myers, 1977). Furthermore the process of bankruptcy is itself costly for the suppliers of debt finance as well as the managers. Bankruptcy removes control of the firm from the incumbent management and transfers it to the suppliers of debt. But if there are a large number of such suppliers then the costs of negotiating between them in order to decide whether to liquidate or reorganise the firm will also be large. As well as these legal and administrative costs of the bankruptcy procedure, there will be costs resulting from the impact of bankruptcy on the firm's economic position: customers may be lost or worthwhile investments may not be financed, because of the possibility that the outcome of the bankruptcy process will be the liquidation of the firm. For all these reasons, therefore, it will not be efficient for a firm raising external finance from a large number of small suppliers to have a high proportion of debt in its total finance.

We have seen, therefore, that when there is a small number of suppliers of external finance, equity's control rights are likely to act as a strong incentive for managers to act in savers' interests. But when there is a large number of suppliers of external finance it is not clear that either equity or debt's control rights will act as a very strong incentive for managers. In the case of equity this is because of the public good problem involved in a large number of small savers monitoring managers and the questionable effectiveness of the hostile takeover threat, while in the case of debt it is because the favourable incentive effects of a strong threat of bankruptcy can only be obtained at a high price in terms of costs of financial distress and bankruptcy. The incentives provided by the composition of the firm's financing for managers to act in savers' interests would appear to be considerably weaker in cases when the firm raises external finance from a large number of savers, each of whose contribution is small.

Theoretical analysis of the role of financial intermediaries

The fact that the savers who provide resources to firms for investment will often be small (that is, the contribution made by each individual saver to the external finance raised by a particular firm is a small fraction of the total) has implications which have not been considered in the discussion so far. Savers are likely to be small (in the above sense) both because the scale of the external finance required by a particular firm will often be very large relative to the resources of any individual saver, and because the desire to spread risks will tend to limit the amount that an individual saver will provide to any one firm. When there is a large number of small savers providing external finance to a firm, interpreting firm financing arrangements in terms of the theory of efficient incentive contracts encounters certain problems. This theory usually envisages a principal designing an incentive scheme for an agent (or agents). However, analysing firm finance along these lines requires making the assumption that suppliers of external finance are able to organise and agree among themselves in designing an incentive scheme, a process which, if there is a large number of suppliers of external finance, will involve considerable negotiation costs and free-rider problems. For this reason the efficient incentive contract approach to firm financing decisions usually proceeds in a different way. It envisages managers choosing the firm's financial policy and, for various reasons, being concerned with the market valuation of the firm. The valuation of the firm is determined by suppliers of finance, who are presumed to have a complete understanding of the incentives faced by managers as a result of the firm's financial policy. This means that a financial policy which leads to an efficient incentive contract (subject to the various constraints) will maximise market valuation, and will thus be chosen by managers. However, this way of implementing the efficient incentive contract approach to firm financing is not entirely satisfactory either, for it requires two questionable assumptions: first, that the firm's securities are traded on a market; and second, that managers wish to maximise market value. The efficient incentive contract approach to firm financial policy in the case when a large number of small savers provide external finance to a firm would seem more plausible if the choice of the form of financing which provides the most suitable managerial incentives could be viewed as being delegated to a single decision-maker, acting on behalf of all savers.

Apart from the fact that when a large number of savers delegate the choice of finance the efficient incentive contract approach to firm financing becomes more plausible, there may be benefits for a large number of small savers if they permit actions to be taken on their behalf by a small number of decision-makers. There are likely to be economies of scale in the acquisition of information for the purposes of deciding which firms should have funds provided to them, and of monitoring the performance of the firms once finance has been provided. If one saver were to incur the fixed cost of acquiring this information and use it on behalf of all other savers then in principle there would be no need for the other savers to incur further costs of acquiring the same information. However, this raises the question of the incentives required for one particular saver to acquire this costly information and, having acquired it, to use it in the interests of the other savers, who do not possess it.

This question is analysed by Diamond (1984) in a model in which a firm needs to raise external finance to operate an investment project and there is a fixed cost of monitoring the realised return from the project. If savers do not observe the return on the firm's investment, an efficient incentive contract cannot involve equity finance, since it is always possible for the firm's managers to declare a very low value of profits and keep the difference between actual and declared profits for themselves. Diamond shows that if savers do not monitor the realisation of profits, the efficient incentive contract is a standard debt contract with non-pecuniary bankruptcy costs, that is, a contract in which savers are paid a fixed amount in non-bankruptcy states while in bankruptcy states they receive the return on the project and the firm's managers suffer non-pecuniary penalties. Monitoring the realisation of the firm's profits, at a cost, would in principle permit a more efficient financial incentive contract involving a mixture of debt and equity, along the lines discussed in the previous section. The fixed cost of monitoring means that there are natural economies of scale in this activity: it is cheaper for a single saver, such as a financial intermediary, to monitor the realised value of the firm's profits on behalf of a large number of small savers than it is for each of the small savers to monitor individually. The role of a financial intermediary in this analysis is therefore to act as a delegated monitor for small savers: it raises funds from savers and pays returns to them, while supplying finance to firms and spending resources monitoring and enforcing financial contracts with firms which are more efficient than those available without monitoring. But if small savers delegate the monitoring of the firm's realised profits to a financial intermediary, the private information that the intermediary has in relation to the savers as a result of monitoring may create incentive problems in the intermediary–saver relationship. Diamond shows that, if savers do not observe the firm's profits or the payments made by the firm to the intermediary, the efficient incentive contract for the financial intermediary, which provides it with incentives to monitor properly and make sufficient payments to savers to attract funds, is also a debt contract with non-pecuniary bankruptcy costs. Before it can be established that delegating monitoring to an intermediary is a more efficient way of supplying external finance than is the case with no monitoring at all, it is necessary to take account of the costs of providing appropriate incentives to the financial intermediary. Diamond shows that sufficient diversification by a financial intermediary across firms does result in delegated monitoring being more efficient than no monitoring. The reason is that the greater is the intermediary's diversification the more certain are its aggregate returns, and hence it is more likely to be able to make its promised payments to savers. Thus as the intermediary's diversification increases, its likelihood of incurring the deadweight bankruptcy costs which form part of its efficient incentive contract decrease, so that sufficient diversification will reduce these costs of providing appropriate incentives for delegated monitoring by an amount which means that it is more efficient to supply external finance with delegated monitoring than with no monitoring.

The general point which emerges from the specific example analysed by Diamond is that when the acquisition of information about a firm is costly, finance can be provided to firms in a more efficient manner if savers delegate the collection of information about firms to a financial intermediary, *provided* that the intermediary has appropriate incentives to act in savers' interests. In principle, any form of costly information-collection about firms can be efficiently delegated to a financial intermediary, whether it be the gathering of information about a firm in order to decide whether to provide funds for the firm's investment (screening) or the collection of information about a firm's behaviour after finance has been supplied to it, in order to provide better incentives for the firm's managers to act in the interests of savers (monitoring). The information gathered by a financial intermediary in this context is useful insofar as it improves performance under an efficient incentive contract, which is to say insofar as it induces managers of firms to act in a way which more closely corresponds to the interests of savers. In this sense, the information collected by intermediaries has the effect of increasing the degree of indirect control that savers have over the actions of managers.

The efficiency advantages of delegating information-collection to financial intermediaries may also extend to the delegation to financial intermediaries of savers' explicit rights to control managers by changing the management of a particular firm, although a formal model establishing this possibility does not exist. An intermediary which raises funds from savers in the form of debt (i.e. by borrowing from savers) can presumably improve the incentives for the managers of the firms to which it supplies finance to act in a profit-maximising way by appropriate use of the rights attached to debt and equity to change control of the firm. In the case of equity, this requires that the financial intermediary holds a significant fraction of the equity issued by a particular firm, so that it has a strong influence on the outcome of votes at the equity owners' meeting and corresponding incentives to monitor management performance carefully. In the case of debt finance, control of a firm can be changed when the firm cannot make its promised payments to the suppliers of debt and goes bankrupt. The discussion in the previous section of the effectiveness of debt's control rights as a means of providing incentives for managers to act in savers' interests considered a number of reasons why it would not be efficient for firms to have a very high fraction of debt in their overall financing, as would be required if the threat of bankruptcy were to be an effective constraint on managers. One reason was that if the debt was supplied by a large number of savers it would be very costly for the savers to negotiate and come to a decision as to whether a bankrupt firm should be reorganised or liquidated. But if the debt is supplied to a firm by one financial intermediary, or perhaps a small number of them, then the costs involved in deciding what should happen to a bankrupt firm will be much lower, and the costs to the firm of bankruptcy may also be reduced, because the degree of uncertainty concerning the outcome of the bankruptcy procedure may be smaller. The effectiveness on managerial incentives of debt's control rights may therefore also be increased by delegating them to a financial intermediary. If delegation of debt's control rights to financial intermediaries does lower the costs of bankruptcy, and so make the threat of it a more effective incentive for managers, then it might be worthwhile for financial intermediaries to develop expertise in dealing with firms in, or near to, bankruptcy, since the incidence of bankruptcy would be expected to be higher. This expertise might include an ability on the part of the financial intermediary to manage and reorganise the firm while it was bankrupt, as well as to deal with the financial and legal aspects of bankruptcy, since if bankruptcy occurred more often because firms had a relatively high fraction of debt in their total finance it would be important to ensure that this did not result in a large number of unwarranted liquidations. A high proportion of debt in firms' financing may, as has been noted above, have costs resulting from managerial actions to try to avoid bankruptcy when a firm is in financial distress. These costs could be reduced if financial intermediaries were able to intervene when bankruptcy was imminent but had not yet occurred: for this to be possible, intermediaries must both be able to identify situations of financial distress and have rights to influence managerial behaviour before default has actually occurred.

It is therefore possible that a system in which external finance is supplied to firms indirectly via financial intermediaries is more efficient than one in which it is provided to firms by savers directly. The delegation of both information collection and the exercise of debt and equity's control rights to financial intermediaries by savers will allow managerial behaviour to be more closely aligned with savers' interests, provided that the intermediaries are faced with suitable incentives to act in savers' interests. Such a system of providing finance for investment will be more efficient than one without intermediaries, so long as the costs of these incentives are not too large. But is there any reason why a system in which finance for investment is provided by banks should be superior to one in which finance is provided by other forms of financial intermediary, such as insurance companies or pension funds? By definition, all financial intermediaries, whether banks or non-banks, take in funds from savers in order to supply them to firms (and other final investors); all financial intermediaries would thus appear to be able to specialise in assessing the risks associated with supplying finance to firms and in influencing the way in which firms use finance, by monitoring and using the control rights attached to debt and equity. Banks are distinguished from other financial intermediaries by the fact that some of their liabilities are used as a means of payment. The payments and receipts of a firm are likely to provide information which is relevant for assessing its economic position. A firm that is doing well and making a good return on its investment will tend to have a surplus of receipts over payments: conversely, a firm that is doing badly is likely to have a surplus of payments over receipts. Information about firms' payments and receipts is not generally available, but banks can observe the deposits and withdrawals of firms which hold accounts with them. If, as seems plausible, such observations convey useful information, then banks will have an advantage over other financial intermediaries in their ability to gather information about firms. A case can thus be made that a system of finance for investment in which the financial intermediaries to which savers delegate various actions are banks is superior to one in which other forms of financial intermediary play this role, because there may be an economy of scope in the provision of payments services and the collection of information about firms, enabling banks to gather information more effectively and/or at lower cost than other financial intermediaries.

The efficiency gains available from delegated information collection and control by financial intermediaries are substantially due to natural mono-poly elements in the activity of intermediation. The economies of scale in the gathering of costly information mean that the benefit from delegating such activities is the reduction in the fixed costs of information collection. In order for the costs of providing incentives for the financial interme-diary to act in savers' interests to be small enough that there is a net gain from delegating information-gathering, it is necessary for the financial intermediary to supply funds to a large number of firms whose returns are not perfectly correlated. Diamond shows that increasing returns to scale caused by reductions in the cost of providing incentives for appropriate delegated monitoring is a very general result: so long as firms' returns are not perfectly correlated, the cost of providing these incentives for a given number of firms monitored by a single intermediary is less than the sum of these costs for monitoring subsets of this number of firms by several intermediaries. Furthermore if, as is plausible, different financial inter-mediaries cannot observe the outcomes of other intermediaries' screening of firms applying for finance, each intermediary may fear that firms applying for funds are ones that have been rejected by others as being of poor quality. Competition among financial intermediaries in order to attract new firms may not be sustainable, as Broecker (1990) shows, and an element of natural monopoly may result because a single large finan-cial intermediary can make more efficient decisions about supplying finance to new firms as a consequence of being able to observe the entire population of applicants, rather than facing a potential adverse selection problem as would be the case with competition. The strong natural monopoly elements in financial intermediation that result from the char-acteristics of efficient delegated information-gathering, and which imply that the efficient number of such intermediaries is one, are reinforced by the fact that, as we have seen, the control rights of debts and equity are also used more effectively if the intermediary exercising them on behalf of savers supplies a large fraction of the external finance of firms.

For obvious reasons, however, a single financial intermediary which enjoys a dominant position because of these natural monopoly elements in financial intermediation is likely to act in ways which reduce the efficiency of the system of providing finance for investment. The absence of competition may mean that the dominant intermediary earns monopoly profits by raising the margin between the cost of funds supplied to firms and the return paid to savers above its efficient level, thereby reducing investment below the efficient amount. The absence of competition may also weaken the incentives of the dominant intermediary to collect information about firm performance in order to ensure that managers act in savers' interests. It may also lead to inefficiencies because there are fewer opportunities for firms with new projects to receive independent evaluation, with the outcome that good ideas fail to obtain finance.[7] These problems are simply the standard ones that natural monopolies create for welfare analysis: the most efficient outcome is in principle available under natural monopoly, but in practice does not occur because monopoly power permits price increases and internal inefficiencies.

Government regulation is a possible solution to these problems, but the general difficulties involved in effectively regulating a natural monopoly are well known, and in this particular instance they are likely to be especially severe, since regulation would involve monitoring a financial intermediary which had a natural monopoly because of the economies of scale in collecting information about firms. Competition among several financial intermediaries, if it were feasible, might be superior to regulation of a single intermediary, and might also have the advantage that competition among independent delegated information-gatherers would lead to the discovery of a greater volume of relevant information. Are the increasing returns to scale from the number of firms monitored by a financial intermediary so large that competition among several intermediaries is impossible? Diamond shows that, in his model, if firms' returns are independent and each firm has the same variance of returns, then the costs of providing appropriate incentives for delegated monitoring are a monotonically declining function of the number of firms monitored. Because the costs per firm monitored of providing these incentives are bounded below by zero, the increasing returns to scale from the number of firms monitored become constant returns to scale asymptotically. Hence it is possible for a number of competing financial intermediaries to exist if most of the reductions in the costs of providing incentives for delegated monitoring are achievable by diversification

---

[7] Although a system with only a single financial intermediary is, by comparison with a system with many intermediaries, likely to result in a relatively large proportion of good projects failing to obtain finance, it may also result in a relatively small proportion of bad projects succeeding in obtaining finance. For a general discussion along these lines, see Sah and Stiglitz (1986).

across a number of firms which is not too large relative to the total number of firms. It may therefore be the case that, despite the strong natural monopoly elements present in financial intermediation, the benefits of having competition among intermediaries, in terms of reducing the inefficiencies mentioned above, outweigh the costs which competition imposes by raising the average cost of financial intermediation. The issue is clearly a complex one, which it does not seem possible to resolve by a purely theoretical analysis.[8]

Implications for the assessment of the German system of finance for investment

What light does the theoretical discussion of the previous two sections throw on the widely-held view of the merits of the 'bank-based' German system of investment finance? This view, it will be recalled, has a number of components. It regards German banks as being very closely involved with firms, so that they can provide a substantial amount of loan finance on favourable terms, reflecting the reduction in the agency costs of external finance that results from their close involvement. The banks' ability to monitor management is seen as providing a more effective disciplinary mechanism than the hostile takeovers on which the UK has to rely for this purpose. The close involvement of the banks with firms, and their ability replace inefficient managements, is also seen as enabling them to reorganise firms in financial distress before costly formal bankruptcy procedures come into operation.

The theoretical discussion of the previous two sections suggests that the way to analyse the possible merits of the German system of finance for investment is in terms of the effects of different institutional arrangements on the collection of information about the investors to whom savers provide funds. Diamond's analysis shows that when resources for investment are provided by a large number of small savers, financial intermediaries can economise on the fixed costs of collecting information about investors and supply external finance more efficiently, provided that the costs of providing intermediaries with appropriate incentives to act in

---

[8] It should be noted, that, given the natural scale economies in monitoring which are a central part of Diamond's argument for the efficiency of financial intermediation, it is not clear that competition among intermediaries will lead to an equilibrium with the efficient number of intermediaries. Yanelle (1989) analyses a model of Bertrand competition among intermediaries in the markets for funds from savers and for supplying finance to firms, and shows that, if intermediaries compete first for funds from savers, the equilibrium under Bertrand competition may not involve financial intermediation even though it is in principle more efficient than direct finance, and even if equilibrium does involve intermediation the form of intermediation that results may be less efficient than direct finance.

savers' interests do not outweigh the reduction in costs which results from delegating the information collection to the intermediaries. One purpose for which a financial intermediary might gather information is the evaluation of managerial performance, which suggests a natural link between information-collection and the exercise of the rights attached to debt and equity to change the managers of a firm. The discussion in the second section of this chapter suggested that debt and equity's control rights would not be effective mechanisms for constraining managers to act in savers' interests if the debt and equity were held by a large number of small savers. Delegating the exercise of these control rights to financial intermediaries would therefore also appear to have potential efficiency advantages, as long as the costs of providing appropriate incentives for the intermediary are not too large, although in the absence of a formal model establishing this possibility it must remain a conjecture. The general theoretical argument for the greater efficiency of a system in which savers supply finance for investment indirectly via financial intermediaries rather than directly from savers to firms is that there are potential advantages in savers' delegating information collection and the exercise of control rights to intermediaries. The financial intermediaries can then supply external finance to firms in that combination of debt and equity which, by its effect on managerial incentives through debt and equity's return streams and control rights, minimises the agency costs of finance.

If the German system of investment finance was an intermediated one while the UK system was unintermediated then, from this perspective, the theoretical basis for regarding the German system as superior would be clear. It should be noted that if this were the case one would expect to observe a greater use of debt finance in the UK system. As we have seen, if it is costly to collect information about firms' returns, then individual savers are unlikely to do so, and in such circumstances the efficient form in which to supply external finance is debt.[9] By contrast, the role of financial intermediaries is to collect information of this sort, and so they can supply external finance to firms in that mixture of debt or equity which has the best incentive effects on the managers of firms. But the UK system of finance for investment is, of course, one in which financial intermediaries do play a significant role – there are, as well as commercial and investment (merchant) banks, insurance companies, investment trusts, pension funds and unit trusts. Given that the UK system of investment finance is not an unintermediated one, why might the German system be superior?

Two different answers might be given to this question. One is simply to

---

[9] See, in addition to Diamond (1984), Townsend (1979) and Gale and Hellwig (1985).

say that German banks are better at supplying funds to firms than are UK financial intermediaries. For example, German banks might have a greater ability to assess the risks of lending, whether as a result of using superior credit assessment methods or as a result of having specialist information departments. This sort of answer implies that there are no significant differences between the *systems* of finance for investment in Germany and the UK: the supposedly greater contribution of the German system to economic performance is due to deficiencies in the *operation* of UK financial intermediaries relative to German ones. There is another possible answer, however, which is to say that the particular institutional features of the German system of investment finance lead to better outcomes in terms of economic performance than do the institutional features of the UK system. These two answers are not mutually exclusive, but the second, if supported by evidence, would appear to offer a more solid basis for deriving policy recommendations aimed at improving the contribution of the UK system of investment finance to economic performance.

Two major differences exist between the institutional features of the German and UK systems of finance for investment. The first is that, broadly speaking, financial intermediaries in the UK are more specialised than is the case in Germany. Historically, UK banks, unlike German ones, have not been universal banks, providing a complete range of commercial and investment banking services, although this difference has been steadily diminishing, particularly in the 1980s, as the large UK clearing banks have become more involved in investment banking. The second major difference concerns the institutional arrangements for corporate governance. Public limited companies in Germany, in contrast to those in the UK, have to have a supervisory board, the function of which is to monitor the management of the company. German banks have the ability to exercise proxy votes on behalf of shareholders who have deposited shares with the banks for safekeeping, which gives them a significant influence on the supervisory boards of companies. Hence banks have the potential to play an important part in corporate governance in Germany. There is no corresponding institutional arrangement in the UK which enables financial intermediaries to monitor and replace inefficient managements; hence the UK has to rely on the hostile takeover mechanism to perform this task.

Does the theoretical analysis of the previous two sections provide any basis for thinking that the institutional arrangements of the German system of finance for investment are superior to those of the UK system? The argument suggested by the theoretical discussion is that there are economies of scope in the collection of information about firms for different purposes, which the characteristic universal nature of German banks may enable them to exploit, and which may be reinforced by the German institutional arrangements that result in banks having an important role in corporate governance via their supervisory board representation. To spell out this argument in more detail, the reason that external finance can be supplied more efficiently via financial intermediaries is that the intermediaries can in principle economise on the fixed costs of collecting information about firms. If there are economies of scope in the provision of payments services and the collection of information about firms, then the financial intermediaries which can most efficiently supply external finance will be banks. If, furthermore, there are economies of scope between the collection of information about firms for different purposes – for example, for screening of loan applicants, monitoring of firms which have received loans, and screening of firms which wish to issue equity shares – then a system in which universal banks are the dominant financial intermediaries will be more efficient than one in which banks and other financial intermediaries specialise in particular functions. As has been noted, an argument can be made for delegating both the exercise of the control rights of debt and equity and the collection of information to financial intermediaries. It is very likely that there is an economy of scope in the monitoring of firm managements and the exercise of the control rights of debt and equity. The German institutional feature whereby banks are represented on company supervisory boards enables this economy of scope to be fully exploited, by giving banks the ability to subject managers to detailed monitoring. It also has implications both for the form in which banks supply external finance in Germany, and for the terms on which it is supplied. If bank supervisory board representation enables banks to monitor managements closely, then banks will be able to limit the costs of financial distress which arise from actions managers take to try and avoid bankruptcy; this removes one of the drawbacks of having a high proportion of debt in a firm's total finance as a means of creating incentives for managers to act in savers' interests. The information which banks may obtain about firms from their supervisory board representation is also likely to enable them to screen loan applicants more efficiently, reducing the need for credit rationing or collateral, and so making loans available to firms on better terms.

In this view, therefore, German banks are seen as financial intermediaries which, by virtue of the particular institutional framework in Germany, deal efficiently with the problems of asymmetric information that are inherent in the supply of external finance for investment. Universal banking and bank representation on supervisory boards enable

German banks to exploit economies of scale in costly information collection, and economies of scope between various different forms of information collection and the exercise of delegated control rights. If the German institutional framework does permit German banks to act in this way then it would be natural for German banks, in addition to monitoring managements closely, to take an active managerial role in circumstances such as bankruptcy. Furthermore, this view can explain why it might be efficient for particular firms to receive all their external finance from a single bank that also provides all the firm's other financial services, which is how the German house bank relationship has been portrayed.[10] The potential efficiency of the monopolistic supply to a firm of external funds and other financial services can be understood as arising from the ability to economise on information-gathering costs, from the economies of scope in universal banking, and from the potential to economise on the costs of negotiation between lenders in circumstances when the firm is bankrupt.

It is, therefore, possible to provide a theoretical basis for the claims about the superiority of the German system of finance for investment over the UK one. But the theoretical argument that has been given is not without its limitations. One relates to the fundamental point of Diamond's analysis. Financial intermediaries can economise on the fixed costs of information-collection, but in so doing they acquire private information which savers do not have. In order to argue that an intermediated system of providing finance to investors is more efficient than an unintermediated one, it is necessary to take account of the costs involved in creating incentives for the financial intermediaries to use their private information in savers' interests. The theoretical argument that has been advanced in support of claims about the merits of the German system of investment finance neither explains what the incentives are for banks to exercise the control rights which have been delegated to them in savers' interests, nor considers the costs of providing such incentives. This is clearly a subject for which empirical investigation of the German system is important.

A second, related, limitation of the theoretical argument is that it takes no account of the possibility that a lack of competition may offset the efficiency advantages that are claimed to result from the institutional features of the German system of finance for investment. The theoretical argument is essentially based on there being strong elements of natural monopoly in the activity of financial intermediation: an efficient system of investment finance is seen as being attainable with a small number of large

---

[10] See the quotation from Kocka on p. 9.

universal banks exploiting economies of scale and scope in information-collection. But a small number of large universal banks may exploit the monopoly power that results from economies of scale and scope, and so fail to produce an efficient system of finance for investment. The efficiency costs that may result from an absence of competition include restriction of investment below the efficient level and lack of incentives for banks to gather information, as discussed on p. 41. The lack of competition between banks may also reduce their incentives to use their private information in savers' interests. A further cost of a system of investment finance in which a firm receives external finance from a single bank arises if banks are risk-averse. The theoretical analysis above has been based on the implicit assumption that banks are risk-neutral, so that there is no risk cost involved in a bank supplying a given total amount of funds to a smaller number of firms for which the bank is the sole provider of external finance, rather than supplying the same total finance to a larger number of firms for each of which the bank is one of several providers of external finance. But if banks are risk-averse, and the returns on firms' investments are not perfectly correlated, then there is such a cost, and banks will benefit by diversifying their total funds across a larger number of firms, reducing their exposure to any one firm. Note that the diversification required to reduce the cost of risk for risk-averse banks is different from the diversification required for the costs of providing incentives for banks to act as delegated information-collectors to be low enough to make delegated information-collection efficient. In the former case, diversification reduces the riskiness of the expected return on a bank's total portfolio; in the latter case, diversification reduces the costs of providing appropriate incentives for delegated information-gathering by banks. The balance between competitive and monopolistic elements in an efficient system of finance for investment is another subject for which empirical investigation of the German system is important.

Conclusion

This chapter has reviewed theories of business finance and financial intermediation in order to provide an analytical foundation for the view that the German system of investment finance is superior to the UK one. It is necessary to have such a foundation in order to understand the functions that a system of finance for investment performs, and hence the reasons why the particular set of institutional arrangements that characterise the German system might lead to that system producing better economic results than other systems do. This chapter has shown that there is a coherent analytical foundation for the various components of the widely-held view of the merits of the German system of investment finance. It is based on the idea that there are economies of scale and scope in information collection and the exercise of the control rights attached to debt and equity finance, which the German system of universal banks with representation on supervisory boards is especially well suited to exploit. If this is true, then German banks may be well-informed about the firms to which they supply funds, and in a position to exert significant influence on the managements of these firms, not simply through the finance they supply, but also because of their role in corporate governance. The banks' role as monitors of management not only enables the control rights of equity to be exercised effectively, but also does the same for debt's control rights, since the close monitoring of management by banks, and the typical house bank relationship, reduces the costs of supplying a large fraction of a firm's total finance in the form of debt.

A major reason for attempting to provide such a theoretical basis is that it suggests a number of issues, in addition to those identified in chapter 1 as comprising the widely-held view, on which empirical evidence can usefully be brought to bear. There are several areas suggested by the theoretical framework where empirical evidence would be very helpful. Economies of scope between information-collection and the exercise of delegated control rights are an important part of the overall analytical foundation for the claims about the superiority of the German system. Empirical investigation of the relationship between bank lending and bank supervisory board representation, and of the relationship between bank lending and bank ability to manage firms in financial distress, can throw light on the significance of such economies of scope. There are also some issues for which the theoretical analysis could arrive at no clear conclusion. Whether there exist suitable incentives for German banks to use the delegated equity control rights they possess by virtue of the proxy-voting system in shareholders' interests, and what is the appropriate degree of competition among universal banks in a system of investment finance, are two questions for which empirical information about the German situation will also be very enlightening.

The chapters that follow attempt to assess the empirical evidence in support of the widely-held view of the merits of the German system of finance for investment. They address both the various components of this view, as set out in chapter 1, and the questions suggested by the theoretical analysis in the present chapter. We turn first to an examination of the claim that bank loans constitute a particularly large part of the finance for investment in Germany.

3 The significance of bank loans in the finance of aggregate investment in Germany

Introduction

Perhaps the most basic component of the view that a 'bank-based' system of finance for investment, such as is claimed to operate in Germany and Japan, is superior to a 'market-based' one is the belief that the close involvement of banks with firms in a 'bank-based' system reduces the agency costs of supplying debt finance. The lower cost of bank-supplied debt is seen as enabling firms to finance a higher level of investment, with a larger proportion of bank loans, than in a 'market-based' system. The following statement by *The Economist* (1990, p. 21) highlights the common perception that the system of investment finance in Germany, together with that of Japan, involves a greater use of bank loan finance: 'Public companies in Japan and West Germany have traditionally relied more on debt than on equity, so their gearing has typically been twice or three times as high as that of Anglo–American [companies].'

This chapter undertakes a detailed analysis of the financing of aggregate investment by non-financial enterprises in Germany in order to assess whether bank loans are a particularly important source of finance for investment. The second section discusses the problems involved in making international comparisons of the financing of investment, and argues that the most useful comparisons are those based on flows of funds. The third section discusses the German system of pension provision, because one distinctive aspect of the finance of investment in Germany is the use by enterprises of pension contributions on behalf of their employees as a source of finance for investment within the enterprise. The fourth section analyses the finance of aggregate investment by German non-financial enterprises in the period 1950–1989, using flow of funds data. The fifth section compares the sources of finance for investment by non-financial enterprises in Germany with those in the

49

Table 3.1. *Structure of liabilities of non-financial businesses, Germany and the UK, end 1971 and end 1981, %*

	Germany			UK	
	End 1971	End 1981		End 1971	End 1981
Equity capital	26	19	Equity capital	47	49
Debt	74	81	Debt	53	51
of which			of which:		
short-term	42	48	bank loans	8	14
long-term	20	19	bonds	13	8
provisions	10	14	trade and other credit	21	25

Source: Bank of England (1984).

UK, again using flow of funds data. The sixth section draws a brief conclusion.

Capital gearing ratio and flow of funds measures of the financing of investment

As the statement from *The Economist* quoted in the previous section illustrates, the claim that bank loans are a particularly important source of investment finance in Germany is usually based on international comparisons of capital gearing ratios (the proportion of total assets financed by debt) for the aggregate non-financial enterprise sector. Comparisons of this type consistently suggest that the debt-equity ratio of non-financial enterprises in Germany is significantly higher than that in the UK. The *Bank of England Quarterly Bulletin* (1984), for example, gives the figures in table 3.1 for the structure of liabilities of non-financial businesses in Germany and the UK (the figures are percentages of total liabilities, and are derived from aggregations of individual firm accounts). According to these figures, the debt-equity ratio of non-financial enterprises is much higher in Germany than in the UK. Given that most firm debt in Germany takes the form of bank loans, these figures suggest that bank lending to non-financial enterprises is also much higher in Germany than in the UK. An immediate complication to be noted when comparing the German and UK figures is that the provisions figure for Germany, which is part of the debt total, includes households' claims on enterprise pension funds. As is discussed more fully below, it is not clear whether it is more appropriate to categorise these claims as a debt or an equity item. Certainly classifying them as a debt item accentuates the difference between German and UK debt-equity ratios, given the UK system in which private pensions are provided by pension funds or insurance companies. The *Bank of England Quarterly Bulletin* (1984) estimates that if all provisions for staff superannuation within German enterprises' balance sheets at the end of 1981 had been funded by pension funds or insurance companies, and if their pattern of investment were similar to that in the UK, the proportion of equity capital in the total liabilities of German firms would have risen from 19% to nearer 25%.

There are, however, some more fundamental problems with the use of capital gearing ratios derived from firm accounting data as a basis for international comparisons of the finance of investment. One concerns the correct measurement of equity capital under inflationary conditions. If assets are not revalued to take account of inflation, the book value of equity capital can be substantially underrecorded. In the UK, land and buildings are periodically revalued, but in Germany all assets are valued at true historic cost with no revaluations; this makes comparisons of UK and German capital gearing ratios rather hazardous. Another problem is that the book values of assets and reserves are sensitive to depreciation schedules, and accounting conventions on depreciation vary appreciably across countries, partly in response to differences in tax regimes. A striking illustration of the influence of different accounting systems on international comparisons of capital gearing ratios is provided by Perlitz *et al.* (1985), who showed that, once adjustments were made to put the two accounting systems on a roughly equal basis, the difference in the share of equity in total capital between Germany and the UK for a sample of very large corporations in 1979 and 1980 vanished.

The difficulties involved in making international comparisons of the finance of investment based on balance sheet data have led Mayer (1988, 1990) to argue that such comparisons can be made more accurately by using data on flows of funds rather than stocks of assets and liabilities. The flow of funds statement shows the sources of funds in a particular year, and the uses to which these funds were put in that year. From this flow of funds statement it is straightforward to establish how enterprises' investment in a particular year has been financed. Because the flow of funds statement describes current cash transactions, it is naturally suited to answering the question of how investment has actually been financed, avoiding the complications involved in using balance sheet data which arise from differing accounting valuation conventions.

An important point to note when using flow of funds data to analyse the financing of investment is that the amount that is actually spent on fixed assets and stockbuilding in any year, and which must therefore be financed, is given by gross capital formation before the subtraction of depreciation. The subtraction of depreciation from gross capital formation to give net capital formation is an accounting adjustment to the actual flow of expenditure on fixed assets and stockbuilding which, while important for some purposes (in particular for establishing the extent to which investment has increased the capital stock rather than simply maintained it), is not relevant to the question of how the total expenditure on capital goods has been financed. It follows that, as depreciation is not subtracted on the uses side of the flow of funds statement, it is also not subtracted on the sources side. Internal finance is therefore appropriately measured as the sum of retained profits and depreciation.

The uses of finance by enterprises in a particular time period include the acquisition both of fixed capital assets and stocks and of financial assets. Some of the sources of enterprises' funds therefore go towards the accumulation of financial rather than physical assets. To identify the finance associated with investment in physical assets, it is therefore necessary to subtract enterprises' acquisitions of financial assets from equivalent increases in liabilities. The finance of physical investment is thus measured in terms of the net amount that has been provided from various sources. However, it can be argued that analysing the finance of investment by an aggregate sector such as non-financial enterprises in terms of net sources of finance for physical investment understates the importance of particular sources of finance, at least in certain circumstances. Suppose, for example, that some non-financial enterprises are borrowing from banks while others are depositing equivalent amounts of funds with banks. The net contribution of bank borrowing to the finance of investment in physical assets by the non-financial enterprise sector is zero, but this may not accurately reflect the significance of bank loans as a source of finance. Even if they are simply lending to some non-financial enterprises the funds deposited with them by others, the banks may be making an important contribution to the finance of the sector as a whole if they have a comparative advantage over non-financial enterprises in screening loan applicants and monitoring loans made. For this reason, we use flow of funds data in two different ways to show the pattern of finance of investment by the German non-financial enterprise sector. The first way is to analyse the sources of finance for non-financial enterprises in terms of their share of investment in physical assets, subtracting enterprises' acquisition of financial assets from their corresponding increases in liabilities. We describe sources of finance for investment analysed in this way as 'net sources of finance'. The second way is to present the sources of funds for enterprises in terms of their share of investment in physical and financial assets; we describe these as 'gross sources of finance'.

Pension contributions as a source of finance for investment in Germany

It was noted in the previous section that one complicating factor in a comparative analysis of the financing of aggregate investment by non-financial enterprises in Germany and the UK arose from differences in the system of pension provision in the two countries. In this section the features of the German system of pension provision, and its implications for the finance of investment, are discussed in greater detail.

The German system of pension provision has three components. The most important in terms of the share of total pensions received is the state pension, which forms part of the German social security system. However the statutory pension insurance funds which finance the state pension operate on a pay-as-you-go basis, in which current pensions are paid for by the contributions of the current workforce, so that these contributions are not available to finance investment.

The second component of the pension system in Germany involves personal provision of pensions by saving in the form of contributions to life assurance enterprises and private pension funds. The significance of this form of household saving has increased over the period 1960-1989. The assets of life assurance enterprises account for about 65% of the total assets of insurance enterprises shown in the capital finance account of the Deutsche Bundesbank. In 1960, funds placed with insurance enterprises made up 18.1% of households' total net acquisition of financial assets; by 1989 the corresponding figure was 32.7%. This increase in the significance of funds placed with insurance enterprises generally, and particularly contributions to life assurance enterprises, as a share of total household saving has not, however, led to an increase in the significance of life assurance enterprises as a source of funds for non-financial enterprises, as tables 3.2 and 3.3 below show. The reason for this is the investment policy followed by German life assurers. According to the Gesamtverband der Versicherungswirtschaft (1988), roughly 50% of the gross new investment by life assurers over the period 1980–1987 was in the banking sector, 20% in the government sector, 20% in the housing sector, and only 12% in the producing enterprises sector. A breakdown of direct investment by life assurers in the producing enterprises sector into debt and equity is not available. However, the capital finance account of the Deutsche Bundesbank shows that in 1987 all insurance enterprises held 4.5% of their total assets in the form of shares and 10% in the form of loans to producing enterprises. The corresponding figures for 1960 were 4.9% in shares and 29.3% in loans. The increased flow of funds from households to insurance enterprises has not resulted in an increase in loans by insurance enterprises

Table 3.2. *Net sources of finance for investment, German producing enterprises sector, 1950–1989, %*

	1950–1989	1950–1959	1960–1969	1970–1979	1980–1989
Internally-generated funds	75.4	75.4	74.1	71.3	80.1
Provisions for pensions by enterprises	3.7	3.2	2.0	4.3	4.9
Capital transfers from government	5.5	1.2	4.0	7.9	9.0
Bank borrowing	11.7	11.8	13.4	12.0	10.2
of which:					
long-term[a]	12.1	9.0	11.5	15.6	12.6
short-term[a]	−0.4	2.8	1.9	−3.7	−0.4
Funds from insurance enterprises	0.5	1.2	0.9	0.5	−0.4
Bonds	0.5	2.3	0.7	−0.4	−0.7
Shares	1.5	1.9	2.4	0.6	1.1
Other	1.2	3.0	2.6	3.9	−4.1
of which:					
foreign trade credit	−1.2	0.0	−1.1	−1.5	−2.2
Total	100.0	100.0	100.1	100.1	100.1

Note: [a] 'Short-term' is defined as a loan with an original maturity of less than one year, while 'long-term' is a loan with an original maturity of more than one year.
Source: Own calculations based on the capital finance account of the Deutsche Bundesbank.

to producing enterprises: such loans have in fact fallen as a proportion of the total assets of insurance enterprises.

Insurance enterprises mainly lend to non-financial enterprises in the form of loans against borrowers' notes (Schuldscheindarlehen). These are long-term loans, usually with a minimum size of DM 1 million, which can be sold, with the borrower's consent, to another party. Borrowers' notes have largely replaced bonds as a means of raising long-term finance by non-financial enterprises in Germany as they do not incur issue costs and their capital value does not alter with interest rate changes since they are not traded. However, insurance enterprises lend more in the form of borrowers' notes to banks than they do to non-financial enterprises (see Wiegers, 1987, p. 230). The capital finance account of the Deutsche Bundesbank shows that funds placed with insurance enterprises by the domestic non-financial sector have increased, as a proportion of bank deposits by the domestic non-financial sector, from 17.8% in 1960 to 56.4% in 1989. This increase in insurance enterprises' share of funds

Table 3.3. *Gross sources of finance for investment, German producing enterprises sector, 1950–1989, %*

	1950–1989	1950–1959	1960–1969	1970–1979	1980–1989
Internally-generated funds	61.0	64.1	62.6	55.6	61.7
Provisions for pensions by enterprises	3.0	2.7	1.7	3.3	3.8
Capital transfers from government	4.5	1.0	3.4	6.1	6.9
Bank borrowing	18.1	17.5	19.2	20.8	15.7
of which:					
long-term[a]	7.4	10.0	8.0	7.2	4.7
short-term[a]	10.7	7.5	11.2	13.6	11.0
Funds from insurance enterprises	1.4	1.8	1.7	1.5	0.6
Bonds	1.5	3.0	1.3	0.7	1.1
Shares	2.4	2.3	3.1	2.1	2.5
Other	8.1	7.7	7.0	9.9	7.8
of which:					
foreign trade credit	2.5	4.6	1.4	2.6	1.1
Total	100.0	100.1	100.0	100.0	100.1

Note: [a] 'Short-term' is defined as a loan with an original maturity of less than one year, while 'long-term' is a loan with an original maturity of more than one year.
Source: Own calculations based on the capital finance account of the Deutsche Bundesbank.

flowing into the financial institutions sector has, however, largely been absorbed by greater flows to banks from insurance enterprises, in the form of both deposits with banks and purchases of bank bonds. Insurance enterprise loans to the domestic non-financial sector have actually fallen, as a proportion of bank loans to the domestic non-financial sector, from 9.3% in 1960 to 6.4% in 1989. The overall conclusion is that the component of the German system of pension provision which involves contributions to life assurance enterprises and private pension funds is not directly a significant source of finance for investment by non-financial enterprises, although it provides investment finance indirectly via the banking system.

The third component of the German pension system involves enterprise pension schemes, of which there are four types. The first, and most important, takes the form of a direct commitment by a firm to its employees: an enterprise makes pension provision for its employees by investing its contributions to employee pensions within the enterprise itself. The pension payments are financed by making provisions in the enterprise's balance sheet, calculated by the expectancy-cover principle, and using (since 1981) a 6% interest rate. When the provisions are made by the firm they reduce its profits, and hence its tax, while when the pensions are paid out provisions are adjusted with no effect on profits. Employees incur no personal income tax liability when the provisions are made, but when the pensions are paid the recipients are liable to pay income tax on them after deduction of an allowance. In practice, however, the pensions are often tax-free because they are usually received together with the social security pension, most of which is not liable to income tax, so that the taxable component of pensions received is not large enough to make the recipients subject to income tax.

The next most important type of enterprise pension scheme is one in which a firm commissions a legally independent pension fund to operate its pension scheme. The contributions of the enterprise, which are calculated on the expectancy-cover principle, reduce its profits and hence tax, but in contrast to direct commitments these contributions are treated as employee remuneration and hence are subject to income tax. However, when the pensions are paid out they are subject to the same income tax treatment as the social security pension, and only a small part is liable to tax. An enterprise can borrow from the pension fund which operates its pension scheme, but the pension fund's investment policy is subject to the standard regulation of insurance enterprises which precludes large exposures to any single firm.

A third and similar type of enterprise pension scheme is direct insurance, in which a firm concludes a contract with a life assurance enterprise in favour of its employees. The tax treatment of the contributions is the same as for independent pension funds. This form of pension scheme is more important for smaller firms because the size of the financial burden is known precisely, with the risks of pension provision being assumed by an insurer outside the enterprise, in contrast to either direct commitments or pension funds, where enterprises have a legal obligation to provide the stated pension benefits.

Finally, enterprises may commission a legally independent provident fund to handle its pension scheme. This arrangement is very similar to that in which a pension fund operates the enterprise pension scheme, but since the introduction of the Occupational Pensions Act in 1974 only a very limited part of an enterprise's contributions to a provident fund have been tax-deductible as operational expenditure, and hence this type of enterprise pension scheme has become rather unimportant.

Only limited data is available on the quantitative significance of these various enterprise pension schemes. According to the Deutsche Bundesbank (1984b), at the end of 1982 the total capital formed in the context of enterprise pension schemes amounted to DM 200 billion, of which almost DM 140 billion was in the form of provisions for pensions in direct commitments and about DM 40 billion was in claims on pension funds. This compares with a total capital stock formed by life assurance enterprises of approximately DM 200 billion in the same year. A more recent estimate[1] puts the volume of different forms of enterprise pensions in 1987 at DM 181.3 billion for direct commitment provisions, DM 68.0 billion for pension funds, and DM 28.7 billion for provident funds. No estimate was available for direct insurance. It is clear that provisions for pensions in the form of direct commitments are quantitatively much the most important type of enterprise pension scheme in Germany.

The range of benefits available under enterprise pension schemes varies considerably, largely because each enterprise has to finance its pension scheme from its own resources. The Occupational Pensions Act does, however, specify some minimum requirements for such schemes, of which one of the most important is that expectations of enterprise pensions become non-forfeitable if the employee reaches the age of 35 and the pension commitment has been in being either for ten years or for at least three years if the employee has been with the firm for at least twelve years. The amount of pension right that is non-forfeitable depends on the ratio of years of actual employment to the maximum possible years of employment with the firm. This non-forfeitable regulation mitigates the possible barrier to job mobility that enterprise pension schemes might create.

For enterprise pension schemes that take the form of direct commitments, contributions to pension funds, or contributions to provident funds, the liability for all claims remains with the enterprise. The question thus arises of what happens to such pensions if a firm becomes insolvent. The Occupational Pensions Act of 1974 established the Pensionssicherungsverein (PSV)[2] to protect employee pension rights in the event of a firm becoming insolvent. The PSV is a privately run mutual insurance fund of which every firm offering a pension scheme subject to insolvency risk has to be a member. The PSV takes over the pensions and unforfeitable pension claims of all firms which go bankrupt or enter official settlement in court procedures. It can also take over the pensions of firms in financial distress but not yet in insolvency procedures although, for obvious moral hazard reasons, this is rare (less than 2.5% of all cases in which the PSV took over firms' pensions in 1975–1987 were ones where the firm was not in insolvency procedures). All members have to inform the PSV of the

---

[1] From the Annual Report of the Pensionssicherungsverein 1987 and Gesamtverband der Versicherungswirtschaft (1988).
[2] Pension Guarantee Association.

present value of their pension obligations each year. These present values serve as the sole basis for calculating the contributions required to cover the pensions of insolvent firms: no risk premia reflecting the possible different likelihood of insolvency for different firms are used. The absence of any risk premia minimises administration costs in terms of collecting information about member firms and possible legal disputes about risk assessments, but it does create potential moral hazard problems. The total contributions in any year are equal to the present value of pensions of all retired persons whose firm went bankrupt in that year plus the present value of pensions of those who worked for a firm which has already gone bankrupt and are reaching retirement age in that year. The PSV, therefore, protects pension rights in the event of an enterprise becoming insolvent, but does not monitor the investment of pension provisions within enterprises.

This discussion of the German system of pension provision reveals the difficulties of arriving at an appropriate classification of provisions for pensions in the form of direct commitments by enterprises when analysing the sources of finance for investment. If an enterprise makes pension provision for its employees in the form of direct commitments, some part of its internally-generated funds are treated as pension contributions on behalf of its employees, and the enterprise's accounting profits are correspondingly reduced. But the funds which constitute these pension provisions do not leave the enterprise: they remain at the enterprise's disposal for the finance of its investment. Although these pension provisions involve a liability to pay out pensions in the future, the use of these provisions by the enterprise is not subject to any external monitoring, and the liability involved is typically a long-term one, with no requirement to make regular annual payments until employees reach retirement. This form of investment finance does involve an eventual liability to pay out funds, but in other respects its characteristics are different from those of debt finance. Since the appropriate classification of these pension provisions is not obvious, they are shown as a separate source of finance in the analysis of the following section. The reader can make his or her own decision as to whether they should be regarded as internally-generated funds or debt.

The finance of aggregate investment by German non-financial enterprises, 1950–1989

In this section, national accounts flow of funds data is used to analyse the finance of investment by German non-financial enterprises over the period 1950–1989. The source of this data is the capital finance account of the Deutsche Bundesbank, which shows the sources and uses of finance by different sectors in the German economy, and the channels through which individual sectors have supplied and demanded funds. The transactions shown in the capital finance account are valued at current purchase and sales prices.[3]

In the capital finance account of the Deutsche Bundesbank, the non-financial enterprise sector consists of all economic units whose main function is that of producing goods and non-financial services for sale: it is divided into producing enterprises and housing. 'Producing enterprises' include private and all public enterprises (regardless of their legal form): self-employed persons and partnerships are also included if their transactions relate to production and capital formation. 'Housing' is defined along functional lines: it comprises the industrial and non-industrial construction and letting of dwellings, and hence all financial operations relating to new housing and the stock of existing dwellings. Since the finance of investment in housing involves rather different considerations than does the finance of investment for the production of other forms of output, we base our analysis of the finance of investment by German non-financial enterprises on data for the producing enterprises sector. An important point to note about the definition of the producing enterprises sector in Germany is that it is extremely broad by comparison with the definition of corresponding sectors in other countries, particularly because it includes unincorporated businesses.

Tables 3.2 and 3.3 show summary details of the finance of investment by producing enterprises over the period 1950–1989.[4] Table 3.2 shows the net sources of finance – the contribution of different sources of funds to the finance of physical investment only – and table 3.3 shows the gross sources of finance – the contribution of different sources to the finance of physical and financial investment. The importance of different sources of finance over the period 1950–1989 as a whole, or in individual decades, is measured in terms of weighted average figures. The figure for a particular source of finance is an average given by weighting the contribution of that source to physical investment (in the case of net sources) or to physical and financial investment (in the case of gross sources) in a year by the constant price value of physical, or physical and financial, investment in that year. Thus the weighted average figure for a particular source of finance over the period 1950-1989 is computed as follows:

---

[3] Full details of the capital finance account of the Deutsche Bundesbank can be found in Deutsche Bundesbank (1988).
[4] We are very grateful to Ian Alexander for his help with the calculations reported in Tables 3.2 and 3.3.

$$\sum_{t=1950}^{t=1989} i_t^j \frac{P_t}{P_{1960}} \bigg/ \sum_{t=1950}^{t=1989} I_t \frac{P_t}{P_{1960}}.$$

where i_t^j denotes the amount of finance of type j in year t (measured in current prices of year t), $I_t = \sum_{j=1}^{n} i_t^j$ (there are n different types of finance), and P_t denotes the capital goods price index in year t. The weighted average figures for the individual decades are computed in the same way, with appropriate changes of years. Hence the weighted average figure for a particular source of finance shows the contribution of that source of finance (measured in constant prices) over the relevant period to either total physical investment (measured in constant prices), in table 3.2, or total physical and financial investment (measured in constant prices), in table 3.3. This way of computing an average over a number of years seemed to be the most suitable one for identifying the importance of different sources of finance for investment over a reasonably long period. The broad conclusions drawn in the analysis below are not, however, sensitive to this particular choice of average. The figures for the importance of different sources of finance obtained from an unweighted, current price average are very similar to those shown in tables 3.2 and 3.3.

We begin detailed analysis of the financing of investment by the producing enterprises sector with a comparison of the net and gross figures in tables 3.2 and 3.3 for the entire period 1950–1989. If a sector undertakes any investment in financial assets, it is inevitable that internally-generated funds will be a smaller gross source of finance than it is a net source. Tables 3.2 and 3.3 show that over the period as a whole internally-generated funds were, indeed, a considerably smaller percentage of producing enterprises' investment in physical and financial assets than of physical investment alone. Long-term bank borrowing was also noticeably smaller as a gross than as a net source of finance. The two sources of finance which, correspondingly, were considerably larger as a percentage of investment in physical and financial assets than of physical investment were short-term bank borrowing and the category 'other', which mainly comprises financial transactions with foreigners. The significant differences between the net and gross sources of finance for the producing enterprises sectors over the period therefore arise for two reasons. One is that the producing enterprises sector tended to accumulate foreign financial assets which, when netted off the foreign financial liabilities it also accumulated, made this a relatively small net source of finance. The other is that the producing enterprises sector tended to deposit more short-term funds with banks than it borrowed short-term from banks. Netting short-term deposits from short-term borrowing obscures the fact that short-term bank borrowing was quite an important source of finance for some producing enterprises even though it was more than offset by short-term deposits with banks by other producing enterprises. As a consequence, overall bank borrowing was more important as a gross than as a net source of finance over the period 1950–1989.

Analysing the finance of investment by the producing enterprises sector in terms of the net sources of finance may, therefore, understate the importance of short-term bank borrowing and financial transactions with foreigners. But the fundamental question that is being analysed is how producing enterprises' investment in physical assets (i.e. gross fixed capital formation and stockbuilding) has been financed, and for this question it is the net sources of finance figures which are the most useful. Bearing the above qualifications in mind, we now focus on table 3.2.

Over the period 1950–1989, internally-generated funds (the sum of retained profits and depreciation) were by far the largest net source of finance for investment in physical assets by the producing enterprises sector. Indeed, it can be argued that the internally-generated funds figures in tables 3.2 and 3.3 underestimate the importance of this source of finance. As we saw in the preceding section, provisions for pensions by enterprises, although carrying with them a liability in the form of commitments to pay pensions to employees in the future, are effectively equivalent to internally-generated funds as a source of investment finance. Provisions for pensions by enterprises were a non-trivial source of finance for producing enterprises over the period 1950–1989, amounting to more than 30% of the net bank borrowing figure.

Long-term bank borrowing was the next most important net source of finance after internally-generated funds over the period 1950–1989. Overall bank borrowing was a slightly smaller net source of finance, reflecting the negative figure for short-term bank borrowing as a net source of funds for producing enterprises. However, it should be remembered here that the net source of finance figures may understate the significance of short-term bank borrowing for particular firms. Capital transfers from the government were the next most important net source of finance for the producing enterprises sector. This item needs to be interpreted carefully. It includes government subsidies to farmers, mining and shipping firms, the Federal Railways, and other public enterprises. It also includes some fictitious flows when parts of the assets of a single sector have to be recorded in different sectors because of the definition of sectors in the capital finance account: for example, the profits of public enterprises are shifted from the government sector to the producing enterprises sector by means of a capital transfer. Hence the internally-generated funds of government-owned enterprises such as the Federal Railways and the Federal Post Office are contained in the capital transfer figures. The capital transfers from government figures therefore overestimate the significance of government subsidies as a source of finance.

Internally-generated funds, provisions for pensions by enterprises, bank borrowing, and capital transfers from government together accounted for 96.5% of the net sources of finance for the producing enterprises sector over the period 1950–1989. The remaining net sources shown in table 3.2 – bonds, shares, funds from insurance enterprises,[5] and 'other' – together accounted for only 3.5% of the total investment in physical assets over this period. One qualification which must be noted here is the possible understatement of the significance of the category 'other' by the net source of finance figures. Another qualification is that the figure for shares refers only to external equity issued by public companies, and so underestimates overall external equity finance: external equity raised by private companies is not identified separately, and instead appears in the category internally-generated funds, the computation of which includes residuals arising from lack of data.

The weighted average sources of finance figures in tables 3.2 and 3.3 for the four decades separately show that the relative importance of different sources of finance did not alter very much over the period 1950–1989 as a whole. Internally-generated funds were relatively less important as a net source of finance in 1970–79, and relatively more important in 1980–89, than in the period as a whole. The importance of internally-generated funds in the individual decades was somewhat different in terms of gross sources: they were relatively most important in 1950–59, and least important in 1970–79. The importance of overall bank borrowing changed only slightly over the period: both as a net and as a gross source of finance, it was somewhat more important in 1960–69 and 1970–79 than in 1950–59 and 1980–89. The relative stability of the overall bank borrowing figure, however, conceals more pronounced variation in the short- and long-term bank borrowing figures. Capital transfers from government grew noticeably in importance over the period as both a net and a gross source of finance, while provisions for pensions by enterprises were a little more important (in terms of both net and gross sources) at the end of the period than at the beginning.

Internally-generated funds, provisions for pensions by enterprises, bank borrowing, and capital transfers from government together contributed a steadily rising proportion of the net sources of finance for investment by the producing enterprises sector over 1950–1989, increasing from 91.5% in 1950–59 to 104.2% in 1980–89. The decline in the contribution of all

---

[5] This category also includes funds from private pension funds and building and loan associations.

other net sources of finance over the period is mainly accounted for by the category 'other' which, as has been noted, corresponds to financial transactions with foreigners. There has also been a steady decline in the importance of bonds and funds from insurance enterprises as net sources of finance over the period, although these have always been very small net sources of finance. Shares, which have also been a small net source over the period as a whole, were somewhat less important in 1970–79 and 1980–89 than in 1950–59 and 1960–69, although there is no clear downward trend in their importance.

The overall conclusion which emerges from tables 3.2 and 3.3 is that over the period 1950–89 German producing enterprises have financed most of their investment with internally-generated funds. This conclusion is unambiguous, even though the figures shown in the two tables are subject to various biases as estimates of the true significance of internally-generated funds. On the one hand, the figures are underestimates, because some part of capital transfers from government consists of the internally-generated funds of public enterprises. It could also be argued that the provisions for pensions by enterprises are, in effect, equivalent to internally-generated funds. On the other hand, the figures are overestimates, because the capital finance account of the Deutsche Bundesbank only records as new equity finance that part of this source of funds which takes the form of sales of shares by public limited companies. New equity finance raised by private limited companies is contained in the internally-generated funds figure, which is measured as a residual. With several possible biases operating in different directions, it is impossible to say whether the figures in tables 3.2 and 3.3 are maximum or minimum estimates of the true importance of internally-generated funds. However, these biases are not large enough to alter the conclusion that the majority of German producing enterprises investment has been financed by internally-generated funds.

Although bank borrowing is the largest external source of finance for investment in Germany, it is very much less significant quantitatively than internally-generated funds, particularly as a source of finance for physical investment, of which only 11.4% over 1950–89 was financed by bank loans. Whether bank loans are nevertheless a relatively more important source of investment finance in Germany requires a comparison with other countries, to which we turn in the next section.

Before making international comparisons, however, there is one further question about the importance of banks as suppliers of finance for investment in Germany which needs to be discussed. The flow of funds data that have been analysed reveal the magnitude of bank borrowing, but they say nothing about what proportion of bank finance for investment is provided in the form of equity rather than debt. Is the amount of equity finance provided by banks in Germany large enough to make the bank loan figures in tables 3.2 and 3.3 a significant underestimate of the importance of total external finance for investment supplied by banks?

The only available data on the relative importance of equity and debt finance supplied by banks comes from the banking statistics collected by the Deutsche Bundesbank, which is balance sheet rather than flow of funds data. This data source shows, for various dates, the book value of bank loans to domestic non-bank enterprises and self-employed persons (excluding housing loans),[6] and the book value of bank holdings of equity in domestic non-bank enterprises. Bank holdings of equity are classified under two headings: marketable equities and participations.[7] 'Marketable equities' are equity holdings purely in the form of a portfolio investment by banks, without an intention by the banks to use the ownership stake conferred by the equity holding to participate actively in the enterprise. 'Participations' are equity holdings by banks where such an intention exists. As a proportion of the book value of bank lending to domestic enterprises and self-employed persons (excluding housing loans), the sum of the book value of bank holdings of marketable equities in domestic enterprises and bank participations in domestic enterprises was 3.20% in 1970, and 3.05% in 1988.[8] This suggests that bank equity finance is very small by comparison with bank loan finance. Since these proportions are obtained from balance sheet data it is necessary to consider the possibility that they do not correctly reflect the relative importance of the flows of bank equity and bank loan finance. For both equity and loans, the book value will reflect the flows of finance which have given rise to the stocks held at a particular date. Since bank loans invariably have a finite term, while bank equity holdings do not, it would seem likely that any bias involved in making inferences about the relative magnitudes of flows of finance from the relative size of the stock figures will exaggerate the importance of equity finance. It is, therefore, reasonable to conclude from these balance sheet proportions that the supply of finance for investment by German banks in the form of equity is very small compared to that in the form of debt, and hence that the bank borrowing figures in tables 3.2 and 3.3 do not significantly underestimate the overall importance of bank finance for investment in Germany.

[6] Data on this are published in the statistical section of the *Monthly Report of the Deutsche Bundesbank*.

[7] Data on bank holdings of marketable equities in domestic enterprises are published in the *Monthly Report of the Deutsche Bundesbank*; data on bank participations in domestic enterprises was kindly provided to us by the Bundesbank.

[8] Data are not available for the period before 1970.

The finance of investment by non-financial enterprises in Germany and the UK

We have argued above that international comparisons of the finance of investment are best made using flow of funds data. In this section we assess whether bank borrowing is an especially important source of investment finance in Germany, by comparing the pattern of finance for investment by the aggregate non-financial enterprise sector in Germany with that in the UK on the basis of national accounts flow of funds data.

Although the flow of funds approach provides the best basis for international comparisons, there are still a number of problems involved in making such comparisons. One problem concerns the definition of the non-financial enterprise sector. The German producing enterprises sector includes all public enterprises and all unincorporated enterprises. UK national accounts data do not permit a precisely comparable definition of the non-financial enterprise sector in the UK. It is possible to identify all privately- and publicly-owned corporations from UK national accounts data, but unincorporated enterprises are included in the UK household sector and cannot be identified separately. The comparisons which follow are therefore based on a definition of the aggregate non-financial enterprise sector which, for Germany, includes unincorporated enterprises but, for the UK, excludes them. A second problem arises from the fact that all national accounts flows of funds data obtain some figures as residuals from other components of the national accounts. This reduces the reliability of national accounts flow of funds data generally and, because the allocation of such residuals is not standardised across different countries' national accounts, it creates another complication when making international comparisons. The UK figures have a single large statistical adjustment to allow for problems with the quality of national accounts-based flow of funds data, while Germany allocates balancing items to several financing categories. Despite these problems, however, it is still possible to use national accounts flow of funds data to make international comparisons, although care must be exercised when so doing.

The data available for the UK only cover the period 1970–1987. Table 3.4 therefore shows weighted averages, over the period 1970–1987 for the UK and 1970–1989 for Germany, computed in the same way as for tables 3.2 and 3.3, for net and gross sources of finance for investment by the non-financial enterprise sector in the two countries. There are some differences in the financing categories shown for Germany and the UK in table 3.4. UK companies do not retain funds set aside for employees' pensions for their own use, so there is no UK entry corresponding to the German provisions for pensions. The UK data do not distinguish between

Table 3.4. *Net and gross sources of finance for investment by the non-financial enterprise sector in Germany (1970–1989) and the UK (1970–1987), %*

A Net sources			
Germany (1970–1989)		UK (1970–1987)	
Internally-generated funds	76.0	Internally-generated funds	87.9
Provisions for pensions	4.6		
Capital transfers	8.5	Capital transfers	8.3
Bank loans	11.0	Loans from financial	15.4
Insurance enterprise loans	0.0	institutions	
Bonds	−0.6	Bonds	0.1
Shares	0.9	Shares	−1.3
Trade credit	−1.9	Trade credit	−2.1
Other	1.5	Other	2.4
		Statistical adjustment	−10.7
Total	100.0	Total	100.0

B Gross sources			
Germany (1970–1989)		UK (1970–1987)	
Internally-generated funds	58.8	Internally-generated funds	59.9
Provisions for pensions	3.6		
Capital transfers	6.6	Capital transfers	5.7
Bank loans	18.0	Loans from financial	27.2
Insurance enterprise loans	1.0	institutions	
Bonds	0.9	Bonds	2.4
Shares	2.3	Shares	6.5
Trade credit	1.8	Trade credit	3.2
Other	7.0	Other	2.4
		Statistical adjustment	−7.3
Total	100.0	Total	100.0

Source: Germany, own calculations based on the capital finance account of the Deutsche Bundesbank; UK, own calculations based on OECD, *National Accounts*, vol. II.

loans made by banks and those made by other financial institutions. As is shown in chapter 5, the definition of the banking sector in Germany is much wider than in the UK so that, as is clear from table 3.4, almost all loans to non-financial enterprises in Germany are made by banks. The fact that bank loans cannot be distinguished separately in the UK does not, therefore, cause any serious problems of comparability. As we have noted, the UK data have a single explicit statistical adjustment figure, while the German data have balancing items included implicitly in several financing categories. Table 3.4 shows that the size of this adjustment for the UK is quite large.

Internally-generated funds were the largest net and gross source of finance in both Germany and the UK. At first glance it appears from table 3.4 that internally-generated funds were a larger net source of finance in the UK. However, the large statistical adjustment for the UK must be borne in mind: if this negative adjustment is allocated proportionately across the financing categories, the figure for internally-generated funds as a net source of finance falls from 87.9% to 79.4% – not much above the German figure. There are two other possible reasons why the figures in table 3.4 may overestimate the difference between Germany and the UK in the importance of internally-generated funds as a source of finance. One is that, while the capital transfers figure for the UK includes only subsidies, the figure for Germany includes both subsidies and the internally-generated funds of public enterprises.[9] The other is that provisions for pensions in Germany can be argued to be effectively an internal source of funds, as we have noted. However, the fact that the German internally-generated funds figure also includes new equity raised by private limited companies must also be borne in mind: this acts to offset the two factors just mentioned. Although it is not possible to be absolutely definite, it seems likely that there was little difference in the importance of internally-generated funds as a net source of finance between Germany and the UK. As a gross source of finance, internally-generated funds may have been somewhat less important in the UK than in Germany. The figure for internally-generated funds as a gross source of finance falls from 59.9% to 55.8% – less than the German figure – if the negative statistical adjustment is allocated proportionately across the categories.

After internally-generated funds, the next most important source of finance in both countries (on either a net or a gross basis) was loans from banks and other financial institutions. Contrary to conventional wisdom, table 3.4 shows that these loans were more important as a source of finance in the UK, accounting for 15.4% as a net source, compared to 11.0% for the sum of bank and insurance enterprise loans in Germany,[10] and 27.2% as a gross source, compared to 19.0% for the sum of German bank and insurance enterprise loans. The negative statistical adjustment figures for the UK may overstate the difference, but if these adjustments are allocated proportionately across the financing categories, the loans from financial institutions figure for the UK becomes 13.9% as a net

[9] See discussion on p. 61 above.
[10] The actual figure for insurance enterprise loans as a net source of finance was 0.01%.

source and 25.3% as a gross source, still larger than the corresponding German figures.

In both Germany and the UK the other sources of finance shown in table 3.4 were rather unimportant for the aggregate non-financial enterprise sector. One point which is worth noting is that as a gross source of finance shares were more important in the UK, but as a net source of finance shares were more important in Germany, though the difference was not large in either case. In the UK, shares were actually a negative net source of finance, reflecting the funds spent by UK companies on the acquisition of other companies' shares in mergers and takeovers.

Given the difficulties involved in making international comparisons of the finance of investment, it would be inappropriate to attempt to draw anything more than broad conclusions from the figures shown in table 3.4. The broad conclusions which can be drawn are, however, striking. The sources of finance for investment by the aggregate non-financial enterprise sector in Germany and the UK in the 1970s and 1980s were remarkably similar. In particular, there is no evidence to support the widely-held view that bank loans are a more important source of finance for investment in Germany than in the UK. If anything, this comparison of the flows of funds involved in financing investment by non-financial enterprises in the 1970s and 1980s suggests that loans by financial institutions were a more important source of finance in the UK than were loans by banks and insurance enterprises in Germany. It is clear that, in terms of the overall importance of loans from financial institutions as a source of finance for investment, there is no more reason to categorise Germany as having a bank-based system of investment finance than there is to categorise the UK in this way.

Corbett (1993) has analysed the sources of finance for investment of the Japanese non-financial enterprise sector over the period 1970–1989 using the same approach that we have adopted in this chapter, based on national accounts flow of funds data. It is therefore possible to compare the sources of finance for investment by non-financial enterprises in Germany and Japan. As always, there are some comparability problems: the Japanese non-financial enterprise sector excludes unincorporated enterprises and large public enterprises. But these problems are not large enough to weaken the main conclusion that results from a comparison of the sources of finance for investment in Germany and Japan. Corbett finds that the weighted average figure for loans (predominantly direct loans from banks) as a net source of finance for Japanese non-financial enterprises was 30.5%, while as a gross source of finance it was 34.5%. These figures are much higher than the German figures for loans from banks and insurance enterprises, which are 11.0% (net) and 19.0%

(gross). Internally-generated funds were correspondingly less important as a source of finance in Japan. This comparison shows that, in terms of the importance of bank loans as a source of finance for investment in the period 1970–1989, it is quite incorrect to categorise Germany and Japan together as having bank-based systems of investment finance.

Conclusion

The analysis in this chapter has shown that there is no evidence to suggest that the aggregate non-financial enterprise sector in Germany finances an especially large proportion of its investment using bank loans. Over the period 1950–1989, bank borrowing accounted on average for 11.7% of the investment in physical assets by the producing enterprises sector, and 18.1% of that sector's investment in physical and financial assets. There was some variation in the contribution of bank loans to investment finance over the four decades – bank borrowing was relatively more important in the 1960s and the 1970s than in the 1950s and the 1980s – but this variation was not large. Although the problems of comparability of data mean that great care has to be exercised when making international comparisons of the finance of investment, the evidence discussed in this chapter suggests that in the 1970s and 1980s loans from financial institutions have been a more important source of investment finance for the UK non-financial enterprise sector than loans from banks and insurance enterprises have been for the German one. Furthermore, the evidence available on the relative importance of loan and equity finance supplied to enterprises by German banks, though limited, suggests that bank equity finance is only a very small proportion of bank loans. It cannot, therefore, be argued that the bank loan figures in this chapter significantly underestimate the overall importance in Germany of bank-supplied external finance for investment.

The similarity between the sources of finance for investment of the German and UK aggregate non-financial enterprise sectors revealed by the analysis in this chapter, and in particular the lack of any evidence that bank loans are more important in Germany, casts a great deal of doubt on one of the basic components of the conventional view of the German system of investment finance. It is, however, necessary to go beyond an aggregate analysis of German banks' role as suppliers of external finance before definitely concluding that the conventional view is mistaken. German firms may prefer, if possible, to finance investment with internally-generated funds, but find that bank finance is more easily available in circumstances when it is required – such as major expansion, financial distress, or starting-up – than do firms in other economies. It is possible that such a difference between the German system of finance for investment and, say, that in the UK would not be apparent in the aggregate finance for investment data analysed in this chapter. The following chapters consider various aspects of German banks' supply of external finance to firms at a more disaggregated level.

4 Legal forms of enterprise in Germany, and their implications for the role of the German financial system

Introduction

In chapter 3 the finance of investment by the aggregate non-financial enterprise sector in Germany was analysed and compared to that in the UK. It is, however, important to examine the finance of investment by German firms at a more disaggregated level. A distinctive feature of the organisation of production in Germany, by comparison with the UK, is that a much larger proportion of the output of the German economy is accounted for by partnerships and sole proprietorships as opposed to limited liability companies. This is the reason for the difference, noted in chapter 3, between the German and UK national accounts definitions of the non-financial enterprise sector. Unincorporated enterprises are included in the household sector in the UK, but in Germany the capital finance account of the Deutsche Bundesbank includes self-employed persons and partnerships in the producing enterprises sector if their transactions relate to production and capital formation. The implications for the German system of investment finance of the difference between Germany and the UK in the relative importance of various types of firm are the subject of this chapter.

The German system of universal banks with representation on supervisory boards was argued, in chapter 2, to create the potential to exploit economies of scale and scope in information-collection and the exercise of the rights attached to debt and equity finance to change the management of a firm. A particular component of this general argument concerns the delegated exercise of equity's control rights by banks. If the equity capital of a firm is widely dispersed among a large number of savers, each owning a very small fraction of the total, and each protected by limited liability, then the incentives for these savers to monitor the performance of the firm's managers will be weak. The threat of dismissal at the annual meeting of the suppliers of equity finance will consequently not be an effective mechanism for inducing managers to act in the interest of the firm's owners. The question then arises what other mechanisms might constrain the managers of such firms to run them in the interests of the suppliers of equity finance. The widely-held view of the merits of the German system of investment finance sees the proxy voting rights and supervisory board representation of German banks as enabling them to exercise equity's control rights on behalf of individual equity holders. The role of German banks in thus constraining the managers of firms with a widely-dispersed equity ownership is seen as superior to the alternative on which the UK has to rely, the hostile takeover mechanism.

The extent to which there is a role for German banks as delegated exercisers of equity's control rights depends, of course, on the importance in the German economy of firms for which the problem of inadequate monitoring and control of managers by suppliers of equity finance arises. Such firms are those for which it is possible to buy and sell ownership claims in an active market – listed public companies. As the present chapter shows, however, listed public companies are much less important in Germany than in the UK. This suggests that there is less scope for agency problems in the relationship between owners and managers of firms to arise in Germany, and hence that the benefits to the German economy of German banks' delegated exercise of equity's control rights may not be large.

The second section of this chapter discusses the different legal forms which business enterprises can take, with particular reference to how a firm's legal form may affect its access to finance and the extent to which agency problems between its owners and its managers are likely to arise. The third section describes the different legal forms of enterprise in Germany and their importance in the German economy. The fourth section compares the relative importance of different legal forms of enterprise in Germany and the UK. The fifth section analyses the available evidence on the sources of finance of different legal forms in Germany. The sixth section draws a brief conclusion.

Legal forms of business organisation

Business enterprises typically take one of three major forms: a sole proprietorship, a partnership, or a limited liability company. As its name suggests, the first of these is a single-person firm, in which one individual both owns and manages the business. The single owner-manager of a sole proprietorship has unlimited liability for its debts. A partnership is an association of two or more individuals who own the firm and share in its profits in agreed proportions. Some members of a partnership may have limited liability for the partnership's debts, but such limited partners are subject to restrictions on the extent to which they can be involved in the active management of the firm. A partnership thus has the defining characteristic that its managers are also owners, and they have unlimited liability for its debts. A limited liability company is an association of individuals who own the firm and share in its profits according to the proportion of the firm's capital they own: the owners of a limited liability company have limited liability for the debts of the company. The most they can lose is the amount they have contributed, or undertaken to contribute, to the company's capital – they cannot be called on to pay any of the company's debts out of their personal assets.

How are the possible sources of investment finance for a firm affected by the legal form it takes? A sole proprietorship can raise equity finance from the resources of the firm or its owner. It cannot, by definition, raise equity finance from any other source. External finance (that is, from sources other than the owner of the firm) has to be raised in the form of debt. A sole proprietorship can borrow either from individuals or from financial intermediaries. For reasons concerned with asymmetric information and the costs of information-collection, as discussed in chapter 2, a sole proprietorship's borrowing from individuals is likely to be from the owner-manager's family or close friends, while its borrowing from a wider range of individuals is likely to take place through a financial intermediary.

In the case of a partnership, there are more possible sources of finance. In addition to raising funds from the resources of the firm or the existing partners, and by borrowing from individuals or financial intermediaries, a partnership can also raise external finance by increasing the number of partners. In the absence of limited liability, however, the scope for raising finance by taking on new partners is not great. Without limited liability, an individual saver cannot reduce the risk of his or her portfolio by spreading his or her holdings across a large number of firms, because however small an individual's holding in a firm, all the individual's wealth could be lost if the firm was unable to pay its debts. In the absence of limited liability, there is a strong incentive for an individual saver to supply funds only to a very small number of firms, since this enables the individual to monitor the firm's affairs closely and to have a large enough ownership stake to be able to control its actions. The absence of limited liability in a partnership also creates risk for the existing partners when they raise finance by taking on new partners. Since all partners are jointly liable for the debts of an unlimited partnership, raising funds by taking on new partners means that the existing partners are exposing themselves to the risk of losing not only their investment in the firm but also their personal assets as the result of a poor decision by the new partners.

Because of these difficulties, limited liability is usually regarded as an essential condition for a firm to be able to raise significant amounts of external finance in the form of equity. Limited liability reduces the risks faced by individual savers when supplying funds to a firm which, because of its size, they will find difficult to monitor or control. It also reduces the risks faced by existing owners of a firm in taking on new owners. Limited liability thus makes it easier for a firm to raise external equity finance for its investment. One consequence of limited liability, however, is that the number of owners of a firm may be so large, and their individual holdings in the firm so small that, as was discussed in chapter 2, the management of the firm is not subject to any control by the owners.

Although limited liability may result in the separation of ownership from control in large firms, it is important to realise that limited liability is only a necessary, not a sufficient, condition for this problem to arise. The limited partners in a limited partnership have limited liability, but are prevented from taking any active part in managing the firm. The managers of a limited partnership are unlimited partners: they are owners of the firm, with unlimited liability for its debts. Hence the agency problems which result from the separation of ownership and control will not be significant for firms of this type. Such agency problems are also unlikely to be serious for private, as distinct from public, companies. A private company is one in which the owners of the company can control the transfer of ownership of the company, thus enabling a family firm, for example, to retain ownership within the family. Private companies cannot offer shares for sale to the public. These features of the private company mean that it is unlikely to be able to raise a significant amount of external finance in the form of sales of equity to individual savers, since restrictions on transferability of ownership imply that a holding in a private company is an illiquid asset for an individual saver. Private companies are therefore likely to depend largely on financial intermediaries as a source of external finance for investment. The consequence of these features of a private company is that such a company is unlikely to have a large number of owners, so the agency problems arising from the absence of incentives for owners to monitor managers are unlikely to arise. It is only for public companies, which cannot restrict the transferability of their shares, are able to offer shares for sale to the public, and therefore can raise significant amounts of external equity finance from individual savers, that such agency problems are likely to be serious.

We now turn to a more detailed consideration of the different legal forms of enterprise in Germany, and their relative importance within the German economy.

Table 4.1. *Turnover accounted for by different legal forms of enterprise in Germany, 1950, 1972 and 1986, %*

Type of legal form	1950	1972	1986
AG	16.5	19.1	21.1
GmbH	15.4	17.1	25.5
OHG	{ 18.6	{ 32.1	6.8
KG			24.0
Sole proprietor	36.9	23.8	15.4
Other[a]	12.6	7.9	7.2
Total	100.0	100.0	100.0

Note: [a] Includes publicly-owned enterprises and cooperatives.
Sources: 1950 from *Statistiches Jahrbuch für die BRD*, 1955, p. 201; 1972 from *Wirtschaftsstatistik*, 1976 (7), p. 418; 1986 from Federal Statistical Office, Series 14, Subseries 8, 1986, Table 5, p. 134.

Legal forms of enterprise in Germany

The most basic distinction between legal forms of enterprise in Germany is that between sole proprietorship (Einzelfirma) and corporate bodies (Gesellschaften). Within the broad category of corporate bodies there are limited liability companies (Kapitalgesellschaften) and partnerships (Personengesellschaften), each of which in turn can take a number of different legal forms. Limited liability companies fall into two main types – the Aktiengesellschaft (AG), which is a public company, and the Gesellschaft mit beschränkter Haftung (GmbH), a private company. The two main types of partnership are the Offene Handelsgesellschaft (OHG) – a general partnership – and the Kommanditgesellschaft (KG) – a limited partnership. These various legal forms of enterprise are described more fully below. First, however, table 4.1 shows the proportion of total turnover in the German economy accounted for by each form as an indication of their relative importance. The appropriate criteria by which the importance of different legal forms of enterprise should be measured are not obvious – clearly the size of enterprises can be measured in terms of assets, employees, or value-added – but the limited availability of data is usually what determines the measure used, and such is the case here. The only available data with which to measure the relative importance of different legal forms of enterprise in Germany concern turnover.

It is clear from table 4.1 why partnerships and sole proprietors are included together with companies in the national accounts definition of the German non-financial enterprise sector. In both 1950 and 1972 these unincorporated enterprises accounted for a larger share of total turnover than companies did, and even in 1986 the share of the latter was only a little larger than that of the former. Companies are relatively more important forms of enterprise in German manufacturing than they are for the German economy as a whole. In 1986 the shares of different legal forms of enterprise in manufacturing industry turnover were as follows: AG 35.3%, GmbH 24.4%, OHG 4.2%, KG 25.1%, sole proprietor 7.4%, and other 3.6%.[1] AGs were therefore more important in manufacturing than in the economy as a whole in 1986, while sole proprietors and 'other' enterprises were less important in manufacturing than in the economy as a whole. There was, however, little difference in the importance of partnerships: in 1986 they accounted for 29.3% of manufacturing turnover as compared to 30.8% of total turnover.

Companies

Aktiengesellschaft

The Aktiengesellschaft, literally 'stock corporation', is broadly comparable to the public limited company in the UK and is one of two types of business enterprise in Germany which issues shares that are legal evidence of ownership. The other such form of enterprise is the Kommanditgesellschaft auf Aktien (KGaA), a partnership partly limited by shares. There is no legal form in the UK that is comparable to the KGaA, which has elements of both a stock corporation and a partnership. It is a legal entity with legal rights and obligations separate from those of its partners. The capital is divided into shares, and the liability of shareholders is limited to the amount of their investment in the company. However, a KGaA must have at least one partner who is a manager of the company and has unlimited liability. There are very few enterprises of this form in Germany: there were 21 in 1960, and 29 in 1982.

AGs may issue shares in both bearer and registered form, but bearer shares are by far the most common, in contrast to the situation in the UK. Both ordinary and preference shares may be issued. Preference shares may be issued with or without voting rights, but they must carry a preferential right to cumulative dividends when profits are distributed. Ordinary shares entitle their holders to a proportionate share of total distributed profits after preference shareholders have been paid, and to voting rights. The voting rights of any single shareholder, individual or firm, may, depending on the particular AG's articles of association, be subject to restrictions which limit the maximum number of votes that a single shareholder can exercise. Table 4.2 shows the total number and

[1] Source: Federal Statistical Office, Series 14, Subseries 8, 1986, Table 5, p. 134.

Table 4.2. *Number and nominal capital of AGs (and KGaAs)[a], 1954–1989*

End year capital	All AGs (and KGaAs)		Listed AGs (and KGaAs)	
	No.	Nominal capital DM billion	No.	Nominal capital DM billion
1954[b]	2,530	20.2	677	10.6
1962	2,560	37.6	643	19.0
1970	2,304	55.6	550	29.7
1980	2,141	91.1	459	45.6
1989	2,508	132.0	486	65.6

Notes: [a] Figures are only for enterprises with registered capital in Deutsche Marks.
  [b] 1954 data exclude West Berlin and the Saar.
Sources: Statistiches Jahrbuch für die BRD, 1955 and 1963; Monthly Report of the Deutsche Bundesbank, 1984a; Statistical Supplements to the Monthly Report of the Deutsche Bundesbank, Series 2: Securities Statistics, December 1990.

nominal capital of AGs (and KGaAs), and the corresponding figures for those which were listed on the stock market, in various years. The listed AGs have consistently represented about 50% of the nominal share capital of all AGs during this period. However the number of listed AGs as a proportion of all AGs fell from 26.8% in 1954 to 19.4% in 1989. The number of listed AGs fell steadily from the mid 1950s until 1983, since when it has started to rise.

Data for the relative shares of listed and unlisted AGs in total turnover are not available. Fritsch (1978) gives details of the 1975/76 turnover of 982 unlisted AGs in industries other than banking and insurance, which in total amounted to DM 209,818 million. The Monopolkommission (1978) estimated that in 1974 the turnover of all AGs was DM 426,128 million. Since the total number of unlisted AGs in 1976 was 1,708, an estimate of 209,818/426,128 = 49.2% for the share of total AG turnover accounted for by unlisted AGs in 1975 seems likely to be a conservative figure.

AGs are subject to a general legal requirement to disclose their financial results. They have to prepare both an annual balance sheet and a profit and loss account, which must be audited, and these financial statements must be publicly announced, by filing them with the Commercial Register. Since 1987 'small' and 'medium' AGs have been able to file their financial statements in a modified form (see the discussion of the disclosure requirements for GmbHs below).

A general meeting of the shareholders in an AG must be held at least once a year. Several decisions about the operations of an AG have to be made by means of a vote at the shareholders' general meeting. Such decisions include the approval of the distribution of profit proposed by management; the appointment of auditors; changes in the articles of association; increases or decreases in equity capital; and merger and liquidation decisions. The most important decision made at the shareholders' general meeting, in terms of corporate governance, is the election of shareholders' representatives on the supervisory board, which is discussed in detail in the next paragraph. The shareholders' general meeting also votes on the dismissal of members of the supervisory board or the management board before their term of office expires.

A distinctive institutional feature of AGs (and KGaAs) is that they are required to appoint a supervisory board (Aufsichtsrat) as well as a management board (Vorstand). If the AG has 2,000 or fewer employees, one-third of the supervisory board members must be elected by its employees, with the remainder being elected by its shareholders. If the AG has more than 2,000 employees, then one-half of the supervisory board members must be elected by its employees.[2] In the latter case the chairman of the supervisory board, who is elected either by a two-thirds majority of all members or, if such a majority cannot be achieved, by the shareholders' representatives, can cast a second vote to break ties in supervisory board decisions. The shareholders' representatives on the supervisory board are elected, usually for the legal maximum of a five year term, at the shareholders' general meeting. Employees' representatives are elected by the workforce. Typically the majority (about two-thirds) of employees' representatives are members of the works council (Betriebsrat), while about one-third are external trade union representatives. Employees' representatives also usually serve for the five year legal maximum term. The size of the supervisory board is legally fixed for AGs with more than 2,000 employees: there must be 12 members for an AG which has between 2,000 and 10,000 employees; 16 members for one with between 10,000 and 20,000 employees; and 20 members for one with more than 20,000 employees.

The Aktiengesetz (Stock Corporation Act) specifies that the main function of the supervisory board is the control of management. This includes the right to appoint and dismiss members of the management board, which directly manages an AG, and to fix their salaries. A member of the management board is appointed for a term of up to five years, with the

---

[2] This arrangement has operated since 1976, before which one-third of an AG's supervisory board members were elected by its employees irrespective of the total number of employees.

possibility of reappointment, and cannot sit on the supervisory board. The management board is obliged to inform the supervisory board about future business polices, the performance of the AG, and the conduct of business. The supervisory board can, furthermore, obtain any other information about the AG from the management board if it deems this is necessary. The supervisory board is not directly involved in management decisions, which are the responsibility of the management board, but it may, depending on the particular AG's articles of association, be required to approve certain major decisions of the management board.

Gesellschaft mit beschränkter Haftung

The Gesellschaft mit Beschränkter Haftung, literally 'limited liability company', is broadly comparable to the private company in the UK. The capital of a GmbH is divided into business interests (Geschäftsanteilen) rather than shares (Aktien). A GmbH does not ordinarily issue share certificates unless permitted to do so by its articles of association: even if share certificates are issued, they are not legal evidence of ownership. Transfer of ownership of a GmbH requires formal action before a German notary. Depending on the articles of association, a transfer of ownership may require the consent of the other owners of the GmbH. The liability of the owners of a GmbH is limited to the amount of their investment in the company. A GmbH must have at least two owners when it is founded, but subsequently all equity may be transferred to one party. It must have one or more managers, who may also be owners of the company. Managers are appointed and dismissed by the general meeting of the owners. A GmbH is required to have a supervisory board as well as a board of managers if the number of its employees regularly exceeds 500, but the rights of a GmbH's supervisory board are not as extensive as those of an AG's supervisory board: in particular it does not appoint the managers. A smaller GmbH may provide for a supervisory board in its articles of association if it so wishes. The rules concerning employee representation on supervisory boards that apply to AGs also apply to those GmbHs for which a supervisory board is mandatory.

Until 1987 neither an audit nor a public announcement was in principle required for the annual accounts of GmbHs. The only GmbHs which had to publish annual accounts were those which met the criteria for large enterprises according to the Disclosure Law (Publizitätsgesetz), which requires all enterprises meeting certain size criteria to publish their accounts, irrespective of legal form.[3] In 1976 a total of 143 GmbHs were

---

[3] This requirement has applied for fiscal years beginning after 31 December 1970. A large enterprise is defined, for this purpose, as one for which two of the following three conditions were met on three consecutive balance sheet dates: (i) balance sheet total

Table 4.3. *Number and nominal capital of GmbHs, 1954–1989*

End year	No.	Nominal capital (DM billion)
1954[a]	29,107	6.8
1962	43,801	19.9
1970	80,146	43.0
1980	255,940	99.1
1989	401,687	180.7

Note: [a] 1954 data exclude West Berlin and the Saar.
Source: Statistiches Jahrbuch für die BRD, 1955, 1963, 1971, 1981, 1990.

required to publish their accounts for this reason.[4] Since 1987 the disclosure rules for GmbHs have been altered, in line with the European Community's Fourth Company Law directive on harmonisation of national requirements for financial statements, so that the same disclosure rules now apply to GmbHs as to AGs. All GmbHs, as well as AGs, must now file annual financial statements with the Commercial Register. However, 'small' AGs and GmbHs are not required to file their profit and loss statements, and the balance sheet may be filed in abbreviated form; 'medium' AGs and GmbHs may file their profit and loss statements in abbreviated form; and only 'large' and 'medium' AGs and GmbHs are required to have their accounts audited.[5]

Table 4.3 shows the total number and nominal capital of GmbHs in various years. Both the number and nominal capital of GmbHs have grown consistently over the period 1954–1989, and this growth is reflected in the figures for the share of total turnover accounted for by GmbHs in table 4.1. By 1986, GmbHs accounted for a larger share of total turnover in Germany than did AGs. All limited liability companies together

exceeded Dm 125 million; (ii) annual sales exceeded DM 250 million; (iii) average number of employees exceeded 5,000.
[4] Fritsch (1978), Anhang III.
[5] A 'small' AG is required to have its accounts audited if it is listed. For these purposes, 'small' and 'medium-sized' AGs and GmbHs are those which in the last two financial years have not exceeded two of the following three criteria:

	Small	Medium
Turnover (DM million)	8	32
Total assets (DM million)	3.9	15.5
Average no. of employees	50	250

accounted for 31.9% of total turnover in 1950, and 46.6% in 1986, but the greater part of the overall increase of 14.7 percentage points in the share of companies in total turnover took the form of an increase in the share of GmbHs, by 10.1 percentage points.

Two main reasons have been advanced as explanations of the preference for the GmbH over the AG as the form by which German enterprises have acquired limited liability status (see Deutsche Bundesbank, 1984a). One is that AGs must have a supervisory board, while GmbHs are required to have a supervisory board only if they have more than 500 employees. Smaller enterprises which wish to preserve their entrepreneurial independence will therefore choose to obtain limited liability status in the form of a GmbH rather than an AG. The other reason relates to the disclosure rules applicable to AGs and GmbHs. As we have seen, GmbHs were until 1987 subject to much less stringent disclosure rules than AGs. The ending of differences in the disclosure requirements for AGs and GmbHs appears to have had some effect on the number of AGs. From the end of 1975 to the end of 1986 the number of AGs was consistently between 2,100 and 2,200, but from the end of 1986 to the end of 1989 the number increased from 2,190 to 2,508. However, the number and nominal capital of GmbHs also continued to grow strongly in the late 1980s.

The GmbH sector contains a wide range of companies of different types and sizes. Some GmbHs are large enterprises which are similar in most respects to AGs. Examples of these are Robert Bosch GmbH (the 22nd largest German firm in 1972, and the 6th largest in 1988, according to the Monopolkommission) and Friedrich Krupp GmbH (the 13th largest firm in 1972 and the 20th largest in 1988). The great majority of GmbHs are, however, medium-sized and small enterprises. A significant number of GmbHs are either subsidiaries of other companies, both AGs and GmbHs, or are majority-owned by other companies. In 1988, Daimler–Benz AG, for example, the largest German firm in that year, wholly-owned 10 GmbHs, while Robert Bosch GmbH wholly-owned 9 GmbHs and had majority holdings in 3 others. But there are also a large number of GmbHs in which management and ownership are in the same hands.

Partnerships, sole proprietors, and other forms of enterprise

There are two main types of partnership in Germany. The Offene Handelsgesellschaft is a general partnership of two or more parties for the purpose of conducting business. Profits and losses are divided according to a partnership agreement. All partners have unlimited liability for the debts of the partnership. The death of a partner results in the dissolution of the partnership unless otherwise specified in the partnership agreement.

The Kommanditgesellschaft is a limited partnership. It has at least one general partner, who has unlimited liability and is usually the senior manager. It also has one or more limited partners, who are liable only to the extent of their capital subscriptions. Limited partners may not usually take part in management of the KG, although their consent may be required for unusual business transactions. The death of a general partner results in the dissolution of the partnership unless, as usually happens, the partnership agreement provides otherwise. A special type of limited partnership is the GmbH & Co. KG, in which the general partner with unlimited liability is a private limited company (GmbH), so that in effect the partnership has completely limited liability.

Table 4.1 shows that partnerships have accounted for about 30% of total turnover in the German economy for most of the period 1950–1989. An article published in the *Monthly Report of the Deutsche Bundesbank* (1977) gives some information about the importance of partnerships relative to companies in different branches of economic activity in the early 1970s. In 1972 partnerships accounted for 33.6% of the total turnover of all enterprises covered in the study, and 32.7% of manufacturing turnover. The corresponding figures for incorporated enterprises were 37.6% and 50% respectively. Partnerships were relatively less important than companies in those areas of production which have large capital requirements, such as chemicals (partnerships 17.3% of turnover in 1972, companies 75.6%), iron and steel (23.7% and 71.8% respectively), road vehicle building (13.2% and 74.0% respectively), and electrical engineering (20.2% and 73.6% respectively). Partnerships were relatively more important than companies in industrial sectors closer to the consumer stage (metal goods production, wood processing, the textile and clothing industries, and food, drink and tobacco), and especially in the distributive trades and construction.

The share of sole proprietors in total turnover in the German economy has been declining steadily in the period 1950–1989, but was still 15.4% in 1986. The *Monthly Report of the Deutsche Bundesbank* (1977) study showed that in 1972 sole proprietors accounted for 22.5% of total turnover of all enterprises in the study, and 13.5% of manufacturing turnover. As was the case with partnerships, sole proprietors were relatively unimportant in areas of production with large capital requirements. In 1972 sole proprietors were relatively important in the wood processing industry, construction, and the retail trade.

In addition to companies and partnerships there are publicly-owned enterprises, cooperatives, and both mutual insurance and building and loan associations. Some of these enterprises are registered in the AG, GmbH or GmbH & Co. KG form.

This section has examined the different legal forms of enterprise in Germany, and shown that throughout the post-war period limited liability companies have accounted for less than half of total turnover in the German economy. Only AGs, and large GmbHs, are legally required to have supervisory boards. The share of total German turnover accounted for by AGs is not large – just above 20% at most. We have seen that one of the two main reasons advanced for the rapid growth in importance of GmbHs is the desire of enterprises to achieve limited liability status without the requirement to have a supervisory board, so it seems likely that most GmbHs do not have supervisory boards. Consequently only a small number of German firms, accounting for probably 30% of total turnover in Germany at most, have supervisory boards.

To understand the implications of the significance of different legal forms of enterprise in Germany requires a comparison with the UK. This is the subject of the next section.

The importance of different legal forms of enterprise in Germany compared to the UK

Attempts to assess the importance of different legal forms of enterprise in Germany relative to the UK are hampered by a lack of detailed data for the UK. Data showing the proportion of total turnover in the UK economy accounted for by different legal forms are available only for the latter half of the 1980s, and these data do not permit a distinction to be made between public and private limited companies, nor between general and limited partnerships. Table 4.4 gives an estimate of the proportion of total turnover accounted for by the main legal forms of enterprise in the UK in 1986, derived from data published in *Business Monitor*. Comparing the figures in table 4.4 with those for Germany in 1986 in table 4.1 shows that the fraction of total turnover in Germany accounted for by companies was very much smaller than in the UK. Correspondingly, the proportion of total turnover in Germany attributable to partnerships and sole proprietors was much larger than in the UK. It therefore appears that legal forms of enterprise with owners who are not protected by limited liability are much more important in the German than in the UK economy.[6]

Care is, however, required when assessing the importance of enterprises

---

[6] One complication which must be noted here is that a category of unlimited companies exists in the UK. In practice such companies are rare, being usually adopted by professions such as stockbrokers in order to gain the administrative convenience of incorporation while satisfying their professional rules which do not permit limited liability (see Farrar, Furey and Hannigan, 1991, pp. 43, 63).

Table 4.4. *Turnover accounted for by different legal forms of enterprise in the UK, 1986*

Type of legal form	% of total turnover
Companies and public corporations[a]	79.3
Partnerships	11.7
Sole proprietors	8.2
General government and non-profit-making bodies	0.8
Total	100.0

Note: [a] Public corporations are government-owned firms.
Source: Own calculations based on *Business Monitor: Size Analyses of UK Business*, 1986, tables 2, 3A–3D.

with limited liability in Germany relative to the UK. Table 4.1 shows that limited partnerships accounted for 24% of total turnover in Germany in 1986. Included in this category is the GmbH & Co. KG which, as we have seen, is, in effect, a limited liability company. Unfortunately no information is available about the share of total turnover in Germany attributable to enterprises of the GmbH & Co. KG form. Nevertheless at least some of the owners of all the enterprises in the KG category had limited liability. The share in total turnover in Germany in 1986 of enterprises which had *no* owners with limited liability was therefore 22.2%. No information is available about the proportion of total turnover accounted for by limited partnerships in the UK, but according to Paish and Briston (1982, p. 21) only about 2,000 have been registered in the UK since 1908, so that it seems likely that this proportion is very small indeed. If, as appears reasonable, most partnerships in the UK are unlimited ones, the share of enterprises which had no owners with limited liability in total UK turnover in 1986 must have been only a little less than 19.9%, and hence only a few percentage points smaller than in Germany.

On p. 74 above it was argued that only public companies were likely to be able to raise significant amounts of external finance by selling ownership claims to individual savers, and hence only these companies were likely to suffer from the agency problems which result from the existence of a large number of individually small owners of a firm, with no incentives to monitor and control the firm's management. As we have seen, although the share of limited liability companies in total turnover in Germany has been rising, this has mainly been due to the growth in the importance of GmbHs. The share of AGs in total turnover has increased rather slowly, from 16.5% in 1950 to 21.1% in 1986. Unfortunately data on the share of public companies in total UK turnover do not exist, so that it is not possible to compare the relative importance of public companies in Germany and the UK on this basis. The figures for the total number of public companies suggest that they were more important in the UK: in 1962 there were approximately 10,700 public companies in the UK[7], compared to 2,560 AGs in Germany; while in 1986 there were 6,115 public companies in the UK[8], compared to 2,262 AGs in Germany. But comparisons of the numbers of public companies do not really provide much information about their relative economic importance.

It may, however, be argued that the distinction between public and private companies is economically less significant than that between listed (or quoted) and unlisted (or unquoted) companies[9] (see, for example, King, 1977, p. 29). A listed company is a public company the shares of which can be freely traded on a public market. In order for a firm to be able to raise significant amounts of external finance by selling ownership claims to individual savers it must be possible for each individual saver to be able to realise the value of his or her ownership claim relatively straightforwardly, since an individual saver with a small holding in a large firm has no ability to control the firm's actions, and hence needs to be able to withdraw from the firm if it follows policies that the individual saver disagrees with. Furthermore, individual savers are likely to wish to hold shares in a firm for a period which is short relative to the firm's lifetime, and this too means that it must be possible for savers to realise the value of their holdings easily. These requirements can be fulfilled if the firm's shares are traded on a public market. A public company which is not listed, however, is likely to find it difficult to raise much external finance by selling shares to individual savers.

It is possible to compare the importance of listed public companies in Germany and the UK. In 1970 3,418 UK public limited companies were listed,[10] while as table 4.2 shows, 550 AGs were listed in Germany. At the end of 1987 2,135 UK public limited companies were listed.[11] The corresponding figure for the number of AGs in Germany that were listed was 474.[12] This difference in the numbers of listed public companies in the UK and Germany is reflected in their relative importance in economic activity. Hay and Morris (1984) provide quantitative estimates of the contribution of listed and unlisted companies to UK gross domestic product (GDP) in

---

[7] Paish and Briston (1982), p. 20.

[8] *Stock Exchange Official Yearbook, 1988–89*, p. 42.

[9] We use the terms listed and quoted synonymously, as also unlisted and unquoted.

[10] Fritsch (1978), p. 27.

[11] *Stock Exchange Official Yearbook, 1988–89*, p. 17.

[12] *Monthy Report of the Deutsche Bundesbank*, October 1991, p. 23.

Table 4.5. *The contribution of different types of company to GDP arising in the UK company sector, 1975, %*

Listed companies[a]	35.2
Unlisted companies[a]	42.5
Privately-owned companies in agriculture, mining and financial services[b]	7.0
Public corporations	15.3
Total (GDP arising in the UK company sector)	100.0

Notes: [a] Excluding those in agriculture, mining and financial services.
  [b] Consists of all listed and unlisted companies in these sectors.
Source: Own calculations based on Hay and Morris (1984), tables 4.1, 4.4, 4.5, 4.6.

1975. The unlisted companies include both public and private companies, while all the listed companies are public companies. As Hay and Morris explain, the limited availability of data makes it difficult to estimate the relative importance of these two types of companies in all sectors of the economy, and it was not possible to estimate the separate contribution of listed and unlisted companies in agriculture, mining, and financial services to GDP. Table 4.5, which is derived from the results presented in several of Hay and Morris's tables, shows the proportional contribution of listed and unlisted companies to GDP originating in the UK company sector in the sectors for which it was possible for separate estimates to be made. Table 4.5 also shows the contribution of all privately-owned companies in the agriculture, mining and financial services sectors, whether listed or unlisted, and that of public corporations in all sectors. If we assume that the relative importance of listed and unlisted companies in agriculture, mining and financial services is the same as it is in all other sectors, we obtain estimates of 38.4% and 46.3% for the relative contribution of all listed and unlisted companies to GDP arising in the UK company sector in 1975. These proportions, together with the figure of 15.3% for public corporations, can then be used to break down the figure shown in table 4.4 for the proportion of total UK turnover accounted for by companies and public corporations. This procedure yields the following estimates for shares of total UK turnover in 1986: listed companies 30.5%; unlisted companies 36.7%; public corporations 12.1%.

  These estimates of the share of total UK turnover in 1986 accounted for by different types of company are only approximate. They are obtained by breaking down an aggregate turnover figure for companies and public corporations using proportions derived from data on the contribution of different types of company to GDP arising in the company sector. Since turnover and GDP are different concepts there is scope for introducing error by this procedure. Furthermore, the GDP data were for 1975 while the turnover data were for 1986. The UK privatisation programme, which began in the early 1980s, means that the share of total UK turnover in 1986 accounted for by public corporations is likely to be overestimated at 12.1%, and correspondingly the share of listed companies is likely to be underestimated at 30.5%. Despite these qualifications, it is unlikely that the main conclusion which results from comparing the above estimate of the share of listed companies in total UK turnover with the figures for Germany shown in table 4.1 is sensitive to possible errors of estimation. In 1986 all AGs – listed and unlisted – accounted for 21.1% of total turnover in the German economy. Listed companies in the UK in 1986 thus accounted for a larger proportion of total turnover than did all AGs in Germany. On p. 77 an approximate estimate of the share of unlisted AGs in the total turnover of all AGs yielded a figure of about 50%. Table 4.2 also shows that the nominal capital of unlisted AGs has consistently been about 50% of that of all AGs. Using 50% as an estimate of the share of listed AGs in the total turnover of AGs yields a figure of 10.6% for the share of listed AGs in total turnover in Germany in 1986. This estimate is also an approximate one, but even allowing for the approximate nature of the estimates for both countries, it is clear that listed companies account for a much larger proportion of turnover in the UK than they do in Germany.

Three main conclusions emerge from this comparison of the relative importance of different legal forms of enterprise in the German and UK economies. Listed companies which, it has been argued, are the only type of firm for which the problem of inadequate monitoring and control of managers by owners is likely to arise, are more important in the UK than in Germany. Partnerships and sole proprietorships are more important in Germany than in the UK. Many German partnerships are, however, limited ones, so that it is not obvious that enterprises with limited liability are much less significant in Germany than in the UK.

The greater importance in Germany of legal forms of enterprise other than public companies, in particular of unlisted companies, partnerships, and sole proprietorships, raises some interesting questions about the role of banks as suppliers of external finance. If the arguments put forward on pp. 73–74 are correct, private companies, partnerships and sole proprietorships are likely to depend heavily on banks (and other financial intermediaries) in order to raise external finance from individual small savers in general, as opposed to raising it from individual savers who are closely connected to the existing owners of such firms via ties of friendship or family. The importance of private companies, partnerships and sole proprietors in the German economy, by comparison with the UK, might be a consequence of more widespread availability of bank loans. As we saw in chapter 3, however, comparisons based on national accounts flow of funds data do not provide any evidence that bank lending finances a larger share of aggregate non-financial enterprise investment in Germany than in the UK. Evidence on the importance of alternative sources of investment finance for different legal forms of enterprise in Germany would therefore be a very useful supplement to the aggregate data analysed in chapter 3. This is the subject of the next section.

The sources of investment finance for different legal forms of enterprise in Germany

Very little information is available about the finance of investment by legal forms of enterprise in Germany other than AGs since, until 1987, only AGs, and a very small number of GmbHs and partnerships, were required to publish their annual financial statements. The analysis of the annual statements of enterprises which has been conducted by the Deutsche Bundesbank since 1965 is the sole source of such information of which we are aware, and even this source has considerable limitations, as will be seen. Given the importance of legal forms of enterprise other than AGs in the German economy, it is necessary to use even imperfect data sources to attempt an analysis of the relative importance of different sources of finance for different legal forms.

The Bundesbank's analysis is based on the annual financial statements submitted by enterprises whose signatures appear on the bills of exchange offered to the Bundesbank by credit institutions. As a consequence, the enterprises whose annual statements are analysed do not form a representative sample of all enterprises. Credit institutions can only offer the Bundesbank bills issued by enterprises which reach the credit rating prescribed by the Bundesbank Law. The average size of the enterprises analysed is much larger than that of all enterprises, and the sample is biased, given its origin, towards the branches of economic activity in which financing through bills is particularly important. The Bundesbank's analysis thus covers enterprises in manufacturing, mining, gas, electricity and water supply, construction, the wholesale and retail trades, and transport and communications (excluding the Federal Railways and Federal Post Office). Enterprises in agriculture, most services, the professions, and finance are not included.

The Bundesbank's analysis gives details of the balance sheets, profit and loss accounts, and sources and uses of funds of various broad categories of enterprises. It was argued in chapter 3 that sources and uses of funds data is the most appropriate for addressing questions about the finance of investment, and we therefore use the figures for the sources and uses of funds of different legal forms of enterprise as the basis for our comparison of investment finance. The Bundesbank obtains these sources and uses of funds data by first ascertaining the annual changes in assets and liabilities from balance sheets for successive years, and then expanding the account of balance sheet changes to include depreciation from profit and loss accounts, following the capital finance account of the Deutsche Bundesbank in concept and definition. The sources and uses of funds data for successive years thus obtained are based on ranges of enterprises which do not fully coincide. The Bundesbank, however, does not regard the differences between the coverage of enterprises in successive years as large enough to prevent comparisons being made across years.

Unfortunately, sources and uses of funds data for different legal forms of enterprise have been made available by the Bundesbank only for the period 1965–1971. Even within this seven year period, changes in enterprises' accounting caused by the introduction of value-added tax meant that the figures for 1965–1967 are not fully comparable with those for 1968–1971. This problem is ignored in the analysis below, since it was felt that the benefits of having data for seven years exceeded the costs involved in lack of full comparability.

The components of enterprises' sources and uses of funds which the Bundesbank published were highly aggregated. The sources side comprised internal funds and three forms of external financing. For partnerships and sole proprietorships, the internal funds figures included capital increases out of undistributed profits and new capital contributions. The three external sources of funds were new equity capital for AGs and GmbHs, the change in short-term liabilities, and the change in long-term liabilities. The uses side was split between the acquisition of tangible assets and the acquisition of financial assets. Five components of the latter were identified: the change in cash resources; the change in short-term claims; the change in long-term claims; the acquisition of securities; and the acquisition of trade investments (participations). It was not, therefore, possible to identify bank loans as a separate source of finance. Bank loans are the major component of the change in liabilities item, but this item also includes borrowing from sources other than banks, as well as provisions for pensions. On the basis of the data for the financing of the aggregate non-financial enterprise sector reported in chapter 3, borrowing from non-banks is likely to be very small relative to bank borrowing, but pension provisions are a rather larger proportion of bank loans. The change in liabilities item, which had to be used as a proxy variable for bank lending, is therefore only an approximate measure of bank loans. Furthermore, it was not possible to distinguish between firms'

Table 4.6. *Sources of finance for investment of different legal forms of enterprise, 1965–1971, %*

	AGs	GmbHs	Partnerships	Sole proprietorships
Gross sources				
Internal funds	64.9	50.6	55.5	51.3
of which: capital increase by partnerships and sole proprietorships	—	—	11.1	13.1
New equity	7.4	8.8	—	—
New debt	27.7	40.6	44.5	48.7
Total	100.0	100.0	100.0	100.0
Net sources				
Internal funds	92.2	76.6	79.2	73.9
of which: capital increase by partnerships and sole proprietorships	—	—	15.5	18.8
New equity	−1.8	8.2	−3.5	−2.4
New debt	9.6	15.2	24.3	28.5
Total	100.0	100.0	100.0	100.0
For information: average number of enterprises from which sources and uses of funds data obtained	879	3851	11138	6712

Source: Own calculations based on data published in *Monthly Report of the Deutsche Bundesbank*, November/December 1968, January 1971, November 1972, November 1973.

purchases of equity and debt securities on the uses side of the account. In calculating the net contribution of equity to the finance of physical investment it was assumed that the acquisition of securities consisted entirely of equity. This is certain to introduce a bias in the net sources of finance figures analysed below, but since the acquisition of securities item was always a very small proportion of total uses any bias will be small.

Table 4.6 shows the gross and net sources of finance for investment by AGs, GmbHs, partnerships and sole proprietorships over the period 1965–71. The sources of finance over the period are calculated as simple averages of their shares in the total finance of each legal form in each year. Lack of data made it impossible to calculate weighted averages of the type which were used in chapter 3 to analyse the sources of finance for the producing enterprises sector. Table 4.7 shows, for comparison, the gross

Table 4.7. *Net and gross sources of finance for investment by producing enterprises, 1965–1971, %*

Gross	Net	
Internally generated funds	59.5	73.1
Provisions for pensions	1.9	2.3
Capital transfers	3.7	4.5
Bank loans	20.9	12.5
Insurance enterprise loans	1.6	0.5
Bonds	1.1	0.7
Shares	2.8	1.5
Other	8.6	4.8
Total	100.1	99.9

Source: Own calculations based on the capital finance account of the Deutsche Bundesbank.

and net sources of finance for the producing enterprises sector over the period 1965–1971, calculated as simple averages in the same way as in table 4.6.

The figures in table 4.6 show that, during the period 1965–1971, GmbHs, partnerships, and sole proprietorships all used more debt, whether measured as a gross or net source of finance, than did AGs. Debt was most important as a source of finance for investment, on either a gross or a net basis, for sole proprietorships; it was next most important for partnerships; and then for GmbHs. If the relative importance of debt finance can be taken as an indicator of the relative importance of bank finance, table 4.6 supports the argument advanced on pp. 73–74 that bank loans were likely to be more important as a source of finance for investment for legal forms of enterprise other than public companies. But table 4.6 shows that internal funds (which, for partnerships and sole proprietorships, include capital increases by these two types of firm) was the most important source of finance for all four legal forms, particularly when the net sources of finance are analysed. Even though sole proprietorships, partnerships, and GmbHs used relatively more debt finance than did AGs, and hence (to the extent that debt can serve as an indicator of borrowing from banks) depended more on bank loans, these types of firms still financed some three-quarters of their investment in physical assets over this period with internal funds.

Table 4.6 provides no evidence that German public companies – AGs – raise a significant proportion of their investment finance in the form of sales of new equity. On a gross basis, new equity was a little smaller as a source of finance for AGs than it was for GmbHs, while on a net basis new equity was noticeably smaller for AGs than for GmbHs. The most striking difference between the sources of finance for investment of AGs and the other legal forms, especially on a net basis, was that AGs used more internal funds than did the other legal forms. The smaller use of debt finance by AGs was not a result of AGs having access to the share market, but was rather due to the heavier use of internal funds by AGs. The greater importance of new equity as a source of finance for GmbHs than for AGs shown in table 4.6 suggests that new equity may have been somewhat more important as a source of funds for the producing enterprises sector than the analysis in chapter 3 indicated. As was noted on p. 62 the capital finance account of the Deutsche Bundesbank only records new equity finance in the form of sales of shares by AGs. Because internally-generated funds are measured as a residual in the capital finance account, new equity finance raised by GmbHs is contained in the figure for internally-generated funds. It appears from table 4.6 that new equity is a small but not insignificant source of funds for GmbHs, which means that the internally-generated funds figures for producing enterprises derived from the capital finance account are overestimated, and new equity is correspondingly underestimated.

The data from which table 4.6 has been derived clearly have several serious limitations, but they are the only available source of information about the investment financing patterns of different legal forms of enterprise in Germany. The only conclusions we wish to draw from table 4.6 concern the relative importance of alternative sources of finance for different legal forms, and we recognise the qualifications which must be attached to any such conclusions in view of the limitations of the underlying data. However, in our view, table 4.6 yields some useful conclusions. Debt finance is more important for sole proprietorships, partnerships and GmbHs than it is for AGs. The evidence of the financing of the producing enterprises sector in chapter 3 showed that bank loans are by far the most important source of debt finance, so it is reasonable to conclude from table 4.6 that bank loans are more important for legal forms of enterprise other than AGs. Nevertheless, for all legal forms, internal funds are the most important source of finance for investment, particularly for investment in physical assets. Although the data are available only for 1965–1971, table 4.7 suggests that these seven years are reasonably representative of the financing patterns of producing enterprises as a whole over a longer period.

In the introduction to this chapter we noted that partnerships and sole proprietorships were excluded from the UK national accounts definition of the non-financial enterprise sector, but were included in the German definition. This difference in definitions is a complicating factor in comparisons of the sources of finance for investment by non-financial enterprises in Germany and the UK. If the relative importance of bank loan finance is correctly indicated by the relative importance of debt, then the figures in table 4.6 provide no reason to suppose that the difference in the definitions of the non-financial enterprise sector biases downwards the importance of bank loans as a source of finance for investment in Germany relative to the UK. Excluding partnerships and sole proprietorships from the definition of the German non-financial enterprise sector, so that it was exactly comparable to the UK definition, would reduce the importance of bank loans as a source of finance in Germany, given the greater use of debt finance by such firms than by AGs and GmbHs. The analysis in this section therefore reinforces the conclusion drawn in chapter 3 that non-financial enterprises in Germany use less bank loan finance than in the UK.

Conclusion

The forms in which firms are organised have important implications, both for the access of firms to different sources of external finance, and for the problems which arise when firms are managed by individuals who do not have an ownership stake in them and are not subject to monitoring by the owners because there is a large number of such owners. The analysis on pp. 73–74 argued that legal forms of enterprise other than public companies would mainly depend on banks and other financial intermediaries in order to raise external finance from savers beyond a relatively small circle of family and friends. It also argued that the problems of inadequate monitoring and control of managers by owners were only likely to arise for firms organised in the form of a public company.

The chapter then examined the significance of different legal forms of enterprise in the German economy, and compared the importance of different types of firm in Germany and the UK. Partnerships and sole proprietorships account for a much larger proportion of total turnover in Germany than in the UK, and limited liability companies for a much smaller proportion. It is not clear that enterprises without *any* limited liability are much more important in Germany than in the UK, because of the significance of limited partnerships in the former – most strikingly, the GmbH & Co. KG, which is a limited liability company in all but name. There does, however, seem to be less scope in Germany for the occurrence of agency problems due to a lack of monitoring and control of managers by owners. This conclusion follows from the greater importance of partnerships in Germany which (except for the GmbH & Co. KG) always have managers who are also owners with unlimited liability and, perhaps most clearly, from the lesser importance of public companies, especially listed companies, in Germany. The fourth section of the chapter argued that inadequate monitoring and control of managers by owners is a problem primarily restricted to listed companies whose shares can be traded on a public market. There have been between four and five times as many listed companies in the UK than in Germany during the post-war period, and the approximate estimates put forward showed that in 1986 listed companies accounted for about 30% of total turnover in the UK, compared to about 10% in Germany.

One other important point which emerged from this discussion is that most German firms do not have supervisory boards. Only AGs, and GmbHs with more than 500 employees, are required to have such boards. It seems likely that the German firms which have supervisory boards account for no more than 30% of total turnover in the German economy. This observation raises some questions about the significance of represen-tation on supervisory boards for German bank lending decisions, since a large proportion of bank loans must be made to firms which do not have supervisory boards.

The chapter finally analysed the very limited evidence available on the sources of finance for investment by different legal forms of enterprise in Germany. The quality of the available data is poor, and conclusions drawn from it must be tentative, but it is the only information we have about the finance of different types of German firm. The evidence is consistent with the hypothesis (pp. 73–74) that partnerships and sole pro-prietorships would rely proportionately more on bank loans as a source of finance than would limited liability companies. However, the main conclusion from the discussion is that internally-generated funds is the most important source of investment finance for all legal forms of enter-prise in Germany. There is no evidence that the greater importance of partnerships and sole proprietorships in Germany relative to the UK is due to the ability of German firms to raise substantial amounts of external finance in the form of bank loans.

The conclusions of this chapter have two main implications for assessing the widely-held view of the merits of the German system of finance for investment. One is that there seems to be much less scope for problems due to inadequate monitoring and control of managers by owners to arise in Germany than in the UK. The significance of this observation for German banks' role as delegated exercisers of equity's control rights is considered in chapters 8 and 9. The other implication follows from the evidence that, for the different legal forms of enterprise in Germany as well as for the aggregate non-financial enterprise sector, bank loans are

much less important than internally-generated funds as a source of investment finance. It is that the claimed merits of the German system of finance for investment which relate to the supply of bank loan finance are not supported by evidence on the actual financing of German firms. These findings raise serious doubts about that component of the widely-held view which sees German firms as having greater access to bank loan finance because of particular institutional features of the relationship between banks and firms in Germany. Chapters 5–7 continue the investigation of this component, with analyses both of the structure of the banking system in Germany, and of various aspects of the supply of external finance to firms by German banks.

5 The structure of the German banking system

Introduction

The analysis of the aggregate financing of investment by non-financial enterprises in chapter 3 provided no evidence that bank loans constitute a larger proportion of the finance of investment by such enterprises in Germany than in the UK: if anything, the evidence suggested that bank loans were a smaller proportion. This evidence raises serious doubts about one of the major components of the widely-held view of the merits of the German system of investment finance: the claim that the close involvement of German banks with the firms to which they supply funds enables them to deal more effectively with asymmetric information problems and provide a larger proportion of debt finance to firms on favourable terms. But there are several reasons why this evidence is not sufficient on its own to reject the claim that investment funds are supplied more efficiently in Germany because the banks are able to overcome the problems created by information asymmetries between savers and investors.

One such reason is that international comparisons of financing have to be made with great care because of problems with the coverage and reliability of data from different countries, and it would therefore be foolish to use these comparisons on their own as a basis for rejecting a major component of the widely-held view. A second reason is the fact that, because investment by non-financial enterprises has been a higher proportion of GDP in Germany than in the UK,[1] bank loans have been a higher proportion of GDP in Germany than in the UK despite having been no larger as a proportion of investment by non-financial enterprises. This observation is consistent with the following possibility. Internally-generated funds may be the preferred source of finance in both Germany

[1] See p. 16.

and the UK, but bank loans may be available on better terms in Germany (because of German banks' closer involvement with firms), thus enabling more investment to be undertaken, which in turn generates more internal funds so that a higher volume of aggregate investment can be financed, although in proportions similar to those of the UK. A third reason why our evidence so far is insufficient is that German banks are seen, in the widely-held view, as playing an important role in monitoring and replacing inefficient managers of firms. This function of the banks is regarded as making a significant contribution to overcoming the difficulties created by asymmetric information for the efficient allocation of investment funds, and is to some extent independent of the supply of debt finance to firms by banks, although there are possible links between the two. Bank supervisory board representation may, for example, enable loans to be made on better terms by providing banks with better-quality information about firms, or it may permit banks to lend more because they are in a better position to control managerial behaviour in situations of financial distress.

For all these reasons it is necessary to go beyond the evidence of the significance of bank loans in the finance of aggregate investment by German non-financial enterprises, and examine in greater detail various elements of the widely-held view of the superiority of the German system of finance for investment. In this chapter we begin this more detailed investigation by examining the structure of the German banking system. The theoretical analysis in chapter 2 suggested that an efficient system of finance for investment might have monopolistic tendencies. The main purpose of this chapter is therefore to provide *prima facie* evidence on the degree of concentration of the German banking system in terms of the various ways in which banks may be able to influence firm performance. The second section describes the various categories of banks which operate in Germany, and the third section assesses the degree of concentration in the banking system in terms of the overall volume of banking business, bank lending to domestic firms, bank control of equity voting rights, bank supervisory board representation, and bank membership of syndicates for new share issues. The fourth section sums up the implications of these findings.

Universal and specialised banks in the German banking system

As has been noted in chapters 1 and 2, German banks are typically universal ones. The term 'universal bank' does not, in fact, have a single agreed definition. A universal bank is unambiguously one which provides a complete range of commercial and investment banking services.

However it has sometimes been suggested that the definition of a universal bank should include the ability to influence non-banks through equity ownership, the exercise of proxy voting rights, and supervisory board membership (see Krummel, 1980, p. 35). As we will see, the structure of the German banking system looks rather different depending on whether the former (wide) or the latter (narrow) definition of a universal bank is used.

A legal definition of a universal bank in the wider sense of a bank which offers the whole range of commercial and investment banking services is implicitly provided by the German Banking Act.[2] Banks in Germany are enterprises conducting banking business. According to the Banking Act, banking business comprises:

(i)   the acceptance of funds from others as deposits irrespective of whether interest is paid (deposit business);

(ii)   the granting of money loans and acceptance credits (lending business);

(iii)   the purchase of bills of exchange and cheques (discount business);

(iv)   the purchase and sale of securities for the account of others (securities business);

(v)   the safe custody and administration of securities for the account of others (safe custody business);

(vi)   the business specified in Section 1 of the Investment Companies Act (investment fund business);

(vii)   the incurring of the obligation to acquire claims in respect of loans prior to their maturity;

(viii) the assumption of guarantees and other warranties on behalf of others (guarantee business);

(ix)   the performance of cashless payment and clearing operations (giro business).

The Banking Act forms the legal basis for supervision of banks in Germany, and all enterprises which conduct any aspect of banking business as defined above are subject to it, with the exceptions of the Bundesbank, the Federal Post Office, and insurance enterprises.[3] Any enterprise conducting banking business is required to be licensed and supervised by both the Federal Banking Supervisory Office and the Bundesbank. The definition of banking business in the German Banking Act is very wide, and in the UK, for example, some of the activities

---

[2] Deutsche Bundesbank Special Series, no. 2, *Banking Act of the Federal Republic of Germany*, August 1986.

[3] Insurance enterprises are subject to the Banking Act 'in so far as they conduct banking business which is not part of their characteristic business'.

defined as banking business in Germany are carried out by non-banks – stockbrokers conduct securities business, solicitors conduct safe custody business, and unit and investment trusts conduct investment fund business. Clearly one reason why the German financial system is characterised as 'bank-based' is that the legal definition of banking business is so broad that most financial institutions are, by definition, banks.

According to the classification used by the Deutsche Bundesbank, banks in Germany can be divided into a large group of universal banks (on the wide definition of a universal bank) and a smaller group of more specialised banks. The group of universal banks can be further divided into three categories on the basis of ownership and legal form: these categories are the commercial bank sector, the savings bank sector, and the credit cooperative sector. Table 5.1 shows the number of banks in each of the categories used by the Bundesbank, and their share in the overall volume of business for selected years in the period 1950–1988. Although building and loan associations conduct banking business according to the Banking Act, and are included in the monthly reporting banks to the Bundesbank, table 5.2 is based on the definition of the German banking system used in the *Monthly Report of the Deutsche Bundesbank* and the capital finance account of the Deutsche Bundesbank, according to which building and loan associations are treated as being separate from the banking system. The three categories of universal banks together accounted for 79.6% of the overall volume of business in 1950, 74.9% in 1970, and 77.8% in 1988, confirming that, at least on the wide definition of a universal bank, German banks are, indeed, typically universal ones.

All the banks in the commercial bank, savings bank and credit co-operative sectors are universal banks in that they are able in principle to conduct the whole range of banking business as specified in the Banking Act. There are, however, variations in the extent to which the business of individual banks within these categories is composed of the different services, and many of the banks in these sectors do not in practice carry out the full range of banking business. To some extent the widespread growth of universal banking (on the wide definition) in all three of these categories is a post-1945 development, since the historical origins of many of these banks, particularly in the savings bank and credit cooperative sectors, were as providers of specialised banking services rather than as universal banks. In the savings bank sector, for example, the traditional functions of the lowest tier – the savings banks – are implicitly defined by the special savings bank laws passed under Land (state) legislation, with which these banks must comply in addition to the Banking Act. These traditional tasks include offering savings accounts and giro transaction facilities, providing credit to low- and middle-income

Table 5.1. *Numbers and share of volume of business^a of various categories of German banks^b, 1950–1988*

	1950^c	1960		1970		1977		1988	
	Share %	No.	Share %	No.	Share %	No.	Share %	No.	Share %
Universal banks									
Commercial banks of which:	36.4	362	24.4	305	24.9	263	24.9	312	23.6
Big banks	19.1	6	11.3	6	10.2	6	10.4	6	8.9
Regional and other commercial banks^{de}	12.8	108	10.4	112	10.7	109	10.9	163	11.4
Branches of foreign banks ^{d}	–	16	–	24	1.5	51	1.9	57	1.8
Private bankers ^{e}	4.5	232	2.7	163	2.5	97	1.7	86	1.5
Savings bank sector of which:	30.8	880	35.7	844	38.5	634	38.5	596	37.3
Regional giro institutions	10.8	13	13.5	12	15.6	12	16.5	11	15.6
Savings banks	20.0	867	22.2	832	22.9	622	22.0	585	21.7
Credit cooperative sector of which:	12.4	11,642	8.6	7,072	11.5	4,817	14.0	3,364	16.9
Regional institutions of credit cooperatives	3.7	19	2.8	13	3.8	11	4.2	6	4.6
Credit cooperatives ^{e}	8.7	11,623	5.8	7,059	7.7	4,806	9.8	3,358	12.3
Specialised banks									
Mortgage banks of which:	5.9	42	17.2	46	13.6	40	13.0	38	13.9
Private mortgage banks^f	–	26	5.8	29	6.6	26	8.2	27	9.0
Public mortgage banks^f	–	16	11.4	17	7.1	14	4.8	11	4.9
Instalment sales financing institutions ^{ef}	–	262	1.5	180	1.1	123	1.1	–	–
Banks with special functions^f	–	18	10.2	17	8.4	17	6.5	16	6.7
Postal giro and postal savings bank offices^f	–	15	2.4	15	1.9	15	2.0	15	1.5
Total	85.5	13,221	100	8,479	99.9	5,909	100	4,341	99.9

Notes: ^{a} Volume of business is the balance sheet total plus endorsement liabilities on rediscounted bills, own drawings in circulation discounted and credited to borrowers, and bills from the banks' portfolios dispatched for collection prior to maturity.

[b] Banks reporting for the Monthly Balance Sheet Statistics excluding the assets and liabilities of their foreign branches and building and loan associations.

[c] No figures available for number of banks in 1950.

[d] Branches of foreign banks included in regional and other commercial banks in 1950 and 1960.

[e] Category instalment sales financing institutions dissolved in 1986, and the 72 banks in it reclassified as regional and other commercial banks (42), private bankers (22) and credit cooperatives (8).

[f] No figures available for private and public mortgage banks, instalment sales financing institutions, banks with special functions, and postal giro and postal savings banks in 1950.

Source: Monthly Report of the Deutsche Bundesbank, March 1961, April 1962, December 1971, August 1978; Deutsche Bundesbank (1989).

Table 5.2. *The largest German banks by asset size, 1975 and 1988, DM billion*

	Group balance sheet total at end 1975		Group balance sheet total at end 1988
Deutsche Bank	91.5	Deutsche Bank	305.3
Dresdner Bank	74.1	Dresdner Bank	231.0
Westdeutsche Landesbank	67.9	Commerzbank	180.4
		Westdeutsche Landesbank	171.1
Commerzbank	56.6		
Bayerische Vereinsbank	48.7	Bayerische Vereinsbank	162.6
Bayerische Landesbank	45.7	Hypo-Bank	135.2
		DG Bank	131.7
Hypo-Bank	40.2	Bayerische Landesbank	128.0
Hessische Landesbank	39.3		
		Norddeutsche Landesbank	107.8
Norddeutsche Landesbank	35.9		
		Kreditanstalt für Wiederaufbau	97.0
BfG	35.1		

Sources: For 1975 Smith (1983), Table 8.1 (a); 1988 *The Banker*, October 1989, p. 103.

households, particularly for housing, and fulfilling the financial requirements of the local communities which are usually their owners. Although the savings banks have been genuine universal banks (on the wide definition) since 1945, their particular strengths in banking business reflect their traditional functions. The same is true of the lowest tier of the credit cooperative sector, the credit cooperatives, whose historical origins were as cooperative banks intended to support their urban or agricultural members. But although the structure of the banking business of both the savings banks and the credit cooperatives reflects their traditional functions, both categories of banks conduct all forms of banking business.

The data on the German banking system published by the Bundesbank record as separate banks those which have significant ownership links with other banks: for example, most private mortgage banks are at least partially owned by commercial banks. Table 5.2 shows the largest ten German banks by asset size at the end of 1975 and 1988 when account is taken of such ownership links. The data in table 5.2 are taken from the consolidated balance sheets shown in banks' accounts and therefore include the assets of foreign subsidiaries, so that they are not directly comparable with the Bundesbank's volume of business data on which table 5.1 is based.

We turn now to a brief description of each of the main categories of German bank identified in the Bundesbank's analysis of the banking system.

Commercial banks

As table 5.1 shows, the commercial banks as a whole accounted for 36.4% of the domestic volume of business of all banks at the end of 1950, but since then their share has been considerably lower, and fairly steady at around 24–25%. There are four distinct classes of banks in this category.

The big banks – Deutsche Bank, Dresdner Bank, Commerzbank and their Berlin subsidiaries[4] – are each stock corporations (AGs), and operate nationally through a network of local branch offices. Although they are the largest German banks in terms of balance sheet totals, as table 5.2 shows, their share in the domestic volume of banking business is not overwhelming, according to table 5.1. However, table 5.1 does not take account of the big banks' large ownership interests in other financial institutions. These interests are particularly significant in private mortgage banks because, with a very small number of exceptions, the issuing of mortgage bonds and granting of mortgage loans are restricted to mortgage banks. Table 5.1 also fails to reflect the major role played by the big

---

[4] The big three banks were broken up into a number of 'Successor Banks', each limited to operating in one Land (state), by the Occupation Forces in 1946/7. However, by 1952 the Federal Republic was divided into three banking areas, and in each area a 'Successor' of the former big three banks operated. The three 'Successors' of each of the big three acted in an increasingly uniform manner, and in recognition of the reality a law to terminate the 'Restriction of the Regional Scope of Credit Institutions' was passed on 24 December 1956. The big three banks reconstituted themselves in 1957 and 1958. In each case the Berlin affiliates were excluded from the amalgamation because Berlin business was felt to require separate and independent arrangements given the political and economic situation.

banks in securities and safe custody business, which will be discussed in the next section of this chapter.

The second class of commercial banks is made up of the regional and other commercial banks, which comprise all banks other than the big banks that are organised as AGs, partnerships limited by shares (KGaAs), or private limited companies (GmbHs). These banks concentrate on providing universal banking services in their particular regions, but some maintain systems of branches which allow them to operate on a multi-regional or national basis. Two such banks with an extensive branch network are the Bayerische Vereinsbank and the Hypo-Bank (Bayerische Hypotheken- und Wechselbank) which, as table 5.2 shows, are among the largest ten German banks. These two Bavarian banks are, in contrast to almost all other commercial banks, permitted to operate as mortgage banks. Another bank with an extensive branch network is the Bank für Gemeinwirtschaft (BfG), which was originally owned by the trade unions and the cooperative movement, but was sold to the Aachener und Münchener insurance group in 1987. As table 5.1 shows, the share of this class of banks in the domestic volume of business of all banks has been fairly constant over the period 1950–1988.

The other two classes of bank in the commercial bank group – branches of foreign banks and private bankers – are not very significant in the German banking system as a whole, as table 5.1 shows. Foreign bank branches are permitted to participate in the same range of banking activities as domestic banks. Private bankers consist of all banks organised as general partnerships (OHGs) or limited partnerships (KGs) (banks have been prohibited since 1976 from organising as sole proprietorships). Although private bankers conduct all banking activities, they tend to specialise in particular types of banking business, such as export finance, securities trading, industrial finance, property management or housing finance.

Savings bank sector

Table 5.1 shows that the savings bank sector had the largest share of any category of bank in the domestic volume of business of all banks in all the years shown except 1950. The savings banks were originally conceived not as commercial profit-making concerns but rather as state institutions with obligations to provide banking services to less well-off members of the community, to furnish credit on favourable terms to public authorities, and to finance local investment of benefit to the region in which the savings bank was located. Although the savings banks still have these obligations, they have developed into universal banks which compete with the commercial banks for most forms of banking business.

There are three tiers within the savings bank sector. The lowest tier comprises the local savings banks (Sparkassen), which are municipal or district institutions incorporated under public law as independent legal entities. Each state (Land) has its own Savings Bank Act which specifies the structure and organisation of savings banks in that state, provides for their supervision by state authorities, and imposes full liability for their debts on the founding municipality or district. A local savings bank is usually permitted to operate only in its own region, and its investments in securities and certain other assets are subject to restrictions. Local savings banks within a state are members of a state savings bank association.

The second tier of the savings bank sector consists of the state savings banks or central giro institutions (Landesbanken-Girozentralen). Each state savings bank is incorporated under public law and is owned, in varying proportions, by its respective state government and state savings bank association, both of which have unlimited liability for its debts. The state savings banks serve as clearing houses for their member local savings banks, function as state bankers in their respective states, and conduct banking business on an interregional and international basis. The largest state saving bank is the Westdeutsche Landesbank Girozentrale which, as table 5.2 shows, is roughly comparable to Commerzbank in terms of consolidated balance sheet assets. Table 5.2 also shows that three other state savings banks were among the largest ten German banks at the end of 1975 – Bayerische Landesbank Girozentrale, Hessische Landesbank Girozentrale, and Norddeutsche Landesbank Girozentrale – and two of these were also among the largest ten banks at the end of 1988.

The third tier of the savings bank sector is the central savings bank, the Deutsche Girozentrale (DGZ), which serves as the central clearing bank for the savings bank system and holds the liquidity reserves for the state savings banks. The DGZ is similar to the state savings banks in terms of the banking business it conducts, but it is smaller in size than many of them. In the Bundesbank data on the German banking system, the DGZ is included with the state savings banks in the category regional giro institutions.

Although both local savings banks and state savings banks are universal banks, certain activities, such as securities trading, underwriting, and international business, are more important for the latter than for the former. The local savings banks raise large amounts of funds from non-banks in the form of sight deposits and bank savings bonds, while the regional giro institutions raise relatively small sums from non-banks. The local savings banks tend to have a surplus of funds and so have relatively large holdings of securities, consisting to a considerable extent of bonds issued by regional giro institutions, which are the single most important source of finance for these institutions. As far as lending to firms is concerned, the local savings banks in a particular region tend to concentrate on making loans to small firms, while the regional giro institutions tend to lend more to medium- and large-sized firms.

Credit cooperative sector

Table 5.1 shows that the share of the credit cooperative sector in the volume of domestic business of all banks fell from 1950 to 1960, but since then has been steadily rising. The credit cooperatives originated simply as cooperative banks providing credit for their members, but have since developed to become universal banks.

The organisation of the credit cooperative sector is similar to that of the savings bank sector. There is a large number of local credit cooperatives and a system of larger regional banks headed by a central clearing house institution. The first tier of this sector comprises local banks organised as cooperatives, whose members are local individuals and businesses. Members of local credit cooperatives contribute capital: there are usually provisions which limit the share of the capital which can be held by any individual member of a credit cooperative, with the result that the capital is almost always widely held. Membership of the credit cooperative used to be a requirement for obtaining a loan, but this is no longer the case. In the event of insolvency the liability of a local credit cooperative's members usually exceeds the capital already contributed by an amount laid down in the bank's statutes: this amount varies, but is commonly equal to the capital already paid in.

The local credit cooperatives are headed by a second tier consisting of regional central cooperative banks, which are either stock corporations or registered cooperatives owned by the local credit cooperatives, and a third tier consisting of a federal clearing house institution, the Deutsche Genossenschaftsbank (DG Bank), which is a stock corporation mainly owned by the regional credit cooperatives. In the Bundesbank data these two tiers are combined to form the category regional institutions of the credit cooperatives. In contrast to the savings bank sector it is the DG Bank that is the most important in this category: as table 5.2 shows, it was the seventh largest German bank in terms of consolidated balance sheet assets at the end of 1988. The regional central cooperative banks are typically much smaller than the state savings banks.

The relationship between the local credit cooperatives and the regional institutions of the credit cooperatives is similar to that between the local savings banks and the regional giro institutions. The local credit co-operatives raise relatively large amount of funds in the form of personal savings deposits, while the regional institutions of the credit cooperatives do relatively little deposit banking business and raise the majority of their funds by borrowing from other banks, in particular from the local credit cooperatives. The regional institutions also participate more than the local credit cooperatives in securities and foreign exchange markets, handle investment and international transactions for their local member banks, and serve as clearing houses for the payments transactions of the local credit cooperatives.

Mortgage banks

Among those banks in Germany which provide a specialised range of banking services rather than universal services, the most important group consists of the mortgage banks. The share of the mortgage banks as a whole in the volume of domestic business of all banks rose sharply from 1950 to 1960, fell somewhat from 1960 to 1970, and has subsequently remained fairly constant. Mortgage banks may be organised as either private or public institutions under a special set of laws which govern activity in this sector of the banking system. These laws generally limit mortgage banks to making long-term mortgage loans and loans to muni-cipalities and other public authorities. Mortgage banks fund their loans mainly by issuing bonds backed by mortgage and municipal loans, and also by long-term deposits. Since with a very few exceptions other banks are prohibited from issuing mortgage bonds, most private mortgage banks are at least partly owned by commercial banks wishing to enter this segment of the market. In some cases the holdings of commercial banks in private mortgage banks are very large indeed: at the end of 1989 Com-merzbank, for example, owned 97% of Rheinische Hypothekenbank AG (the largest private mortgage bank), Deutsche Bank owned 93.1% of Frankfurter Hypothekenbank AG (the second largest private mortgage bank), and Dresdner Bank owned 94.8% of Deutsche Hypothekenbank Frankfurt AG (the third largest private mortgage bank).

Banks with special functions

The group of banks with special functions comprises various public and private institutions which have been formed to offer specialised banking services. The largest such institution is the government-owned Kredit-anstalt für Wiederaufbau (KfW), which was set up in 1948 to administer Marshall Aid funds for the reconstruction of German industry, and now provides loan finance in a number of specialised areas, such as export finance, finance of projects in less developed countries, environmental programmes, and loans to small- and medium-sized German firms. A little under half of the KfW's funds comes from government loans: the remainder comes from bank loans, other loans, and bond issues. As table 5.2 shows, at the end of 1988 the KfW was the tenth largest German bank in terms of consolidated balance sheet assets. Another government-owned bank is the Deutsche Ausgleichsbank, which specialises in the provision of start-up finance for German enterprises. Industriekreditbank AG – Deutsche Industriebank is a privately-owned bank which was established by German industry to serve the financing needs of small- and medium-sized enterprises, and it specialises in providing medium- and long-term loans to these enterprises. The share of banks with special functions in the volume of domestic business of all banks has declined from 10.2% at the end of 1960 to 6.7% at the end of 1988.

The degree of concentration in the German banking system

Chapter 2 proposed a theoretical foundation for the various components of the widely-held view of the merits of the German system of investment finance. It was argued that the German system of universal banks with representation on supervisory boards might be particularly well suited to the exploitation of economies of scale and scope in information collection and in the exercise of the control rights attached to debt and equity finance. This argument suggests that an efficient system of investment finance may be one with strong elements of natural monopoly, in which a small number of universal banks become dominant because of the economies of scale and scope that exist in information-gathering and the exercise of control rights. But if economies of scale and scope mean that there is a lack of competition in the system of finance for investment, it is also possible that the dominant universal banks will exploit their monopoly power and hence an efficient system will not result. This section begins investigating the extent to which such dominant universal banks do, in fact, exist in Germany, by assessing the degree of concentration in various parts of the German banking system.

Domestic volume of banking business

The data presented in table 5.1 above suggest that, in terms of the share of the domestic volume of business of all banks accounted for by individual categories of banks, the German banking system over the period 1950–1988 was not highly concentrated. The largest three banks (the big banks)

Table 5.3. *Share of largest five German banks in balance sheet total of all German banks, end 1987*

Bank	Group balance sheet total DM million	Share of all German banks' balance sheet total %
Deutsche Bank	268,341	7.3
Dresdner Bank	206,938	5.6
Commerzbank	161,731	4.4
Westdeutsche Landesbank	152,504	4.1
Bayerische Vereinsbank	149,663	4.0

Source: Own calculations based on *Die Bank*, 11/88, pp. 645–647.

accounted for 19.1% of the domestic volume of business in 1950,[5] but from 1960 onwards this share was only about 10%. However, as has been noted, table 5.1 is based on the Bundesbank data on the banking system, which does not take account of the strong ownership links that exist between some banks, and thus underestimates the extent to which the overall volume of business of German banks is concentrated. To overcome this problem, it is possible to use consolidated balance sheet data taken from banks' annual reports to measure concentration. These data take account of the subsidiaries owned by banks, although they have one drawback in terms of measuring concentration within the banking system in Germany, which is that they also include holdings in foreign subsidiaries. Table 5.3 shows the share of the balance sheet total of all German banks accounted for by the largest five German banks at the end of 1987. The share of the largest five German banks was 25.4%, while that of the three big banks was 17.3%. These figures suggest that although the degree of concentration in the domestic volume of business of German banks is underestimated by table 5.1, the broad impression given by that table is accurate: this is a banking system in which the three big banks are significant in terms of the volume of business of all banks, but not dominant. If concentration is measured in this way, the German banking system is in fact less concentrated than is the UK system. Unfortunately it is not possible to compare the shares of the largest German and UK banks in the balance sheet total of all banks in the respective countries, due to the absence of comprehensive data for the UK. However a limited comparison is possible using data published in *The Banker* for October 1989. At the end of 1988, the share of the largest three German banks in the consolidated balance sheet total of the largest 25 German banks was 30.4%, while

[5] Strictly speaking, the 'Successor Banks' of the big banks accounted for this share in 1950.

the share of the largest five German banks was 44.6%. By contrast, at the end of 1988 the largest three UK banks made up 57.0% of the balance sheet total of the largest 25 UK banks, and the largest five made up 73.7%.

Lending to domestic firms

The Bundesbank has published data on bank lending to domestic non-bank enterprises and self-employed persons by different categories of banks since 1969. The form in which this data was published, however, was changed at the end of 1980. From 1969 to 1980 the figures for bank lending to domestic non-bank enterprises and self-employed persons excluded mortgage loans secured by housing sites, but included other housing loans and mortgage loans secured by real estate used for industrial purposes. After 1980 the exclusion of mortgage loans secured by housing sites was ended, so that the figures from that date onward included all forms of lending to domestic non-bank enterprises and self-employed persons for housing purposes, as well as mortgage loans secured by industrial real estate. A direct comparison between the lending data under the two different definitions is only possible for the end 1980 figures. Table 5.4 shows the shares of different categories of banks in total bank lending to domestic non-bank enterprises and self-employed persons in 1980 according to both definitions, as well as in 1970 and 1988 according to the pre- and post-1980 definitions respectively. As we saw in chapter 3, the capital finance account of the Deutsche Bundesbank divides the enterprise sector into producing enterprises and housing, because housing finance involves rather different considerations from the finance of investment by producing enterprises. The pre-1980 definition of bank lending to domestic non-bank enterprises and self-employed persons, which excludes most, but not all, housing loans, is therefore the most appropriate one for the purposes of the questions investigated in this book.

Table 5.4 shows that the big banks' share of total bank lending to domestic non-bank enterprises and self-employed persons was somewhat larger than their share of the domestic volume of bank business. The share of the big banks appears to have fallen from 1970 to 1980, and then risen again from 1980 to 1988. If the relationship between the big banks' share of lending excluding and including mortgage loans secured by housing sites in 1980 is assumed to apply to the 1988 figure for the big banks' share (including mortgage loans for housing), an estimate of 14.3% is obtained for the big banks' share of loans to domestic non-bank enterprises and self-employed persons (excluding mortgage loans for housing) in 1988, as

Table 5.4. *Bank lending to domestic non-bank enterprises and self-employed persons by various categories of bank, 1970, 1980 and 1988, %*

	End 1970[a]	End 1980[a]	End 1980[b]	End 1988[b]
Commercial banks	36.3	30.0	25.9	28.7
of which:				
Big banks	16.0	12.5	10.5	12.0
Regional and other commercial banks	16.5	13.4	12.0	13.6
Branches of foreign banks	–	1.7	1.4	1.1
Private bankers	3.8	2.4	2.0	2.0
Savings bank sector	32.3	35.6	36.9	34.9
of which:				
Regional giro institutions	14.5	13.6	14.4	11.9
Savings banks	17.8	22.0	22.5	23.0
Credit cooperative sector	12.7	17.7	15.3	15.8
of which:				
Regional institutions of credit cooperatives	1.9	2.7	2.2	2.0
Credit cooperatives	10.8	15.0	13.1	13.8
Mortgage banks	7.1	7.3	14.7	14.5
of which:				
Private mortgage banks	4.9	5.9	8.6	9.4
Public mortgage banks	2.2	1.4	6.1	5.1
Instalment sales financing institutions	1.2	1.4	1.1	–
Banks with special functions	8.1	5.1	3.6	4.0
Postal giro and postal savings bank offices	2.4	2.8	2.3	2.1
Total	100.1	99.9	99.8	100.0

Notes: [a] Excluding mortgage loans secured by housing sites (see text for details).
[b] Including mortgage loans secured by housing sites (see text for details).
Sources: Statistical Supplements to the *Monthly Reports of the Deutsche Bundesbank*, Series 1, Banking Statistics, Table 6, December 1971, April 1981, August 1989.

compared with 16.0% in 1970. Neither of these figures suggests that the big banks dominate the market for bank lending to domestic non-bank enterprises and self-employed persons. Of course, the big banks own several large private mortgage banks, so the figures in table 5.4 somewhat underestimate the overall importance of the big banks in lending to domestic firms. But if, in a rough attempt to take account of this feature of the German banking system, half the figure for the private mortgage banks in table 5.4 is added to the figures for the big banks, the resulting estimate of the overall share of the big banks in lending to domestic firms in 1970 is still only 18.5%.

It is clear from table 5.4 that the main effect of the 1980 shift in the definition of bank lending to domestic non-bank enterprises and self-employed persons (from excluding mortgage loans secured by housing sites to including them) was to increase the share of the mortgage banks and lower the share of the commercial bank sector. This is because, as we have seen, most commercial banks are prevented from making mortgage loans. If the procedure described in the previous paragraph to estimate the big banks' share in 1988 of total bank loans to domestic firms (excluding mortgage loans for housing) is applied to the commercial bank sector as a whole, the following figures are obtained. In 1988, the estimated share of the commercial banks in bank lending to domestic enterprises and self-employed persons, excluding mortgage loans for housing, was 33.2%, of which the big banks accounted for 14.3%, the regional and other commercial banks 15.2%, foreign banks 1.3%, and private bankers 2.4%.

The corporate governance role of banks

Our assessment of the degree of concentration in the German banking system so far has focused on the overall volume of business and bank lending to domestic non-bank enterprises and self-employed persons, both of which are reflected in banks' balance sheets. There are, however, some aspects of German banking business which are not reflected in banks' balance sheets, such as securities and safe custody business. These aspects of banking business are very important for an understanding of German banks' role in corporate governance, and must be considered before a satisfactory assessment of the degree of concentration in German banking can be achieved. The data available for examining the extent of concentration in these aspects of banking business is, unfortunately, much less comprehensive than the balance sheet statistics used in this chapter up to now.

The important role that German banks can play in corporate governance in Germany derives from their control of equity voting rights at shareholders' meetings. As we saw in chapter 4, the supervisory board has the function of controlling the management of AGs, and shareholders' representatives on the supervisory board are elected at the annual general meeting of the shareholders. Hence, depending on the extent of their control of equity voting rights, banks can have a significant influence on the outcome of votes at shareholders' meetings, and in particular on shareholder representation on supervisory boards.

Because the vast majority of German shares are unregistered bearer ones, many shareholders, particularly private individuals, use the banks' securities deposit service for the safe custody and administration of their shares. Banks which hold shares for depositors can exercise the voting rights attached to these shares under the direction of the depositors. Before 1965 the Depotstimmrecht (deposit voting right) of banks took the form of depositors being able to authorise banks to exercise their voting rights for periods of 15 months at a time. Depositors could issue voting instructions to banks during this period, but banks were not required to ask for such instructions. Since a change in the law in 1965, a bank to which a 15 month proxy voting right has been given must indicate to the depositor how it intends to vote on the various issues on the agenda at a particular shareholders' meeting, and ask the depositor for directions as to how the bank should exercise the proxy votes. If no directions are given by the depositor, the bank can exercise the proxy votes according to its stated intention to vote. The bank may only depart from casting the proxy votes according to its original statement of intent if it can safely assume that, under the circumstances, the depositor would have agreed to the change. In this case the bank must inform the depositor of the change, and give reasons for it.

The proxy votes exercised by banks on behalf of shareholders are the major source of banks' ability to control the outcome of votes at shareholder meetings. The sum of the nominal value of shares deposited with banks and the nominal value of banks' own shareholdings has been consistently estimated at between 55 and 60% of the total nominal value of shares in those years for which data is available. According to the Bundesbank, in 1964 50.5% of the total nominal value of German shares (excluding insurance enterprise shares) was deposited with banks, while banks' own holdings were some 5% of this total, giving a combined figure of 55.5% (Deutsche Bundesbank, 1965, p. 4). Immenga (1978) estimated that in 1976 50.7% of the total nominal value of shares in Germany was deposited with banks while banks' own holdings were 7.5%, giving a combined figure of 58.2%. In 1988, according to Bundesbank figures,[6] 53.5% of the total nominal value of German shares (excluding insurance enterprise shares) was deposited with banks, and banks' own holdings were 8.1%, giving a combined figure of 61.6%. Clearly banks have the potential to exert a great deal of influence on the outcomes of votes at shareholders' meetings, although the actual extent of their influence

---

[6] Supplement to *Statistical Supplements to the Monthly Reports of the Deutsche Bundesbank*, Series 1, Banking Statistics by Category of Banks, July 1989, no. 7, p. 3.

Table 5.5. *Nominal value of deposits of domestic shares with banks by category of bank, end 1977 and end 1988, % of total*

	End 1977	End 1988
Commercial banks	76.4	77.7
of which: Big banks	47.5	44.6
Regional and other commercial banks	21.5	27.2
Branches of foreign banks	0.3	0.2
Private bankers	7.1	5.7
Savings bank sector	18.6	16.3
of which: Regional giro institutions	9.0	7.8
Savings banks	9.6	8.5
Credit cooperative sector	3.1	4.7
of which: Regional institutions of credit cooperatives	0.6	1.6
Credit cooperatives	2.5	3.0
Other banks	1.9	1.3
Total	100.0	100.0

Note: [a] Figures for 1988 are for domestic shares excluding insurance enterprise shares.
Sources: Gessler Commission and Supplement to *Statistical Supplements to the Monthly Reports of the Deutsche Bundesbank*, Series 1, July 1989, no. 7.

depends on the proportion of the shares deposited with them for which they can control the proxy voting rights.[7]

Table 5.5 shows the distribution of deposited shares between various categories of banks in 1977 and 1988. The 1977 figures come from the report[8] of the Commission for Fundamental Problems of the Credit Sector, or Gessler Commission, while the 1988 figures come from the Bundesbank's security deposit statistics.[9] In both years the commercial banks as a whole held just over three-quarters of all shares deposited with German banks. Well over half of the commercial banks' holdings of deposited shares were accounted for by the three big banks, which held 47.5% of all deposited shares in 1977 and 44.6% in 1988. The big banks in

---

[7] It may seem reasonable to suppose that, for obvious reasons connected with the costs of deciding how to vote, most depositors would not make any use of their right to instruct the bank how to vote, so that most of the voting rights attached to the shares deposited with them are at the banks' disposal. But many of the shares deposited with banks are owned by non-financial enterprises or government (in 1988 17.5% and 4.3% of the total nominal value of shares respectively), and it is not obvious that these shareholders have no incentives to instruct the banks how to vote.

[8] Gessler Commission (1979).

[9] See n. 6 above.

particular, and the commercial banks in general, were proportionally far more important in terms of their holdings of all shares deposited with German banks in 1977 and 1988 than they were in terms of the overall volume of business or total lending to domestic non-bank enterprises and self-employed persons.

It is not possible to obtain such detailed figures concerning the distribution of shares deposited with banks for earlier years, but it is possible to obtain from the Bundesbank's security deposit statistics a breakdown of deposited shares, although this does not distinguish between the different classes of banks within the category of commercial banks. At the end of 1962, commercial banks held 82.6% of all domestic shares (excluding insurance enterprise shares) deposited with banks. The corresponding figures for the savings bank sector were 14.7% (regional giro institutions 7.2%, savings banks 7.5%); for the credit cooperative sector 1.7% (regional institutions of the credit cooperatives 0.1%, credit cooperatives 1.6%); and for other banks 1.0%.[10] Comparing these figures with those shown in table 5.4 suggests that the shares deposited at German banks in 1962 were also likely to be concentrated at the three big banks.

The equity owned by German banks is also concentrated in the hands of the big banks. This is true for equity held in the form both of portfolio investments and of participations.[11] For the former, the *Monthly Report of the Deutsche Bundesbank* (May 1987) showed that the big banks held 50% of all German banks' holdings of domestic shares (excluding participations) in 1970, and 51.3% in 1986. The regional and other commercial banks accounted for 25.4% in 1970 and 22.2% in 1986. For bank equity holding in the form of participations, table 5.6 gives some impression of the degree of concentration. This table shows the results of a comprehensive investigation by the Gessler Commission into the holdings by individual banks of 10% or more of the equity of non-bank companies, including large GmbHs as well as AGs, on 31 December 1974. Here again, the big banks accounted for more than 40% of the total nominal value of bank equity holdings. However, in contrast to the figures for deposited shares and pure portfolio investments, the figures for participations show a significant proportion held by the regional giro institutions. The Gessler Commission investigation showed that the largest 10 bank holders of

[10] Source for these figures *Monthly Report of the Deutsche Bundesbank*, July 1965, p. 10.
[11] According to the banking statistics published by the Bundesbank, a participation comes into being if an 'intention to participate' exists, that is, if the equity owner intends to be significantly involved with the company on a long-term basis. In doubtful cases this includes a shareholding with an aggregate par value equal to one-quarter of the company's nominal capital (see *Monthly Report of the Deutsche Bundesbank*, May 1987, p. 25).

Table 5.6. *Ownership of non-bank companies by type of bank, 1974*

	No. of banks in survey	No. of banks with equity holdings in non-banks	Holdings in non-banks		
			No.	Nominal value DM million	% of total nominal value
Big banks*a*	6	6	87	1489.4	41.0
Regional banks and other credit banks	112	41	211	740.5	20.4
Private banks	123	35	101	188.7	5.2
Regional giro institutions	12	12	135	901.8	24.8
Savings banks	53	25	62	72.6	2.0
Regional institutions of credit cooperatives	12	11	45	158.8	4.4
Banks with special functions	18	8	21	80.5	2.2
Total	336	138	662	3631.8	100.0

Note: *a* Including Berlin subsidiaries.
Source: Gessler Commission, para. 295.

non-bank equity stakes of 10% or more accounted for 75.8% of the nominal value of all such bank holdings.

The evidence presented here shows that bank control of equity voting rights is to a large extent concentrated in the hands of the big banks. This concentration is reflected in bank representation on supervisory boards. A government enquiry into concentration in the German economy[12] surveyed 425 AGs in 1960, and found that there were 795 bank representatives on their supervisory boards, 211 of which were chairmen of the supervisory board. The three big banks accounted for 423 of the bank representatives (53.2%) and 119 of the supervisory board chairmen who were bankers (56.4%). Table 5.7, taken from a report of the German Monopoly Commission, provides details of bank representation on the supervisory boards of all AGs, KGaAs and GmbHs in 1974. The big banks had over 40% of the total bank representation on the supervisory boards of AGs, and the commercial banks as a whole accounted for 83.9%. For GmbHs, bank representation on supervisory boards was less concentrated than for AGs, and the individual category of banks with the largest share of bank representation on the supervisory boards of GmbHs was not the big banks but the regional giro institutions. As a consequence,

[12] *Bericht über Ergebnis einer Untersuchung der Konzentration in der Wirtschaft*, Bonn, Deutscher Bundestag, Drucksache IV/2320, 1964.

Table 5.7. *Bank representation on supervisory boards by bank group, 1974*

	AGs		GmbHs		All AGs, KGaAs, GmbHs	
	No. of rep-resentatives	%	No. of rep-resentatives	%	No. of rep-resentatives	%
Big banks	405	41.1	71	20.4	483	34.5
Regional and other commercial banks	252	25.6	55	15.8	314	22.4
Private bankers	170	17.2	14	4.0	185	13.2
Regional giro institutions	86	8.7	82	23.6	170	12.2
Savings banks	29	2.9	66	19.0	119	8.5
Credit cooperative sector	19	1.9	31	8.9	73	5.2
Banks with special functions	25	2.5	29	8.3	55	3.9
Total	986	99.9	348	100.0	1399	99.9

Source: Monopolkommission (1976), Table 48, p. 256.

the concentration of bank representation on supervisory boards in the hands of the big banks was less pronounced for all companies than it was for AGs alone. However, it must be recalled that it is for AGs that German banks' corporate governance role is potentially most important. The ability of banks to influence the management of AGs through control of equity voting rights and supervisory board representation is concentrated among the big banks, and more generally within the commercial bank sector.

Underwriting of new share issues

Another aspect of securities business in which the big banks, and especially Deutsche Bank, have a dominant position is the underwriting of new share issues by AGs. The usual procedure by which a listed AG in Germany issues shares, whether as an initial public offering or as an issue by an already-listed company, involves a syndicate of banks first buying the issue from the company at a price negotiated between the company and the syndicate. As a second, separate, step, the syndicate then offers the shares to the market. The syndicate therefore bears the risk of placing the issue. The details of the issue are arranged by the leader of the syndicate, which is usually the house bank of the company. All the

Table 5.8. *Importance of various categories of banks in syndicates for new share issues by domestic firms, 1966–1975*

No. of banks in category	Category of banks	Proportion of	
		Leaders of syndicates	Total no. of cases of participation in syndicates
6	Big banks	60.3	30.7
29	Regional and other commercial banks	25.1	32.5
28	Private bankers	8.6	27.7
13	Regional giro institutions and DG Bank	6.0	9.1
	Total	100.0	100.0
		(537 cases)	(2,925 cases)

Note: ^a Including Berlin subsidiaries.
Source: Gessler Commission, Tables 17 and 25.

members of the syndicate receive a fee for the risk they bear in under-writing the issue, and the leader receives an additional fee for arranging the details of the issue. The composition of a particular AG's syndicate typically does not change very much over time.

The report of the Gessler Commission provides the most detailed infor-mation available about the share of different banks in underwriting business. The Gessler Commission conducted a survey of the 76 banks which formed the issuing syndicate for government bonds to obtain information concerning these banks' participation in issuing syndicates between 1966 and 1975. In this period there were 537 issues of new shares by domestic firms, and the 76 banks surveyed reported a total of 2,925 cases of participation in syndicates for these issues. The average number of banks in a syndicate, according to these figures, was therefore 5.45. This estimate is biased downward somewhat, since the issuing syndicates also included banks which were not members of the syndicate for govern-ment bond issues; however, this bias is not large.

Table 5.8 shows the importance of various categories of banks among the 76 surveyed by the Gessler Commission both as participants in syndicates for new share issues by domestic firms and as leaders of such syndicates. Syndicates for new share issues by domestic firms in the period 1966–1975 were dominated by banks from the commercial bank sector. The big banks were especially important as leaders of these syndicates, acting as syndicate leaders for 60.3% of the new share issues by domestic firms in this period. The dominant position of the big banks, especially

Table 5.9. *Membership of various categories of banks in issuing syndicates of 71 large listed AGs, 1974/75, %*

No. of banks in category	Category of banks	Proportion of syndicates of 71 AGs of which bank was	
		Leader	Member
3	Big banks	81.7	98.6
	of which: Deutsche Bank	54.9	97.2
	Dresdner Bank	25.4	84.5
	Commerzbank	1.4	73.2
3	Largest regional and other commercial banks [a]	4.2	62.0
14	Savings bank sector	5.6	33.8
1	DG Bank	–	9.9
74	Other banks [b]	8.5	94.4

Notes: [a] Bayerische Vereinsbank, Bayerische Hypotheken- und Wechsel Bank, Bank für Gemeinwirtschaft.
[b] Regional and other commercial banks and private bankers.
Source: Gessler Commission, Table 27.

Deutsche Bank, was most marked in the issuing syndicates for large listed AGs. Table 5.9 shows the results of an investigation by the Gessler Commission into the composition of the issuing syndicates of 71 large listed AGs in 1974 and 1975. The big banks as a group were members of the issuing syndicates of 70 of the 71 large listed AGs, and leaders of the syndicates of 58 of them. Deutsche Bank alone was a member of the syndicates of 69 of these AGs, and syndicate leader for 39.

The underwriting of new share issues by domestic firms is, therefore, concentrated in the hands of the big banks, especially so far as the leadership of issuing syndicates for large listed AGs is concerned. Evidence of concentration can, of course, only be suggestive of a lack of competition and the existence of monopoly profits. The report of the Gessler Commission did not state unambiguously that underwriting was a part of German banking business in which restrictions on competition allowed monopoly rents to be earned. It nevertheless concluded its discussion of securities issuing syndicates by saying that access to these syndicates, especially those for new share issues, was not easy for other banks even if these banks had adequate capital market- and placement-power, and by noting that the relative shares of different banks in syndicates had not changed much over time.[13] It seems reasonable to

[13] Gessler Commission (1979), para. 482.

conclude, as did Krummel (1980) in his review article on the Gessler Commission report, that underwriting business is subject to significant entry barriers, and hence that those banks which are members of new share issue syndicates are in a position to earn monopoly profits from their underwriting activities. Certainly the fees received by German banks for underwriting new share issues seem high by comparison with the fees paid to underwriters of new share issues in the UK.[14] According to the Gessler Commission report, the fee received by the banks in a new issue syndicate for the risk they bear in placing the issue in the market is 3.4% of the nominal value of the issue purchased by each bank. The leader of the syndicate receives, in addition to the fee for risk-bearing, a further 0.6% of the nominal value of the issue for arranging the details of the issue.[15] By comparison, the *Bank of England Quarterly Bulletin* (1986) reports that, in the UK, the issuing house which arranges a new share issue and underwrites it (usually in conjunction with a group of sub-underwriters) receives a fee of 2% of the nominal value of the issue. Out of this 2% fee the issuing house pays the sub-underwriters and the broker to the issue. The former receive 1¼% of the nominal value of the issue which they underwrite, and the latter receives ¼% of the nominal value of the issue.

The concentration both of bank representation on the supervisory boards of AGs and of leadership of syndicates for new share issues by AGs in the hands of the big banks suggests another way in which German institutional arrangements may lead to improved supply of external finance to firms. Representation on the supervisory board of an AG may give a bank information about the firm which would not otherwise be available and hence enable the bank more effectively to screen firms wishing to issue new shares. If this were the case, then the superior information available to the lead underwriter of German new share issues, the syndicate leader, might give German AGs greater access to new equity as a source of finance, because the informational imperfections which, it has been argued, limit firms' use of new equity (see, for example, Myers and Majluf, 1984) are reduced by the German system of investment

---

[14] Although the formal procedures by which already-listed companies make a new share issue are different in Germany and the UK, in effect the methods used in the two countries are similar. In the German procedure, the banks in a syndicate purchase the new shares from the company at a fixed price below the current market price and then sell the shares on the market. In the UK procedure, new shares are issued pro rata to existing shareholders at a price below the market price, and underwriters are paid a fee to take up any shares not subscribed. In both countries the price at which the new shares are issued is typically 15 to 20% below the market price, and the risk borne by the underwriters is that the price of the existing equity falls below the price of the new issue over a maximum period of three weeks around the time of the issue.

[15] Gessler Commission (1979), Table 30, p. 460.

finance. However, the evidence on the use of new equity finance by German AGs is not consistent with this hypothesis. Table 4.6 showed that AGs, all of which have supervisory boards, made proportionately less use of new equity to finance their investment than did GmbHs, most of which do not have supervisory boards. Mayer and Alexander (1990) used company accounting data to compare the sources of investment finance over the period 1982–1988 of 77 non-financial AGs chosen from the largest 115 companies quoted on the Frankfurt Stock Exchange with 73 non-financial UK companies chosen from the largest 115 companies quoted on the London Stock Exchange. They found that new equity issues accounted for 8.2% of the German firms' investment in physical and financial assets, compared to 14.3% for the UK firms. As a proportion of investment in physical assets only, new equity was − 10.2% for the German firms and − 11.3% for the UK firms.[16]

One other aspect of German banks' role as underwriters of new share issues which is worth discussing in more detail concerns initial public offerings, when AGs first obtain a listing on the German stock market. As was noted in chapter 1, one strand of the general argument that German banks are superior to UK ones in terms of overcoming information problems in the capital market concerns German banks' role as underwriters of initial public offerings by German firms. The argument here, based on experience in the late nineteenth and early twentieth centuries, is that the underwriting banks were able to screen firms which wanted to obtain a listing on the stock market, and hence prevent adverse selection problems from reducing, or eliminating, this potential source of finance.[17] Is there any evidence that close relationships between German banks and firms in the post-1945 period have enabled the banks to perform this screening function, and have hence promoted an active market for initial public offerings by German firms?

The exclusive right of banks to apply for the admission of a new security to the primary stock market tier (the official market) is laid down in Section 36 of the Stock Exchange Act. In the other stock market tiers (the regulated and unregulated markets) banks have also had the exclusive right to apply for admission ever since a loophole which enabled a non-bank, Portfolio Management GmbH, to take 10 firms to the un-official market was closed in 1984. Any firm which wishes to have its securities listed on the stock market must, therefore, submit itself to the scrutiny of a bank which will apply for admission and organise the issue. Banks are, therefore, in a position where they can in principle ensure that only good-quality firms receive a listing on the German stock market. In

[16] Mayer and Alexander (1990), Table II, p. 458.
[17] See pp. 9–10.

practice, however, until 1983 the number of initial public offerings on the German stock market was so small that it is not possible to argue that, by screening firms which wanted to list their shares, banks have maintained an active market for newly-listed firms. According to Schürmann (1980), there were only 25 initial public offerings on the German stock market in the entire period from 1959 to 1979. Ten of these 25 occurred between 1977 and 1979, perhaps because of the reform of the German corporation tax system in 1977, which had the effect of reducing the taxation of much equity-financed investment. Of the 15 initial public offerings which took place between 1959 and 1976, several were the result of privatisations, in which the Federal government sold some of its holdings in companies to private investors (for example, Lufthansa, Veba, and Volkswagen). A further 8 initial public offerings occurred between 1980 and 1982, but it was not until 1983 that the rate at which firms achieved an initial listing on the stock market began to increase rapidly, leading to a total of 125 initial public offerings from 1983 to 1989.[18] There has clearly been a marked change in the significance of initial public offerings in Germany in the 1980s, but the total number of new listings of companies on the German stock market over most of the period with which this book is concerned was very small. By comparison, the *Bank of England Quarterly Bulletin* (1986) reports that 102 companies made an initial public offering in the UK listed market during the three years from 1983 to 1985. It cannot, therefore, be argued that by screening firms which wanted to be listed, and hence ensuring that the market for long-term share finance from private investors was not spoiled by poor-quality firms, German banks created an active market for initial public offerings by firms which wanted wider access to supplies of equity finance.

Conclusion

This chapter has examined the structure of the German banking system with particular reference to the extent of concentration in it. In terms of the wide definition of a universal bank, as a bank providing a complete range of commercial and investment banking services, the German banking system has been relatively unconcentrated in the post-1945 period. There are three categories of universal banks – the commercial banks, the savings bank sector, and the credit cooperative sector. Within each of these categories there is a large number of banks, and although

---

[18] The dominant position of the big banks as leaders of issuing syndicates continued to be apparent for these 125 new listings. As a group, the big banks were syndicate leaders for 63.2% of the new listings, with Deutsche Bank being the leader in 52 cases, Dresdner Bank in 13, and Commerzbank in 14.

many of them are rather small banks, there is no evidence that a small number of universal banks is dominant in the banking system, whether in terms of their share of the overall volume of business of German banks, or in terms of their share of total German bank lending to domestic non-bank enterprises and self-employed persons. However, the position is different if we adopt the narrow definition of a universal bank, as a bank with the ability to influence non-banks through equity ownership, the exercise of proxy voting rights, and supervisory board membership. The ability of German banks to play a part in corporate governance through these mechanisms has indeed been concentrated in the hands of the three big banks during the post-1945 period, although these three banks are not the only ones capable of exerting influence on non-banks in these ways. On the narrow definition of a universal bank, it seems reasonable to describe the three big banks as dominant in the German banking system. This impression is reinforced by evidence showing the big banks' dominant position as leaders of syndicates for new share issues by German AGs.

The market for bank lending to firms in Germany does appear to be a competitive one, as is shown by the large number of universal banks (on the wide definition), and the lack of any evidence of lending to domestic non-bank enterprises and self-employed persons being dominated by a small number of banks. But care has to be exercised when drawing inferences about the degree of competition in German banking from a description of its structure. Competition among the numerous banks in Germany is to some extent limited by region. The local savings banks and credit cooperatives operate in only a single regional market, while typically the regional and other commercial banks, the regional giro institutions, and the regional institutions of the credit cooperatives operate in several regional markets. Only the big banks and a few others operate throughout Germany. Furthermore, banks in the savings bank and credit cooperative sectors tend not to compete with other banks in the same sector. A more detailed examination of the market for bank lending to firms in Germany is therefore required before we can definitely conclude that it has been characterised by competitive conditions.

By contrast, bank control of equity voting rights and representation on company supervisory boards in this period has been far more concentrated, with the three big banks having a much greater share in these activities than they did in total bank lending to firms. The big banks were also dominant as leaders of syndicates for new share issues by AGs. However, there was no evidence that supervisory board representation by banks which were leaders of issuing syndicates had enabled a greater supply of new equity finance to be made available to German AGs.

Furthermore, the contradiction between the significant degree of concentration in German banks' corporate governance activities and the lack of any significant degree of concentration in German bank lending to firms raises a number of questions about the hypothesis that there are economies of scope between the monitoring of managements (via supervisory board representation) and the efficient provision of external finance in the form of bank loans. In order to answer these questions, chapter 6 provides a more detailed analysis of bank lending to firms in Germany.

6 Bank supervisory board representation and other aspects of German bank lending to firms

Introduction

This chapter extends the analysis of bank lending to firms begun in chapter 5. In that chapter it was shown that German bank lending to firms was not concentrated in the hands of the three big banks, while bank control of equity voting rights and bank representation on company supervisory boards was. This contrast raises some questions about the hypothesis that a system of investment finance characterised by universal banks with representation on supervisory boards is efficient because it exploits economies of scale and scope in information-collection and in the exercise of control rights attached to debt and equity finance. However, the bank lending data presented in chapter 5 was for loans to all German firms, while only AGs and large GmbHs are required to have supervisory boards. It is therefore possible that, although bank lending to all German firms is not concentrated, bank lending to those firms which have supervisory boards is concentrated among particular banks in a way which reflects the concentration of bank supervisory board representation. In order to evaluate the hypothesis that there are significant economies of scale and scope in information-gathering and the exercise of control rights, it is necessary to examine whether a relatively small number of universal banks have a dominant position in bank lending to German firms with supervisory boards as well as in bank representation on supervisory boards. If bank supervisory board representation reduces information asymmetries, there should also be evidence that bank lending is a more important source of finance for those German firms which have supervisory boards than for those which do not.

The idea that bank supervisory board representation has a favourable effect on the supply of loan finance to firms is an important part of the widely-held view of the merits of the German system of finance for investment. This chapter considers various aspects of German bank lending to firms in order to assess whether such a favourable effect exists. The second section analyses the evidence on the relative use of bank loan finance by German firms that do and do not have supervisory boards. The third section examines the claim that the German economy benefits from having a higher proportion of long-term bank lending than the UK economy has. The fourth section investigates the competitiveness of the market for bank loans, and in particular whether there is evidence of long-term commitment between banks and firms being established through house bank relationships which restrict competition. The fifth section discusses the basis on which German banks make decisions about loans to firms, and the significance of collateral in such decisions. The sixth section draws a conclusion.

Some of the evidence on which this chapter is based comes from interviews conducted by the authors in Germany in 1988. Interviews were carried out with 15 banks, 17 firms, 2 receivers, 1 chartered accountant, and 1 stock exchange employee. These interviews were granted on the condition that full confidentiality was maintained, so that in what follows references to the results of these interviews are intentionally general rather than specific. Further details of these interviews are given in the Appendix to this chapter.

Bank supervisory board representation and bank lending

There are two different, but not mutually exclusive, reasons why bank representation on a company's supervisory board might increase the supply of bank loan finance to that company. The first is that representation on a company's supervisory board may increase the information available to a bank which is relevant for its lending decisions. Supervisory board representation is therefore seen as reducing the extent of asymmetric information between lenders and borrowers, thereby enabling banks which have a presence on a company's supervisory board to supply debt finance to such companies on better terms, involving less credit-rationing and less stringent collateral requirements, than for firms where banks are not represented on the supervisory board. The second reason is that supervisory board representation may enable a bank to monitor management closely and influence decision-making within the company. In particular, this may diminish the costs of financial distress. Other things being equal, financial distress is more likely the higher the proportion of debt in a firm's total finance. It is claimed that the costs of financial distress are reduced by bank supervisory board representation, since this is seen as enabling a bank to prevent managers taking inefficient decisions in an attempt to avoid insolvency, and to reorganise firms before financial distress becomes acute. Hence it is possible for firms with bank representation on their supervisory boards to have a larger proportion of bank debt in their total finance than those without such bank representation.

Many German firms do not have supervisory boards. As was explained in chapter 4, all firms organised in the form of AGs are required to have a supervisory board, as do firms organised as GmbHs if they have more than 500 employees. Smaller GmbHs may have a supervisory board if they wish. The fraction of total turnover accounted for by AGs rose from about 17% in the early 1950s to about 20% in the 1970s and 1980s, while that accounted for by GmbHs increased from about 15% in the early 1950s to 17% in the early 1970s and 25% in the mid 1980s. It is not possible to establish the proportion of total turnover accounted for by GmbHs with greater than 500 employees. A very approximate measure of the importance of firms with supervisory boards in the German economy is provided by the fraction of total employment in Germany accounted for by firms employing 500 or more employees. In 1987 this figure was 34.4%.[1] It seems reasonable to regard one-third as being an upper bound estimate of the fraction of total output in the German economy produced by firms with supervisory boards.

The fact that many German firms do not have supervisory boards suggests a test of the hypothesis that bank supervisory board representation increases the supply of bank loan finance. The only legal form of enterprise in Germany which has to have a supervisory board is the AG. Furthermore, as table 5.7 showed, about 75% of all bank supervisory board representatives sit on the supervisory boards of AGs. If the hypothesis that supervisory board representation by banks increases their lending to firms is correct, we would expect to observe a greater use of bank loan finance by AGs than by other legal forms of enterprise in Germany.

The data on the finance of investment by different legal forms of enterprise analysed in chapter 4 showed that debt finance was less important as a source of finance for AGs than for GmbHs, partnerships or sole proprietorships. However, these data were not sufficiently detailed to enable bank borrowing to be identified explicitly. A clearer picture of the importance of bank loans as a source of finance for AGs compared to other legal forms of enterprise can be derived by comparing the financing of AGs with that of the producing enterprises sector as a whole. Weighted

---

[1] Source: own calculations based on Federal Statistical Office, Series 2, 'Unternehmen und Arbeitsstätten'.

averages over the period 1961–1976 of the net sources of finance[2] of the sample of 100 AGs studied by Geisen (1979) were compared to weighted averages of the net sources of finance for the producing enterprises sector as a whole over the same period. Overall bank borrowing comprised 7.3% of the net sources of finance of the sample of AGs over the period, compared to 13.2% of the net sources of producing enterprises as a whole. Long-term bank loans were 12.4% of the AGs' net sources, compared to 14.3% for producing enterprises. Internally-generated funds were 102.9% of the net sources of the sample of AGs, compared to 74.7% for producing enterprises.

A similar comparison, involving a larger sample of AGs and a more recent time period, is shown in table 6.1, where the sources of finance for investment calculated from aggregate company accounting data for a sample drawn from the population of all AGs in manufacturing over the period 1971–1985 are compared with the sources of finance of the producing enterprises sector as a whole. The size of this sample is constant over two year periods, but declines from 846 in 1971 to 576 in 1985. Given that the total number of AGs throughout this period was roughly 2,200 in any one year, this sample can be taken as representative of all AGs. Over the period 1971–1985 bank loans were significantly less important as a source of finance for AGs in manufacturing than for the producing enterprises sector as a whole. The weighted average figure for overall bank borrowing as a net source of finance for AGs was -2.7%, compared to 11.6% for producing enterprises; for long-term bank loans, the figures were 1.7% for AGs and 14.4% for producing enterprises. As a gross source of finance,[3] overall bank borrowing was 1.1% for AGs and 19.3% for producing enterprises, while long-term bank loans were 1.2% for AGs and 6.8% for producing enterprises. The relatively smaller importance of bank loans as a source of finance for AGs was offset by the relatively greater importance of internally-generated funds for AGs. Internal funds were 88.1% of net sources, and 61.9% of gross sources, for manufacturing AGs, compared to 72.7% net and 56.4% gross for producing enterprises as a whole.

These comparisons show that AGs, which are a subset of the producing enterprises sector as a whole, and all of which have supervisory boards, make less use of bank loans to finance investment than does the producing enterprises sector, which mainly consists of firms without supervisory

---

[2] Net sources of finance are measured as proportions of investment in physical assets, by subtracting acquisitions of financial assets from the corresponding incurrence of financial liabilities. See Chapter 3 for further discussion.

[3] Gross sources of finance are measured as proportions of investment in physical plus financial assets. Again see Chapter 3 for further discussion.

Table 6.1. *Weighted average net and gross sources of finance for investment by manufacturing AGs, 1971–1985, %*

	Net	Gross
Internally-generated funds	88.1	61.9
Provisions for pensions	14.7	10.4
Bank loans	−2.7	1.1
of which: long-term	1.7	1.2
Bonds	−1.4	−1.0
Other long-term debt	0.2	0.2
Other claims/liabilities	−0.4	6.5
Trade credit	9.5	12.0
External equity	12.0[a]	8.5
Cash and short-term financial assets	−6.6	—
Long-term financial assets	−13.6	—
Total	99.8	99.6

Note: [a] This figure does not accurately measure the net contribution of external equity to the finance of physical investment. Purchases of equity by AGs are not identified separately from other purchases of long-term financial assets in the data. According to the Federal Statistical Office the category 'long-term financial assets' is largely comprised of equity purchases. See text for discussion.
Source: Own calculations based on Federal Statistical Office, Special Series 2.1.

boards. It follows that AGs finance a lower proportion of their investment by bank loans than do other types of German firms, most of which do not have supervisory boards. This conclusion casts considerable doubt on the hypothesis that a firm with one or more banks represented on its supervisory board is able to raise more bank loan finance than a firm without such representation.

Of course, the sources of finance for investment may differ between AGs and other types of German firm for reasons that are quite unconnected with supervisory boards. One possibility is that, because AGs are the only legal form of enterprise in Germany which may issue shares, they may use less bank finance than other firms because they raise external finance in the form of new share issues. The data on which table 6.1 is based did not enable AGs' purchases of equity to be identified separately from their other purchases of long-term financial assets. According to the Federal Statistical Office, the category long-term financial assets is largely, though not entirely, composed of equity purchases by AGs. Hence an estimate, inevitably somewhat downward-biased, of the net contribution of external equity to the finance of physical investment can be obtained by subtracting the long-term financial asset figure in the first column of table 6.1 from the external equity figure. It can safely be concluded that external equity is a very small net source of finance for manufacturing AGs. Another possibility is that the lower use of bank borrowing by AGs, which are on average much larger than the average German firm, simply reflects a general tendency for the largest companies not to raise much finance from banks. The existence of such a general tendency is supported by the finding of Mayer and Alexander (1990) that large corporations in the UK raise less bank loan finance than does the UK corporate sector as a whole. But Mayer and Alexander's comparison of the sources of finance of a sample of very large German and UK firms suggests that large German firms use less bank loan finance than do large UK firms. Mayer and Alexander compared the gross and net sources of finance over the period 1982–1988 of a sample of 77 non-financial corporations drawn from the largest 115 German AGs quoted on the Frankfurt Stock Exchange with a sample of 73 non-financial corporations drawn from the largest 115 UK companies quoted on the London Stock Exchange. Loan finance was more important, both as a net and as a gross source of finance, for the UK sample than for the German sample (see Mayer and Alexander, 1990, Table II). Thus, even allowing for any general tendency for large corporations to use less bank loan finance than firms as a whole, it appears that AGs in Germany use a particularly small proportion of bank lending. This evidence casts yet more doubt on the view that German firms with bank representation on their supervisory board are able to raise a large proportion of their finance for investment in the form of bank loans.

One additional piece of evidence which suggests that bank representation on supervisory boards does not promote higher bank lending comes from the interviews carried out with banks. According to these interviews, supervisory board representation is generally insignificant as a source of information used by banks to make loan decisions. One reason for this is that bank supervisory board representatives are legally prohibited from passing on information to others in their bank. Sections 93 and 166 of the Stock Corporation Act state that supervisory board members have to keep information obtained on such boards confidential: breach of this duty is a criminal offence (Section 404, Stock Corporation Act). Another reason is that in many cases supervisory boards have only limited information about the operations of the company. A study by Gerum, Steinmann and Fees (1988), which analysed the articles of association of all 281 AGs with more than 2,000 employees in 1979, gives some idea of the information typically available to the supervisory board about the firm's prospects. This study found that only 20% of the AGs they studied had articles of association which required supervisory board consent for the AG's general product or market strategy, while only 10% required such consent for general business plans or investment finance plans. For 86% of the AGs studied, the supervisory board met only twice a year – the legal minimum number of meetings – which does not suggest that supervisory board members are well-informed about the detailed activities of an AG.

The evidence presented in this section is not consistent with the view that representation of banks on supervisory boards in Germany enables them to provide a large proportion of firms' investment finance in the form of loans. The majority of German firms do not have supervisory boards, yet they use more bank loan finance than do firms which do have supervisory boards.

The maturity of bank lending in Germany

One way in which bank lending in Germany appears to differ from that in the UK is in the maturity of bank loans. The claim that German banks do more long-term lending than UK ones is, as has been documented in chapter 1, a component of the widely-held view of the merits of the German system of finance for investment.[4] On the basis of this claim, it has been argued that German firms have a competitive advantage as a result of being able to take a longer-term perspective and engage in larger-scale investment than comparable UK firms (see, for example, Mayer and Alexander, 1990, p. 451). Bank representation on company supervisory boards has been put forward as one reason for the apparently greater proportion of long-term bank lending in Germany: such representation is seen as giving banks more information about firms, and hence, by comparison with the situation in the UK, reducing the risk to the banks of committing funds to firms over a longer period of time.

The discussion in the previous section has already cast doubt on the general claim that bank representation on supervisory boards is a significant source of information for making loan decisions. As for the specific argument that supervisory board representation enables banks to make a higher proportion of long-term loans, the data shown in table 6.2 suggest that this view is also incorrect. In chapter 5 it was shown that bank supervisory board representation is concentrated among the big banks in particular, and in the commercial bank sector in general. If bank representation on company supervisory boards did permit greater amounts of long-term lending to be made, one would expect that a higher proportion of lending to domestic firms by big banks, and the commercial

---

[4] See the quotations from Carrington and Edwards (1979) and Charkham (1989) on p. 2.

Table 6.2. *Maturity of lending by various categories of banks to domestic non-bank enterprises and self-employed persons (excluding mortgage loans secured by housing sites), end 1970 and end 1980, %*

	End 1970			End 1980		
	Short[a]	Medium[a]	Long[a]	Short[a]	Medium[a]	Long[a]
All banks	42.1	12.8	45.1	37.3	9.8	52.9
Commercial banks	63.2	16.2	22.6	56.2	10.9	32.9
of which:						
Big banks	58.1	17.2	24.7	47.3	12.4	40.3
Regional and other commercial banks	63.8	12.3	23.9	51.8	10.6	37.6
Foreign banks	—	—	—	88.9	4.8	6.3
Private bankers	82.5	8.7	8.8	80.9	9.2	9.9
Savings bank sector	35.4	12.1	52.5	32.4	8.6	59.0
of which:						
Regional giro institutions	23.8	15.9	60.3	21.3	10.8	67.9
Savings banks	44.8	9.1	46.1	39.2	7.3	53.5
Credit cooperative sector	53.4	9.7	36.9	44.4	11.8	43.8
of which:						
Regional institutions of credit cooperatives	56.5	17.6	25.9	49.0	17.3	33.7
Credit cooperatives	52.9	8.2	38.9	43.6	10.8	45.6
Mortgage banks	1.2	5.1	93.7	1.0	2.4	96.6
of which:						
Private mortgage banks	1.5	3.3	95.2	0.9	2.3	96.8
Public mortgage banks	0.6	8.9	90.5	1.6	2.7	95.7
Instalment sales financing institutions	30.1	62.7	7.2	37.3	49.0	13.7
Bank with special functions	6.5	18.0	75.5	5.9	11.3	81.8
Postal giro and postal saving bank offices	0	0	100.0	0.1	—	99.9

Notes: [a] 'Short-term' is defined as having an original maturity of less than one year; 'medium-term' as having an original maturity of between one and four years; and 'long-term' as having an original maturity of more than four years.
Sources: Statistical Supplements to the Monthly Reports of the Deutsche Bundesbank, Series 1, Table 6, December 1971, April 1981.

banks as a whole, would be long-term than was the case for such lending by other banks. Table 6.2 shows that in both 1970 and 1980 the big banks, and the commercial bank sector, had a lower proportion of their lending to domestic non-bank enterprises and self-employed persons in the form of long-term loans than did German banks as a whole. The maturity pattern of lending by different types of banks to domestic firms shown in table 6.2 is not consistent with the claim that supervisory board represen-

Table 6.3. *Maturity of lending to firms in Germany and the UK, 1970–1989, %*

1. Original maturity of bank lending (excluding housing loans) to domestic non-bank enterprises and self-employed persons in Germany

	Short-term[a]	Medium-term[a]	Long-term[a]
1970	42.5	12.2	45.3
1980	39.5	9.3	51.2
1989	34.8	8.1	57.1

2. Residual maturity of lending to industry in the UK

	Short-term[a]	Medium-term[a]	Long-term[a]
a) Clearing bank lending to industry			
1980	67.0	20.0	13.0
1987	63.1	19.2	17.7
b) Total lending to industry			
1980	42.0	12.0	46.0
1987	50.8	15.5	33.7

Note: [a] 'Short-term' means less than one year for both the German and UK data. 'Medium-term' means between one and four years, and 'long-term' more than four years, for the German data. For the UK data 'medium-term' means between one and five years, and 'long-term' more than five years.
Source: German data from various issues of the *Monthly Report of the Deutsche Bundesbank*. UK data for 1980 from Vittas and Brown (1982), and for 1987 from Dicks (1989).

tation permits a higher proportion of bank lending to be long-term. One complication in interpreting the data shown in table 6.2 is that most private mortgage banks are at least partly owned by commercial banks. It could, therefore, be argued that commercial banks' supervisory board representation influences the volume of long-term lending to firms by private mortgage banks. But if the lending to domestic non-bank enterprises and self-employed persons by private mortgage banks is added to that of the commercial banks as a whole, the maturity breakdown of the resulting total still involves a lower proportion of long-term loans than the overall average, as follows: 1970 short 55.9%, medium 12.9%, long 31.2%; 1980 short 47.1%, medium 9.6%, long 43.3%.

The evidence that a much larger proportion of overall bank lending to firms in Germany is long-term than is the case in the UK is also questionable. There is very limited evidence available on the maturity of bank lending to firms in the UK, and what is available is not easily comparable to the German data. Table 6.3 presents the data that are available for comparison. The data for total bank lending to domestic non-bank enterprises and self-employed persons in Germany shown in table 6.3 differs slightly from that in table 6.2, in that all loans for housing are excluded from the loans data in table 6.3, while only mortgage loans secured by housing sites are excluded from the data shown in table 6.2.

There are two serious problems of comparability which must be borne in mind when drawing conclusions from table 6.3. The first of these is that while the German data refer to the *original* maturity of loans, the UK data refer to the *residual* maturity of loans. The difference between these two ways of classifying the maturity of lending is most easily explained by means of an example. Suppose a loan of £100 is made, with repayment due in five equal instalments. Such a loan is classified, in terms of residual maturity, as being five £20 loans with maturities of one, two, three, four and five years respectively. In terms of original maturity it would be classified as one £100 loan with a five-year maturity. After two years the loan would be classified, in terms of residual maturity, as being three £20 loans with maturities of one, two and three years, while in terms of original maturity it would be shown as one £60 loan of five years' maturity. It is clear that classifying loans in terms of residual rather than original maturity will lower the average maturity of lending. Unfortunately the extent of the bias introduced by the different maturity classification of German and UK bank lending is not known; however, it will clearly tend to cause the UK data to represent loans as having a lower maturity than the same loans would appear to have as represented by the German data.

The second problem is that, as was noted in chapter 5, the definition of the banking sector in Germany is much broader than in the UK, and consequently the appropriate basis for comparison is not clear. The UK figures in table 6.3 show the maturity of lending both by the clearing banks, a very narrow definition of bank lending compared to the German one, and by all financial institutions, a wide definition which is more nearly comparable to the German one, although it does include loans by some financial institutions, such as insurance companies, which are not included in the German data.[5] Ignoring the complications created by the different maturity classifications for a moment, UK *clearing bank* lending to firms does involve a much lower proportion of medium- and long-term loans than does German bank lending, but the difference is less marked when *total* UK lending is compared to German bank lending. The

[5] See Vittas and Brown (1982) for a very thorough discussion of the difficulties in making international comparisons of the maturity of bank lending.

difference is also less marked if the maturity of UK clearing bank lending in table 6.3 is compared to the maturity of German commercial bank lending for 1980 shown in table 6.2,[6] which is the most appropriate narrow definition of German bank lending for comparison with UK clearing bank lending. The comparability problems resulting from different definitions of the banking sector, combined with the bias created by different maturity classifications, considerably weaken the empirical basis for believing that there is a greater fraction of long-term bank lending in Germany than in the UK.

Even if it were granted that in Germany a higher proportion of bank lending to firms was long-term than was the case in the UK, the theoretical basis for the argument that an economy benefits from having a higher proportion of long-term bank lending to firms is not obvious. Consider a bank's decision about whether to finance a two-period investment project by a firm with a sequence of two one-period loans, the second being negotiated as the first ends, or with a single two-period loan. From the bank's point of view the difference between the sequence of short-term loans and the long-term loan is that in the former case the bank has a greater ability to influence the behaviour of the firm, since it has the option of not renewing the loan at the end of the first period, while in the latter case the bank is committed to providing finance for two periods. Other things being equal, therefore, it would be expected that a long-term loan would have a higher cost to the firm than would a sequence of short-term loans, in order to compensate the bank for the loss of its option not to renew the loan. This suggests that, in the absence of information about the relative costs of different maturities of loans, it is not possible to analyse whether it is better for lending to be short- or long-term. Unfortunately, there exist no useful data about the relative costs of short- and long-term bank lending in Germany and the UK.

More generally, a number of considerations are relevant for the costs and benefits of short- and long-term lending, as Dowd (1992) points out. Consider again a bank's decision about whether to finance a two-period investment project by a firm with a sequence of two one-period loans or a single two-period loan. Suppose that, as in chapter 2, there are informational asymmetries between the bank and the firm, so that the bank cannot distinguish the firm's characteristics at the beginning of the first period, and the firm's management has some scope to pursue its own interests at the bank's expense. For simplicity, the relevant characteristics of firms are taken to be whether they are one of two possible types – good or bad. At the end of the first period, some information is revealed to the

---

[6] The definition of bank lending in table 6.2 includes housing loans other than mortgage loans secured by housing sites, but the effect of this difference in definition is small.

bank which enables it to distinguish the firm's type. This information is not, however, publicly available. In such a framework, short-term loans have two advantages. One is that, since good firms know that at the end of the first period the bank will be able to identify them as good and thus will be willing to grant them loans on better terms in the second period, good firms will be more willing to use short-term loans than will bad ones. Adverse selection problems are thus mitigated by the use of short-term loans. The other is that, because the firm has to return to the bank for finance to continue the project, the ability of the management of the firm to benefit at the bank's expense is restricted, and furthermore the firm has to provide more information to the bank. However, short-term loans also have disadvantages which can be avoided by using long-term loans. There are costs of renegotiating short-term loans at the end of the first period, and short-term loans also leave the firm open at the end of the first period to opportunistic behaviour by the bank, which may attempt to use its private information about the firm's type to charge a higher interest rate on the second-period loans, enabling it to earn supernormal profits. Given that the use of short-term loans has both benefits and costs, it is far from clear what the optimal maturity structure of lending is. This is especially true when account is taken of the possibility of a bank having incentives *not* to exploit its private information when renegotiating the terms of the second-period loan, in order to build up a good reputation so as to attract future customers. Whether a system of finance for investment in which a high proportion of loans to firms is long-term is superior to one with a lower proportion of long-term loans is clearly an open question, because there are potential benefits as well as costs resulting from the reduced commitment of banks to firms implied by a greater proportion of short-term lending.

Irrespective of the theoretical costs and benefits, there is an important empirical consideration to be taken into account. This is the fact that the long-term lending undertaken by German banks does not involve the banks in an unbreakable long-term commitment of finance to firms. The general business conditions of German banks give them the right to withdraw loans at any time if, in their view, the borrower's position has worsened enough to cause concern. Admittedly, it is difficult for the banks to use this right except when the borrower is clearly in serious financial difficulties. However, in such circumstances German banks do use their rights to withdraw loans, as is shown by the discussion in chapter 7 of bank behaviour when firms are suffering financial distress.[7] The interviews we conducted suggested that most long-term bank lending in

[7] See p. 168.

Germany is made at a fixed rather than a variable rate of interest, but the period for which the rate is fixed is for five years from the start of the loan. After five years, the interest rate payable on the loan is renegotiated, and this also provides banks with an opportunity to end the commitment that long-term lending is taken to imply. The institutional arrangements which apply to long-term bank lending in Germany thus mean that such lending does not in fact involve banks in unshakeable long-term commitments of funds.

The view that the German system of finance for investment benefits the German economy by providing a high proportion of long-term bank loan finance has been shown in this section to lack both solid theoretical foundation and firm empirical support. There is no evidence to support the view that representation on supervisory boards enables banks to undertake more long-term lending, since those categories of German bank which have representation on firms' supervisory boards make a smaller proportion of long-term loans than do those German banks which do not have supervisory board representation. The available data do not permit meaningful comparisons of the maturity of bank lending in Germany and the UK, because of the difference in the way loan maturity is classified in the two countries. Long-term bank loans in Germany do not involve unbreakable long-term commitments, and in any case there is no clear theoretical basis for the view that it is better for an economy to have a system of investment finance which provides a relatively high proportion of long-term loans.

Competition and commitment in the market for bank loans in Germany

So far, this chapter has not considered any evidence on the concentration of bank lending to those firms, primarily AGs, which do have supervisory boards. If representation on firms' supervisory boards gives particular banks advantages in the market for lending to such firms, most of the loan finance raised by these firms should be supplied by the banks which are represented on their supervisory boards. Chapter 5 showed that the big banks and, more generally, the commercial banks account for most bank supervisory board seats. Even the largest German firms do not have very many banks represented on their supervisory boards. A study of the largest 100 AGs in 1974 by the Monopolkommission showed that 75 of them had banks represented on their supervisory boards. The average number of bank seats on the supervisory boards of these 75 AGs was 2.4. In a small number of cases, one bank had two seats, which means that the figure 2.4 is a slight overestimate of the average number of banks represented on the supervisory boards of these 75 AGs.[8] The existence of significant economies of scale and scope in information-collection and the exercise of control rights by banks should, therefore, be reflected in particular AGs raising loans from a very small number of banks, and the market for loans to AGs in general being dominated by the commercial banks, especially the big banks. Evidence of particular firms raising loans from a single bank would be consistent with an interpretation of the house bank relationship, which is seen as being characteristic of bank-firm relationships in Germany, as one in which a particular bank mono-polises the supply of financial services to a particular firm.[9] In this section we therefore examine the competitiveness of the market for bank loans to firms in detail.

Another reason for undertaking a detailed analysis of the extent of competition in the market for bank loans to firms in Germany is the suggestion by Mayer (1988) that there is a central conflict between competition and commitment in the provision of long-term investment finance to firms. Mayer's argument is set in an incomplete contract framework, in which problems of verifiability and enforceability are presumed to make it impossible for firms and banks to conclude complete long-term contracts which, for instance, might include provisions specify-ing the sharing of returns to be realised in ten years' time between a firm and its bank. The inability of banks and firms to write complete and binding long-term contracts may prevent profitable long-term invest-ments being financed because the bank may anticipate subsequent oppor-tunistic behaviour by the firm. Consider, for example, a firm which is currently in financial distress but has good long-term prospects. The firm would like to receive a loan from a bank now and not pay any returns to the bank until its cash flow position recovers as a result of the investment it has financed from the bank. For the bank to be willing to provide the funds and take an initial loss on them, it must be sure that it will share in the future returns that the firm gets from the investment, and that its share will be large enough to compensate for the initial loss. But if a contract which ensures that the bank will share adequately in these future returns cannot be written then, once the firm is financially sound and the bank's contribution is sunk, the firm has an incentive to turn to other suppliers of finance who are willing to provide loans at lower rates than the firm is paying to the bank which financed the investment. Anticipation of such opportunistic behaviour by the firm, which will leave the bank with a loss, may prevent the bank supplying funds to the firm in the first place. Mayer suggests that the problems created for the financing of long-term

[8] See Monopolkommission (1978), pp. 301–303.
[9] See the discussion on p. 9.

investment by the impossibility of writing complete contracts, and the consequent inability of firms to commit themselves not to behave opportunistically, can be overcome by close long-term relationships between banks and firms which establish commitment by restricting competition among banks to provide finance to firms.

Mayer does not show precisely how close bank-firm relationships can establish the commitment required to promote long-term investment. A formal analysis of this question, based on the interpretation of the house bank relationship as one in which a particular bank monopolises the financial arrangements of a particular firm, is provided by Fischer (1990). Fischer shows that it is possible for firms and banks to choose financing relationships which restrict competition, and so establish the required commitment, by giving an informational advantage to the single bank, or house bank, which provides the firm's investment finance. Fischer considers a two-period model in which firms seek finance from banks for a sequence of investments with uncertain returns. Firms are of two types: good, which banks can finance profitably, and bad, which they cannot finance profitably. Banks cannot distinguish firm types when supplying funds for the first-period investment, but as a result of providing finance in the first period they learn the firm's type at the end of the period. It is not possible for banks and firms to write contracts in the first period which commit them to any actions in the second period.

Fischer supposes that in the first period, when banks cannot distinguish firm type, the expected return to a bank from supplying finance to a firm is less than the opportunity cost of bank funds. In order for banks to be willing to supply finance in the first period, they must anticipate receiving an expected return from providing finance to good firms in the second period (when firm type can be distinguished) which is above the cost of bank funds by an amount sufficient to compensate for the expected loss on supplying finance in the first period. If, as a consequence of having provided funds to the firm in the first period, more than one bank knows in the second period that a firm is good, Bertrand competition between the banks lowers their expected profits from financing second-period investment to zero. In such circumstances banks will not be able to earn sufficient expected profits in the second period to compensate for their expected losses in the first period, and hence no finance for investment will be provided in the first period. But if only one bank knows in the second period that a firm is good, competition between banks does not reduce expected profits to zero. The informational advantage of the single bank which exclusively financed the firm's first-period investment means that it can earn positive expected profits from supplying finance for second-period investment which are not competed away by less well-informed banks. The positive second-period expected profits to the bank which exclusively finances the good firm's investment in both periods compensates for the first-period expected loss, and hence permits finance to be provided in the first period. The firm agrees to exclusive finance in the first period, even though this restricts competition in the second period and so results in the firm only receiving second-period funds at a rate yielding positive expected profits to the bank, in order to make the provision of finance for first-period investment feasible. Commitment by the firm to the bank is thus established by giving the bank an informational monopoly in the second period via exclusive financing.

Fischer's formal analysis does not in fact show that the exclusive financing required to establish commitment will be provided by banks rather than by other financial intermediaries, but it is straightforward to see how this can be done. If no saver has sufficient funds to finance a firm exclusively, then the gains from exclusive financing require there to be a financial intermediary which collects funds from savers and then acts as the exclusive supplier of finance to firms. Such an arrangement will be efficient provided that the gains from exclusive financing exceed the costs of providing incentives for the intermediary to act in savers' interests. If there are economies of scope between providing exclusive financing and providing payments services, then banks will have an advantage over other financial intermediaries in supplying exclusive finance.

This section undertakes a detailed analysis of the competitiveness of the market for bank loans to firms in Germany in order to assess both whether large firms receive most of their bank loan finance from the small number of banks represented on their supervisory boards, and whether there is any German evidence to support the claim that commitment between banks and firms can be established by restricting competition among banks. The detailed examination of the degree of competition in the market for bank loans to firms in Germany which follows is based to a large extent on the results of interviews with banks and firms carried out in 1988. The conclusions drawn from these interviews, however, may not be representative of the period 1950–1989 as a whole, because there is some reason to think that the degree of competition in the market for bank loans in Germany has increased over this period. An article in the *Monthly Report of the Deutsche Bundesbank* (Deutsche Bundesbank, 1971), reviewing trends in the business of the various categories of German banks over the period 1960–1970, states (p. 31) that 'certain [bank] groups abandoned the restraint they had previously shown towards certain lines of business and categories of customers ... the widening of the scope of the services offered by the individual groups of institutions was ... a reflection of the greater competitiveness in banking once the total abolition of interest rate controls in early 1967 paved the way for general competition in interest rates'. A similar article, referring to the more recent period of 1978–1988 (Deutsche Bundesbank, 1989), states (p. 14) that 'competition between banks has also been encouraged recently by the fact that major corporate customers in particular, given the marked improvement in their liquidity position and the sophisticated financial management techniques they use, no longer rely to the same extent as they used to do on established and close accounting relationships with "principal bankers". At the same time, the various categories of banks are increasingly canvassing customers from outside their traditional clientele'. These statements suggest that there was a greater degree of competition between banks in the market for loans to firms in 1988 than in earlier years of the post-1945 period, so that some care must be exercised in using the results of the interviews as a basis for assessing the extent of competition in the period as a whole. Unfortunately no other comparable studies which provide a detailed examination of the degree of competitiveness in the German market for bank loans to firms appear to exist for earlier years.

The increase in the intensity of competition over the period 1978–1988 noted in the 1989 article in the *Monthly Report of the Deutsche Bundesbank* was repeatedly confirmed in our interviews with banks and firms. The growing significance of the regional giro institutions and the regional institutions of the credit cooperatives in the market for loans to large firms has led to intense competition between lenders to such firms, and has induced those commercial banks which had previously tended to concentrate on lending to large firms, such as the three big banks and a few other large commercial banks, to compete more actively in the market for loans to medium-sized firms. In turn, this process has increased competition in the market for loans to small firms.

In such a competitive market there is little or no scope for exclusive financing relationships between banks and firms. Indeed, even before the increase in competition over the period 1978–1988, there is little evidence of such exclusive financing relationships. Krummel (1980) refers to a 1974 government inquiry which found that the domestic bank connections of the thirty largest German borrowers, overwhelmingly industrial companies, ranged from a minimum of 53 to a maximum of 132. Table 6.4, taken from Braun (1981), shows the number of bank connections of each firm in a sample of 300 firms in the late 1970s. Even the smallest firms in the sample were unlikely to conduct all their banking business with a single bank, and the larger a firm was, the larger its number of bank connections. Two-thirds of the largest firms in the sample shown in table 6.4 had more than ten bank connections. This evidence shows that it is

Table 6.4. *Distribution of bank connections for firms of different sizes in Germany, late 1970s, %*

| Firm turnover | No. of bank connections | | | |
	1	2–5	5–10	> 10
< 25 million DM	–	75.0	25.0	–
≥ 25 and < 100 million DM	7.7	38.5	38.5	15.3
≥ 100 and < 500 million DM	–	40.4	36.2	23.4
> 500 million DM	–	11.3	21.8	66.9

Source: Braun (1981).

incorrect to characterise bank-firm relationships in Germany during the 1970s (i.e. before the most recent increase in competition noted by the Deutsche Bundesbank) as being either ones in which the financial arrangements of particular firms were monopolised by particular banks, or ones in which a very small number of banks provided all the financial services used by a particular firm.

Fischer's theoretical analysis suggests that a house bank relationship must involve exclusive financing in order to permit long-term investment to be funded. However, such investment might still be facilitated, even if loans are also raised from other banks, as long as a firm can rely on a house bank to provide financial support over the long run. The firm might be willing to pay a higher rate on finance supplied by the house bank in exchange for a long-term commitment, and in a framework where the house bank relationship lasts for many periods, rather than two as in Fischer's model, the firm's incentives to act opportunistically may be reduced. A firm's incentives to commit itself to a long-term house bank relationship may be reinforced in a many-period framework if breaking such a relationship involves costs, for example if it is treated as a negative signal of the firm's quality by all other banks, with consequent difficulties in raising finance. It is therefore worthwhile to investigate the features of the house bank relationship further.

One obvious feature to investigate in this context is whether house banks are able to charge higher rates of interest on loans to 'their' firms. Data on interest rates charged on specific loans to individual firms are not available, so it is necessary to resort to qualitative estimates. In our interviews with banks, we obtained estimates of the interest margin charged on loans to firms. The difference between the prime rate at which banks could raise funds on the interbank market and the highest rate at which loans would be made available to firms was consistently stated to be 0.5–1 percentage points for large firms, and 2–3 percentage points for smaller firms. These margins are similar to those charged on bank overdrafts to firms in the UK. Large creditworthy firms in the UK are commonly charged an interest rate of 1 percentage point above either base rate or the three-month interbank rate (which are very similar) – see the articles in the *Bank of England Quarterly Bulletin* (1983, 1988).[10] The surveys by Binks, Ennew and Read (1988, 1990) report that the average margin charged on overdraft finance to the very small UK firms in their samples was 2.6 percentage points above base rate.

Our interviews with German banks made it very clear that intensive competition in the market for loans to large firms left no scope for house banks to charge a higher interest margin on loans: this was also confirmed by the results of interviews with large German firms. The interviews revealed that the degree of competition to supply loans to large firms in Germany is so great that a large firm typically has between five and ten main banks which share equally in the firm's business. There are more of these main banks sharing equally in the firm's business than there are banks represented on the firm's supervisory board. A large firm will generally have a house bank, but it is most accurately seen as the first among equals in a group of banks rather than a monopoly supplier of financial services. For small- and medium-sized firms, the interviews suggested that house banks were sometimes able to charge slightly higher rates on loans, but the additional margin the house bank was able to charge amounted to at most one-quarter of a percentage point. The interviews provided some evidence that house banks were able to charge higher margins to small firms which were in financial distress and had no other source of finance apart from the house bank. Such cases were, however, invariably described as involuntary involvements by the banks concerned, which had been unable to withdraw from the firm in time. The higher margins that house banks were able to charge to small firms in financial distress cannot therefore be regarded as payments received by house banks for long-term commitments. Evidence on interest rate margins thus fails to provide much support for the view that house banks in Germany provide long-term commitment in exchange for receiving higher rates on loans.

As we have seen, for large German firms the house bank acts as first among equals in a group of several main banks, rather than as the dominant supplier of financial services. The house bank is usually the bank which has had the longest-standing connection with the firm in question. Many medium-sized firms also have a group of main banks in which the house bank is first among equals. The interviews showed,

[10] The *Bank of England Quarterly Bulletin* (1988) suggests that large UK corporate borrowers may be able to borrow at a lower rate than this in some circumstances.

however, that firms with an annual turnover of less than 500 million DM still quite commonly have house banks, in the sense of dominant suppliers of financial services. Such positions are particularly taken on by the big three banks and the largest of the regional and other commercial banks. The interviews made it clear that these banks were very keen to establish house bank relationships of this kind for firms of this size which were good risks, but also that the competition to supply finance to such firms is so great that it is difficult to maintain dominant house bank positions. Our interviews with firms showed that those firms in this size category which were performing well and so were good risks from the banks' point of view did not want to have a dominant house bank, because they desired competitive conditions for loans and other financial services and wanted to prevent the influence of any one bank becoming too large. These firms did not regard the possible benefit of a dominant house bank being more committed to the firm in a situation of financial distress as justifying the cost of restricting competition among banks for current financing requirements.

For banks other than the big three and the largest regional and other commercial banks, dominant house bank positions are much less common, except for cases where because of the very small size of the firm major involvement of more than one bank is inefficient. Judging from the interviews, such banks do not usually wish to become dominant house banks. Savings banks – the lowest tier of the savings bank sector – in particular stated that, for reasons of avoiding excessive exposure to risk, they consciously wish to avoid taking more than 50 per cent of a firm's loans, and that they actively encouraged firms above a certain size to seek another bank. Given that the savings banks are particularly important suppliers of long-term loans to firms,[11] this suggests that there is no causal relationship between the provision of long-term bank finance and the existence of dominant house banks.

Even if a dominant house bank does not charge a higher margin on loans than other banks do, the house bank might be able to obtain supernormal returns because it has superior information about the firm and so faces less risk while making loans at the same rate as other banks. If so, the house bank might be willing to commit itself to the firm to a greater extent than other banks would be. To what extent do dominant house banks have information advantages over other banks?

[11] At the end of 1970, the savings banks accounted for 18.2% of total long-term bank lending to domestic non-bank enterprises and self-employed persons (excluding mortgage loans secured by housing sites), the same proportion accounted for by the entire commercial bank sector. The corresponding figures at the end of 1980 were savings banks 22.2%, commercial bank sector 18.7%.

In the interviews banks were asked how the information available for making loan decisions differed between old and new customers. All banks interviewed except one were of the opinion that the quality of information available improved during the course of a lending relationship with a particular firm. They gave a number of reasons for this. One was the greater ability of the bank to judge the quality of the management in general and the reliability of management forecasts about future prospects in particular. A second was that over time it became possible for the bank to interpret the annual balance sheets more accurately because of having more information about the firm's policy with regard to asset valuation. A third reason was that experience of the firm's use of its overdraft facility, and of its pattern of payments and receipts, provided additional information. This latter point was consistently made in the interviews, and supports the view advanced in chapter 2 that an economy of scope between the provision of payments services and information collection may explain why the most efficient system of finance for investment is one in which banks rather than other financial intermediaries are the dominant suppliers of external funds to firms.

Although the banks interviewed were nearly unanimous in their view that they had better information about firms to which they had already made loans, it is not clear that the differences in information between old and new customers were significant for banks' lending behaviour. Almost without exception the banks interviewed thought that the information available for making decisions about loans to new customers was adequate. Only one bank said that it would initially make smaller loans to firms which were new customers because of having less information. It is not obvious, therefore, that house banks have a great enough information advantage over other banks to enable them to earn supernormal returns on their loans.

There was, however, some indication from the interviews with both banks and firms that the ending of a dominant house bank relationship between a firm and a bank was generally interpreted by other banks as a negative signal of the firm's prospects. In this respect, dominant house banks do seem to have some informational advantage, and this could give them the ability to earn supernormal returns. There were two cases among the firms we interviewed in which the information monopoly of a dominant house bank severely impeded the transfer of the firm to another bank. Both cases concerned medium-sized firms with relatively slim equity bases and a concentration of their loan finance with a single bank. The interviews also made clear, though, that the problems of having a dominant house bank are well understood by German firms. In particular, those firms which are good risks from the banks' point of view –

almost all large firms, and many medium-sized ones – have realised the importance of keeping several banks equally well-informed in order to avoid any one bank having too much influence.

The quality difference in the information that banks have about old customers relative to new ones does not seem sufficiently great to sustain long-term commitments between firms and dominant house banks. Both large firms, and those small- and medium-sized firms that can demonstrate their creditworthiness by means of a large equity base and/or a continuously good profit performance, avoid committing themselves to a dominant house bank. The firms which are willing to commit themselves to a single dominant house bank tend to be the financially weaker and less profitable small and medium-sized firms. Many banks are therefore reluctant to become dominant house banks, as exemplified by the statement by one of the private banks we interviewed that it would not seek a house bank position because such positions are sought after only by firms with lower creditworthiness and a need for 'shelter'. For firms that are good risks, the security of a dominant house bank is less important, and they are thus less prepared to allow a single bank to have an informational monopoly. The firms that are prepared to have a dominant house bank are the bad risks, and many banks clearly do not regard the somewhat higher rates they could charge if they were the dominant house bank as sufficient to compensate for the greater risk involved in lending to these firms. This behaviour can clearly be understood in terms of a concept of adverse selection similar to that used to explain why lenders ration credit rather than raising interest rates until the loan market clears (Stiglitz and Weiss, 1981).

The evidence discussed in this section shows that in the 1980s the market for bank loans to firms was very competitive, and although house bank relationships existed it was rare for the house bank to be the dominant supplier of bank finance to a particular firm. The question that must arise, of course, is whether this conclusion applies to earlier periods. The statements quoted from the *Monthly Report of the Deutsche Bundesbank* suggest that conditions were less competitive in the 1950s and 1960s than subsequently. But no detailed studies appear to be available which might indicate how much less competitive the market for bank loans to firms was. It should be recalled that the evidence both from Krummel and from Braun, which shows the extensive number of firms' connections with banks, refers to the 1970s. The argument that the house bank relationship restricts competition in order to establish long-term commitment between banks and firms is thus lacking in empirical support for roughly half of the period with which this book is concerned. Even if it were true that there was much less competition between banks in the earlier part of this

Table 6.5. *Factors determining a positive decision for short- and medium-term bank loans in Germany*

Factor	Weighted relative frequency %
Good profitability and liquidity	34.1
Quality of management	24.2
First-rank mortgages as collateral	15.3
Nature of project financed by loan	10.8
Debt ratio	7.8
Mobile assets as collateral	6.6
Other	1.1
Negative pledge	0.1

Source: Drukarcyk *et al.* (1985), Table K–35, p. 121.

period, and dominant house bank relationships were therefore more common then, it is not obvious that the increase in competition and the decline in dominant house bank relationships has reduced the amount of long-term investment in Germany. In our interviews with both banks and firms, the responses to questions about the factors determining the maturity of a loan consistently stated that loan maturity was tailored to the nature of the investment. Table 6.3 shows that the proportion of long-term loans in total bank lending to domestic enterprises and self-employed persons has increased over the period 1970 to 1989, so that it is difficult to argue that increased competition over this period has lead to a reduction in long-term investment. But the main conclusion to be drawn from this section is that all available detailed evidence on competition in the market for bank loans is consistent with the concentration data analysed in chapter 5, and presents a picture of a highly competitive market.

The information available for bank loan decisions, and the significance of collateral

The analysis in the previous three sections of this chapter has shown that there is no evidence to support the view that representation on supervisory boards of firms gives banks advantages which permit them to lend more, or longer-term, to these firms. In this section we therefore turn to the general question of the basis on which German banks make decisions about loans to firms in Germany. Because one component of the widely-held view of the merits of the German system of finance for investment is based on the claim that asymmetries of information between banks and firms are much less great in Germany, so that collateral requirements for loans are lower,[12] we give particular consideration to the use of collateral.

Table 6.5 is taken from the study by Drukarcyk *et al.* (1985), and summarises the responses of 281 German banks to a 1983 questionnaire concerning the factors that would determine a positive decision for short- and medium-term loans to firms.[13] Adding together the two entries in table 6.5 which relate to the provision of collateral, we obtain a figure of 21.9%. It appears from this table that the profitability and liquidity of a firm, the quality of its management, and the provision of collateral are by a considerable margin the three most important factors which have a positive influence on German bank lending decisions.

How do German banks establish whether a particular firm which has applied for a loan is characterised by good management and good prospects for profitability and liquidity? According to our interviews, the banks always obtain a firm's accounts for the preceding three years. Other sources of information, such as the firm's internal plans, or chartered accountants' reports, are used much less frequently. Many banks have accounting data banks for a large number of firms, enabling bank loan officers to compare accounting ratios for the firm requesting a loan to the corresponding ratios for the relevant industry. It seems impossible, however, to give a simple and accurate account of how these various ratios are transformed into a lending decision, In our interviews, bankers repeatedly stated that each lending decision had to be made in the light of the individual characteristics of the firms, and that the accounting data was in practice of limited value. It was commonly pointed out that accounting data are historic whereas the bank was interested in the future performance of the loan applicant, and that to evaluate likely future performance there was no real substitute for the loan officer's personal experience and judgement.

According to our interviews, the training given to bank loan officers in Germany occurs mainly on the job: new loan officers spend a significant amount of time in junior positions within the loan department, developing the necessary skills for loan assessment by observing the practices of their superiors. There was no evidence either of bank loan officers in Germany having specialist detailed knowledge of relevant technology or product developments enabling them to make particularly well-informed evaluations of the riskiness of loans, or of German banks possessing departments with the technical expertise to assess whether particular projects for which finance is being sought are likely to be successful. This

[12] See the quotation from Cable and Turner (1983) on pp. 8–9.
[13] Short-term loans have maturities of up to one year, and medium-term loans have maturities of between one and four years.

lack of evidence to support the claim that German banks have ample staffs of technical advisers, capable of assessing industrial prospects and risks, and are thus willing to lend in circumstances when UK banks do not, has been noted by others. Macrae (1966), for example, stated that 'those famous technical and technological departments of the banks turn out to be rather myths; even in the biggest banks, they seem generally to be merely bankers with some knowledge of present trends in particular industries, rather than great innovating boffins in their own right'.

The available evidence therefore suggests that decisions about bank loans to firms in Germany are mostly made by bank loan officers on the basis of accounting data about firms combined with their experience and judgement as loan officers. There is no evidence that loan officers in Germany possess specialist knowledge about particular industries. The basis on which decisions about bank loans to firms are made in Germany thus appears to be very similar to that in other countries (see Corbett, 1987, for evidence of the similarity of UK and Japanese bank loan decision procedures to the German procedures reported here).

One distinctive institutional arrangement which affects the information available to bank lenders in Germany is the Deutsche Bundesbank's credit information exchange for loans of DM 1 million or more. This arrangement originates in the 1934 Banking Act, which provided for the establishment of a credit information exchange at the Reich Commissioner for Banking for loans of Reichsmark 1 million or more. The operation of the credit information exchange has been the responsibility of the Bundesbank since 1957. The Banking Act requires all bank and insurance enterprises to report loans of DM 1 million or more to the Bundesbank on a quarterly basis. If the credit information exchange receives reports on loans of DM 1 million or more to a single borrower from several banks, it notifies each such lender of the overall debt of the borrower and the total number of lenders. It is clearly useful for lenders to be aware of the extent of their borrowers' overall indebtedness in order to decide how closely to monitor borrowers, and the credit information exchange obviously provides valuable information of this kind for loans of DM 1 million or more. To what extent the credit information exchange provides German banks with a significant informational advantage over banks in other countries is, however, unclear. For obvious reasons banks in all countries ask potential borrowers questions about their debts to other lenders. Although the credit information exchange may provide German banks with more comprehensive and reliable details about their borrowers' debts than is the case elsewhere, this information is only available for relatively large loans, and banks receive it only after they have made the loan. Nevertheless, the fact that a bank which is considering making a large loan to a firm in Germany knows that it will receive

Table 6.6. *The significance of various types of collateral for short- and medium-term bank loans in Germany, %*

Type of collateral	Average share of collateral in total volume of loans	Average share of collateral by no. of loans
Real estate (mortgage, etc.)	31.2	26.9
Mobile assets	34.4	48.8
Other forms of collateral	4.0	3.8
Total collateralised loans	69.6	79.5
Unsecured loans	30.4	20.5

Source: Drukarcyk *et al.* (1985), Table K–22, p. 111.

details of other large loans to the firm if the loan is granted may reduce uncertainty, and thus permit some such loans to be undertaken that would not be granted in other countries. The credit information exchange also means that banks with large outstanding loans to a firm will be informed if the firm takes out new large loans from other banks. Such information is likely to be important in situations of financial distress.

How important is the provision of collateral for bank loans in Germany? According to our interviews, long-term loans are very rarely given by German banks without requiring collateral. However, some short- and medium-term lending is made without collateral. The study of Drukarcyk *et al.* (1985) provides a great deal of information about the extent to which collateral is used for short- and medium-term bank lending. Table 6.6, which is based on banks' responses to a question in the Drukarcyk *et al.* study, shows that 69.6% of the total volume of short- and medium-term lending, and 79.5% of the total number of such loans, are collateralised in some form.

There is a certain amount of variation between German banks in their attitude towards the provision of collateral for loans. As table 6.7 shows, just over one-third of the banks questioned by the Drukarcyk *et al.* study gave unsecured short- and medium-term loans 'often', while the remainder did so 'rarely' or 'never'. The reasons given for making unsecured loans by those banks which did so often suggest that in some cases this occurs because the firms are financially so sound that the banks can forego collateral, while in other cases unsecured lending occurs because of a long-term relationship between the bank and the firm. The responses relating to quality of management and, obviously, aid for long-term customers can both be interpreted in this latter way.

The Drukarcyk *et al.* study also provided some information about the

Table 6.7. *Attitude of banks towards the provision of collateral for short- and medium-term loans*

Frequency with which bank makes uncollateralised short- and medium-term loans	No. of banks	% of banks
Never	15	5.4
Rarely	171	60.6
Often	96	34.1
Total	282	100.1

Reasons given for making uncollateralised short and medium term loans by the 96 banks which extended such loans often, %

Creditworthiness test says that firm will remain solvent	41.4
Above average quality of management	22.0
Personal creditworthiness of customer	17.8
Financial aid for long-term customer with short-term liquidity problems	14.8
Other	4.2
of which: reorganisation loans to avoid bankruptcy	0.4
Total	100.2

Source: Drukarcyk *et al.* (1985), Table L–24, p. 113.

variation across firms in the extent to which collateral was required for loans. Of a sample of 123 small- and medium-sized firms, 44.7% had to provide collateral for all their bank loans, and 71.5% had to provide it for three-quarters or more of their loans. A small group of 11.4% of the firms in the sample could, however, do without collateral for any of their loans: these presumably are firms which are very good risks according to the criteria set out in table 6.7.

The importance of collateral for loans in Germany is caused partly by institutional factors. Savings banks are often subject to limits on the amount of uncollateralised loans they can make – for example in Northrhine–Westphalia this limit is 25% of customers' deposits. Furthermore the refinance of mortgage banks, as well as some special purpose banks such as the Industriekreditbank, is tied to their using mortgages to secure their loans. The Banking Act requires that a bank's loans do not exceed 18 times its equity: loans which are secured by a mortgage only count at half their value for this calculation. Accounting rules for banks require that the write-off on a problem loan is equal to the nominal value of the loan minus the sum of what can be recovered beyond any doubt and a careful estimate of the return from selling any collateral which might be attached to the loan.

This evidence on the provision of collateral for loans to firms in Germany shows that, in the 1980s, almost all long-term bank loans, and nearly 70% (by loan volume) of short- and medium-term bank loans, were made on a collateralised basis. Those short- and medium-term loans for which collateral was not required were made to firms that were good risks on standard criteria of being financially sound, having good management, and having been reliable long-term customers of the bank making the loan. No detailed survey exists of the use of collateral requirements by UK banks comparable to that of Drukarcyk *et al.*, but Binks, Ennew and Reed (1988) carried out a survey of 3,487 very small UK firms in 1987, which included a question about the most recent bank loan received. Of those firms which had made a successful loan application, 29.3% had not been required to provide collateral. Comparing this figure with the estimate in table 6.2 that 20.5% of short- and medium-term loans in Germany are made without collateral suggests that collateral is used at least as widely in Germany as in the UK, although this must remain a tentative conclusion in the absence of more detailed UK evidence.

Conclusion

The main purpose of this chapter has been to evaluate the view that bank supervisory board representation has a favourable effect on the supply of bank loan finance to firms. In the course of this discussion, a number of related aspects of German bank lending to firms have also been considered. The main conclusion of the chapter is that the available evidence does not support the view that representation on the supervisory boards of firms enables banks to supply more loan finance to these firms. Those German firms which have supervisory boards make less use of bank loan finance than do either German firms without supervisory boards, which are, on average, smaller in size, or UK firms which are comparable in size but do not, of course, have supervisory boards. Our interviews consistently yielded the response that bank representation on a supervisory board did not increase the information available to a bank for lending decisions. There is no evidence that bank representation on supervisory boards leads to more long-term lending: those German banks which account for most bank supervisory board representatives have a smaller proportion of their total lending in the form of long-term loans than do German banks as a whole. There is also no evidence that bank lending to firms with supervisory boards is dominated by those banks which account for most bank supervisory board representatives. The only available detailed evidence, which covers the period 1970–1989, shows that the market for bank loans to large firms is very competitive indeed.

A number of other conclusions have also emerged from this chapter. The claim that more bank lending to firms in Germany is long-term than is the case in the UK has been shown to have a weak empirical basis, and in any event there is no clear theoretical argument which provides a reason for thinking that it is better for lending to firms to be long- rather than short-term. The evidence available shows the market for bank loans to firms to be competitive generally, with little scope for long-term commitments to be established by means of dominant house bank relationships. The procedures used by German banks to evaluate loan applications seem to be similar to those used in other countries: there is no evidence of banks possessing special technical expertise, and collateral is required for most loans.

This chapter has been concerned with evidence relating to German banks' ordinary lending behaviour. However, an important component of the conventional wisdom about the merits of the German system of investment finance is concerned with bank behaviour when firms to which they have lent find themselves in financial distress, and this is the subject of chapter 7.

Appendix: Interviews with banks and firms

The analysis in chapter 6 is partly based on evidence obtained from interviews carried out by the authors with German banks and firms in 1988. These interviews were granted on the condition that full confidentiality was maintained, so that references to the results of the interviews in chapter 6 are intentionally very general. This Appendix provides some more details of these interviews.

Interviews were conducted with 15 banks, 17 firms, 2 receivers, 1 chartered accountant who specialised in banking, and 1 employee of the Frankfurt Stock Exchange who worked in the admission department.

The issues covered by the interviews with banks are shown by the questionnaire on which these interviews were based, given at the end of this Appendix. The 15 banks interviewed came from the following categories of banks:

Commercial bank sector	7
Savings bank sector	5
Credit cooperative sector	2
Banks with special functions	1

The banks interviewed were mainly large banks, but some small banks were included among those interviewed. The individual bankers interviewed usually belonged to the top or second tier of management in the case of the smaller banks, and to middle management in the case of the large banks.

The 17 firms interviewed were all drawn from the electrical engineering and electronics industry. These firms all fell into the medium-sized or large category. The annual turnover in 1986 or 1987 of the firms interviewed ranged from approximately DM 16 million for the smallest to approximately DM 51 billion for the largest. The interviews with the firms covered a number of issues other than their relations with banks: that part of the questionnaire which concerned bank-firm relationships is also given at the end of this Appendix.

The interviews with the receivers and the chartered accountant focused mainly on the role of banks when firms to which they had lent were suffering a financial crisis, while the interview at the stock exchange concentrated on the role of the banks in initial public offerings by firms.

Questionnaire for interviews with banks

Structure of business with firms

1. What proportion are loans to firms of your total loan volume?
2. What is the structure of your loans to firms in terms of: industry groups; firm size; loan maturity; fixed and variable rate loans?
3. What proportion of your loans to firms are loans in which your bank is the main bank making loans to the firm?
4. To what extent do you undertake leasing finance?
5. To what extent do you undertake participation finance?

Bank strategy with respect to firms

6. What is your view of the general structure of bank-firm relationships in Germany?
   - most firms favour *one* main bank relationship, in which a single bank takes a dominant position with respect to the firm
   - most firms receive banking services from several banks on an equal basis.
7. What relationships with firms does your bank seek to achieve, and what advantages does your bank's strategy have?
8. What are the particular competitive advantages that your bank has over other banks?
9. How do you manage your loans to a particular firm with respect to (a) cost calculations and pricing policy, (b) risk?

Loan decisions

10. How, and by whom, are creditworthiness assessments for new customers carried out?
11. How frequently are the following sources of information used for such creditworthiness assessment: annual accounts, certified accounts, internal firm documents, information agencies, industry data, economy data, other?
12. Are there minimum requirements for the creditworthiness of firms (e.g. satisfaction of particular indicators)?
13. In what way is the available information about existing firm customers essentially different from that about new customers?
14. Who decides whether to grant a loan (description of decision process)?
15. What considerations other than creditworthiness influence the decision whether to grant a loan?
16. Can first-class collateral compensate for a negative decision about creditworthiness?
17. How are the terms of the loan agreed?
18. How does the decision process for rolling-over an existing loan differ from that for making a loan to a new customer?
19. How is the performance of loan officers assessed?
20. In such assessment, are there measurable performance indicators to which the earnings and promotion prospects of the loan officer are linked?
21. Under what circumstances would a loan officer suffer adverse consequences if a loan turned out badly?

Features of ongoing bank-firm relationships

22. How frequently and at what level do you maintain contact with your firm customers?
23. What function does bank representation on supervisory boards play in this context?
24. Under what circumstances would you favour representation on the supervisory board of one of your customers?
25. Do you regard representation of your bank on the supervisory board of one of your customers as a measure which increases your ability to have further business relationships with that customer?
26. What quantitative and qualitative significance would you assign to representation on supervisory boards in the overall framework of bank-firm relationships in Germany?

27. Who carries out the monitoring of loans to firms by your bank?
28. What information is used to monitor loan performance?
29. What additional measures beyond ordinary monitoring do you use for the early detection of insolvencies?
30. What alarm signals would lead to double-checking of the loans to a particular firm? At what stage is a financial crisis typically recognised?

Behaviour of bank in situations of firm financial distress

31. Who decides what the bank should do when a financial crisis is recognised? What measures does the bank take?
32. How does a bank decide whether to implement or participate in a reorganisation attempt?
33. What is the average loss, in percent, suffered by the bank if a firm customer goes bankrupt?
34. What measures does the bank typically take if a reorganisation is attempted?

Questionnaire for interviews with firms

1. What is your current turnover, and how has your turnover developed over the last ten years?
2. What is your firm's ownership structure?
3. To what extent over the last ten years have you used short- or long-term bank loans?
4. What role do bank loans play in the finance of your investment?
5. How do you structure your relationships with banks?
6. What advantages do you see in the structure you have chosen (house bank relationships as opposed to equal relationships with several banks)?
7. How long have your present bank relationships existed?
8. Has there ever been a change in your bank relationships, and, if so, what was the reason for the change?
9. How, in general, would you assess the costs and benefits of a change in your bank relationships?
10. What information about your firm is obtained by your banks (frequency of personal contacts, significance of supervisory board representation)?
11. What influence do your banks have on your investment decisions?
12. If your firm suffered a financial crisis, how would you assess the possibility of resorting to your bank or banks for support?
13. Has there ever been a serious financial crisis in your firm? If yes, how did your banks behave?

7 German bank behaviour when firms are in financial distress

Introduction

One particular aspect of German bank lending behaviour which requires detailed analysis concerns the response of banks to situations of financial distress on the part of firms to which they have made loans. As was noted in chapter 1, the German system of finance for investment is claimed to have the merit that German banks are more ready to support firms in financial distress than are UK banks. Dyson (1986, p. 132), for example, states that

> the solidarity of a Hausbank with the firm's management finds its clearest expression in the bank's sense of duty to organise rescues in times of crisis, using at such times its wide range of industrial, financial and governmental contacts as well as its own expertise and numerous services ... Banks maintain a network of favoured industrial managers and their proteges who can be drafted in to a corporation in difficulties.

According to *The Economist* (1 August 1992, p. 70) 'in Germany ... a company in trouble will usually be coaxed back to health by its supervisory board or its bankers'. As we saw in chapter 6, it is difficult to argue that a greater willingness of German banks to reorganise firms in financial distress, if it exists, is the result of long-term commitments between particular firms and particular banks in the form of an exclusive house bank relationship. Nevertheless, examples such as the role of German banks in rescuing AEG in the late 1970s and early 1980s are often invoked in support of the claim that bank attitudes to reorganisations differ between Germany and the UK. Leaving aside the point that the AEG rescue would not have ultimately taken place without substantial Federal government financial support, so that it is wrong to see it as an example of German banks on their own reorganising a firm in financial distress, the obvious question which arises concerning the AEG example is whether it is typical of German bank behaviour when firms are in financial distress. This is the subject of the present chapter.

The second section provides a brief discussion of the analytical issues involved in financial distress and bankruptcy, expanding on the discussion in chapter 2. The third section sets out the main features of the German legal framework for dealing with insolvencies. The fourth section examines the evidence on German banks' ability to detect financial distress on the part of firms to which they have lent, while the fifth section considers the evidence on how the banks behave once financial distress has been identified. There is a conclusion in the sixth section, which assesses the extent to which the evidence supports the view that German banks are able to reduce the costs of financial distress and bankruptcy by close monitoring of firms and active involvement in managing troubled firms that are being reorganised.

The costs of bankruptcy and financial distress

A firm which cannot make the payments that have been promised to its suppliers of debt finance goes bankrupt, and control of the firm passes from the holders of equity in the firm to the suppliers of debt. The suppliers of debt then decide whether to reorganise the firm or liquidate it. Bankruptcy involves a number of costs. First, there are the direct costs of the bankruptcy procedure – the legal and administrative costs incurred in the formal process of transferring control of the firm to the suppliers of debt. Second, there are the indirect costs of bankruptcy. The indirect costs reflect the difficulties involved in managing a firm which is going through the bankruptcy process. The complexities of the bankruptcy procedure may lead to a fall in the value of the firm's assets, for example because uncertainty about the outcome of the procedure prevents expenditure on maintenance or other worthwhile investments, or because a firm in bankruptcy may lose customers who switch to other firms in anticipation of the firm being liquidated at the end of the procedure.

There are also costs attached to financial distress – the situation in which bankruptcy is imminent but has not yet occurred. In such circumstances the management of the firm, representing the interests of the equity holders, has incentives to take inefficient actions in order to avoid bankruptcy. Suppose, for example, that a firm has debts of 100 due next period, and its returns next period, in the absence of any investment, will be 60. The firm has available 20 which it can invest this period, in one of two projects. The first yields 30 next period with certainty, while the second yields 50 with probability 0.1 and 0 with probability 0.9. For simplicity assume risk-neutrality and a discount rate of zero. The expected value of the first investment is clearly greater than that of the second, and the first investment should be chosen. But the firm's management, acting in the interests of the equity holders, will choose the second, since the firm will go bankrupt with certainty if the first investment is chosen, while if the second is chosen there is a 0.1 probability that the firm will avoid bankruptcy and the equity holders will receive a return. In circumstances where bankruptcy is imminent, the firm's management will only be concerned with that part of an investment project's return which is large enough to avoid bankruptcy, so they will have incentives to choose excessively risky projects and not carry out worthwhile safe ones. These inefficient decisions are the costs of financial distress.

The higher the fraction of debt in a firm's overall finance, other things equal, the more often bankruptcy and financial distress will occur, and the greater will be the associated costs. Although the use of debt finance has some favourable incentive effects on the management of a firm, as was noted in chapter 2, the costs of bankruptcy and financial distress act to limit the extent to which firms raise external finance in the form of debt. Clearly one way of explaining possible differences between countries in the extent to which investment is financed by debt is in terms of differences in institutional arrangements which affect the costs of bankruptcy and financial distress. These costs may be lower in one country than another because of differences either in the legal framework for dealing with bankruptcy, or in the ability of suppliers of debt finance to monitor the behaviour of firms to which they have lent, and to reorganise firms in financial distress. An important component of the conventional wisdom concerning the merits of the 'bank-based' system of investment finance in Germany is based on the view that German banks are able to reduce the costs of bankruptcy and financial distress.

As we have seen, the costs of financial distress arise from the incentives which imminent bankruptcy gives to management to take inefficient decisions which benefit equity holders at the expense of suppliers of debt. If the suppliers of debt finance are able to monitor and control managerial behaviour closely, these costs can be reduced. The role that German banks play in corporate governance via their representation on company supervisory boards might be argued to have just this effect, enabling banks to identify situations of financial distress and giving them rights to influence managerial behaviour before bankruptcy has actually occurred. There are also costs of bankruptcy itself, resulting from the difficulties of managing bankrupt firms. These considerations suggest that if a relatively higher proportion of investment was financed by bank borrowing in Germany than elsewhere, so that, other things equal, financial distress and bankruptcy were more common, it would be worthwhile for banks to develop an expertise not only in dealing with the financial and legal aspects of bankruptcy, but also in the ability to manage and reorganise firms in financial difficulties. Reorganisation of a firm in financial distress or bankruptcy will be easier the smaller the number of lenders to the firm, since the costs of negotiating among the lenders will be reduced. One advantage of there being a single bank lending to a firm is that these coordination costs are minimised. As has been seen in chapter 6, however, there is little evidence that the house bank relationship between banks and firms in Germany is one in which a single bank provides all the loan finance of a particular firm. Nevertheless one possible role of a house bank may be to take the lead in coordinating lender behaviour in a reorganisation. Empirical evidence on German bank behaviour in situations of firm financial distress is obviously necessary in order to assess the view that it results in lower costs of bankruptcy and financial distress.

Many of the costs of bankruptcy and financial distress arise because there is a conflict of interest between the suppliers of equity and the suppliers of debt finance in circumstances when bankruptcy is possible. Equity holders are only concerned with the returns that the firm receives if it is not bankrupt, and they take no account of returns the firm receives if it is bankrupt, since these go entirely to the suppliers of debt. By contrast, if the firm is not bankrupt, suppliers of debt take no account of returns above the payments that have been promised to them, since these go entirely to the equity holders. It follows that if the suppliers of debt are making decisions about a firm they will tend to make inefficient decisions as a result of ignoring the returns which accrue to equity holders when the firm is not bankrupt. Hence it is likely that, following bankruptcy, suppliers of debt will inefficiently liquidate the firm rather than reorganise and continue its operations, and, in circumstances of financial distress, if suppliers of debt are in a position to manage the firm they will choose excessively cautious investments. These costs can be mitigated, either by the equity holders bargaining with the suppliers of debt and making side-payments to induce them to choose different actions, or by the suppliers of debt holding some equity as well, so that they have some interest in returns above the payments to lenders in non-bankruptcy circumstances. German banks do supply some finance in the form of equity, so another empirical question to ask is whether this provides them with incentives to make efficient reorganisation decisions about firms in financial distress or bankruptcy.

Bankruptcy procedures in Germany

Before examining whether the evidence relating to German bank behaviour with respect to firms in financial distress and bankruptcy is consistent with the theoretical analysis of ways in which the costs of financial distress and bankruptcy might be reduced by close bank monitoring and control of management, it is necessary to understand the main features of German bankruptcy procedures. German insolvency law does not distinguish between personal and corporate bankruptcies: in contrast to the UK, the same procedures apply to both. If a firm cannot pay its debts, or if a firm is a corporation and its liabilities exceed its assets, it must apply either for bankruptcy or for settlement in court within three weeks. The insolvency of a firm also gives all creditors the right to start foreclosure proceedings, provided that bankruptcy or settlement in court procedures have not been opened. Once such procedures have begun, however, only secured creditors have this right. This feature of German insolvency law, whereby assets which serve as collateral for loans can be sold outside and independently of legal bankruptcy or settlement in court procedures, gives secured creditors an extremely strong position.

Only the debtor can apply for a settlement in court (Vergleich); a creditor cannot. Approval by the court, whether to continue or to liquidate the firm, requires that all claims involved in the settlement should receive a minimum of 35% of their nominal value. This minimum increases to 40% if the claims cannot be paid within one year. If at any point it appears that this minimum will not be attained, bankruptcy procedures will be opened. Even if the settlement is approved by the court, it must still be accepted by the creditors. The majorities required are more than 50% of the creditors represented at the creditors' meeting, and more than 75% of the value of the claims represented. Note that these creditors are unsecured creditors, since creditors holding collateral have to be treated separately anyway, and have the right to sell the assets on which their claims are secured outside this procedure. A settlement in court has some advantages over bankruptcy for the debtor, since although the court appoints a supervisor (Vergleichsverwalter) with some rights, the authority to run the business remains with the debtor. Furthermore, a settlement in court settles the claims involved once and for all, whereas claims which are not satisfied in a bankruptcy remain valid.[1]

The alternative to a settlement in court is bankruptcy (Konkurs), which can be applied for by either the debtor or the creditors. Whether bankruptcy procedures are opened depends on whether the firm's assets are large enough to cover the legal costs of the procedure. If bankruptcy procedures are opened, the debtor loses control of the firm, and the court appoints a receiver (Konkursverwalter) to take charge of it. The fate of a bankrupt firm depends very much on the receiver's actions. In particular,

---

[1] This distinction is, of course, only significant for partnerships and sole proprietorships, which have unlimited liability.

Table 7.1. *Significance of insolvency procedures in Germany, 1971–1986*

	1971	1976	1981	1986
Bankruptcy				
Number of Konkurs	4255	9221	11580	18793
of which: opened	2087	2702	3162	4098
of which: settled after one year	1813	2336	2452	3420
Liabilities associated with those settled after one year (DM million)	1397	6411	4959	7818
Settlement in court				
Number of Vergleich	182	141	73	49
of which: settled after one year	175	120	63	37
Liabilities associated with those settled after one year (DM million)	210	283	116	128

Source: Statistiches Bundesamt, Fachserie 2, Reihen 4.1 and 4.2.

any attempt to keep the firm in business, or to sell it, will very often depend on the receiver's ability to convince the creditors that such a policy is appropriate. A 50% majority of the value of the claims represented at the creditors' meeting is required to approve such decisions. Again it should be noted that these creditors are the unsecured ones. Secured creditors have to be negotiated with separately, because of their right to sell assets independently of the bankruptcy procedure.

Table 7.1 shows that over the period 1971–1986 bankruptcies were far more common than settlements in court, and that bankruptcies became even more frequent relative to settlements in court as the period advanced. Table 7.1 also shows that the proportion of applications for bankruptcy which were actually opened fell over the period, from 49% in 1971 to 21.8% in 1986. Part of this decline may be explained by a change in the law in 1974, which made social security claims against the Federal Employment Office conditional on an application for bankruptcy, even if there were clearly insufficient assets to cover the costs of the procedure.[2] But there appears to be a general downward trend in the ratio of assets to liabilities in insolvencies, which is also reflected in the fall in the number of settlements in court.

The German legal procedures for dealing with insolvencies make it difficult for an insolvent firm to continue operation. Secured creditors can sell assets on which their claims are secured independently of either the bankruptcy or the settlement in court procedure, even if these assets are essential for the continuation of the business. The settlement in court

[2] See Cuny and Haberstroh (1983).

procedure, which is, relatively speaking, the most suitable for a reorganisation, leaves the control of the firm in the hands of the debtor, and thus, as we have seen, is rarely used. The fate of a firm which has entered the bankruptcy procedure depends very much on the actions of the receiver. In our interviews with receivers, it emerged that only a relatively small number of receivers had a background and experience enabling them to have a chance of keeping a bankrupt firm in business. This conclusion was supported by the study of Gessner *et al.* (1978, p. 209), which found that there was only a small group of receivers who were professional in the sense of spending most of their time dealing with bankrupt firms: the majority of receivers only occasionally handled a case. In addition to this obstacle to receivers being able to keep a bankrupt firm operating, the incentives for receivers to save a firm are not good. A receiver can be held liable for claims incurred after the bankruptcy procedure has been opened if such claims cannot be met in full and, in the priority ordering of creditors' claims, the receiver's fees rank behind claims incurred as a result of transactions undertaken by the receiver on the firm's behalf.

The only real chance of saving a bankrupt firm in Germany is, therefore, to sell it to another firm. Here too there are obstacles, mainly resulting from the strong position enjoyed by the employees of a bankrupt firm. Since 1972 employees who are dismissed in an attempt to continue the firm on a smaller scale have been entitled to compensation according to their age and the number of years they have worked for the firm. This 'Sozialplan' is a preferred claim in bankruptcy, and can act as a considerable financial burden for an attempted rescue.[3] More recently it has become impossible, rather than just expensive, to reduce employment as part of an attempt to continue the operation of a bankrupt firm. §613a of the General Civil Code states that employees may not be dismissed in a merger of two firms, and this has been interpreted by the courts to apply also to the sale of a bankrupt firm to another firm. In our interviews with receivers, and in some of the interviews with banks, this emerged as a very important impediment to the sale of a bankrupt firm. A survey carried out in 1984 by Keller-Stoltenhoff (1986) found that 25% of the attempts to sell bankrupt firms failed because of §613a. Thus it is now only possible to sell bankrupt firms if no employees are dismissed in the process.

Given these difficulties in keeping a bankrupt firm in business, the figures shown in table 7.2 are not surprising. This table summarises the responses of 308 receivers to a questionnaire in the Gessner *et al.* study (1978), and shows that in the experience of 86% of the receivers in the

---

[3] See Gross (1982) for a description of the 'Sozialplan'.

Table 7.2. *Continuation of firms at the conclusion of bankruptcy procedures, according to receivers*

Frequency of continuation	% of receivers giving this response (total no. of receivers questioned = 308)
Often	2
Sometimes	12
Rarely	21
Never	65

Source: Gessner *et al.* (1978), Table II/17, p. 219.

survey firms rarely or never continued to operate, even as part of a different firm, after bankruptcy procedures were concluded.

A slightly different impression of the number of firms which continue to operate at the conclusion of bankruptcy procedures is given by table 7.3, which shows the results of a question in the survey conducted by Hesselmann and Stefan (1990). This survey covered 56 receivers, who in the years 1984–1988 had participated in 2,106 bankruptcies. In 17.4% of these bankruptcies, successful attempts to continue the firm were made. However, care must be exercised in comparing the figures shown in tables 7.2 and 7.3. The proportions in table 7.2 are of the total number of receivers questioned, while those in table 7.3 are of the total number of bankruptcies in which the receivers surveyed had been involved over the period 1984–1988. The receivers in the Hesselmann and Stefan survey are clearly drawn from the relatively small group of professional receivers, since the average number of bankruptcies settled by each over a five-year period was 37.6; professional receivers are more likely to be able to save bankrupt firms than are receivers in general, who are not (as we have seen) usually professional. Finally, the number of continuations shown in table 7.3 refer to bankruptcy procedures that have been opened: as we have seen, these are a relatively small proportion of total bankruptcy applications. Continuation of a bankrupt firm for which bankruptcy procedures are not opened is almost impossible, because in such cases there are hardly any unsecured assets (failure to open procedures means that unsecured assets are worth less than the costs of the procedure), and it is difficult to coordinate the unsecured creditors. Correctly interpreted, tables 7.2 and 7.3 paint a consistent picture, which confirms the view that once a German firm reaches the point where legal insolvency procedures have to be started, it is difficult to avoid liquidation.

Table 7.3. *Continuation and liquidation of bankrupt firms*

	No.	%
Total bankruptcy cases	2106	100.0
Immediate liquidation	1609	76.4
Attempt at rescue by debtor	81	3.8
of which: successful	55	2.6
Attempt at negotiated rescue	416	19.8
of which: successful	311	14.8

Source: Hesselmann and Stefan (1990).

The fact that the German legal framework for dealing with insolvencies makes continuation of a firm so difficult is one of the main objects of reform of the legal procedures.[4] It also means that many attempts to reorganise a German firm in financial distress take place outside the legal system, in the form of out of court settlements. The difficulty of reorganising a firm within the legal framework for insolvency, and the significance of out of court settlements, are both reflections of the fact that secured creditors have rights to foreclose on assets which act as collateral for their claims outside the bankruptcy or settlement in court procedures. Since these assets will usually be essential for the continuation of the business, attempts to rescue the firm take place mainly outside the courts.

Detection of financial distress by German banks

Table 7.4, which is based on the responses of 284 banks to a question in the survey by Drukarcyk *et al.* (1985), shows the significance of different methods used by German banks to monitor loans made to firms. All the banks analyse the accounts of firms to which they have made loans, and most visit the firms. Only just over half the banks check the payment transactions of the firms to which they have lent. This suggests that a significant minority of the banks responding either had made loans to firms that did not use the bank's payments services, or did not think that checking the firms' payments was a useful way of monitoring the firm. In either case this observation raises a question about the importance of the economy of scope between payments services and information collection which, it is claimed, explains why the financial intermediaries that provide external finance to firms are banks.

The figures in table 7.4 give no indication of the quality of the infor-

---

[4] See Bundesministerium der Justiz (1988).

Table 7.4. *Methods of monitoring bank loans to firms in Germany*

Method	No. of banks using method	Proportion of total no. of banks responding (284) using method
Analysis of annual accounts	284	100
Visits to firm	232	81.7
Checking payment transactions	161	56.7
Giving advice to customers	138	48.6
Other	57	20.1

Source: Drukarcyk *et al.* (1985), Table K–41, p. 124.

mation obtained from these various methods of monitoring bank loans to firms. According to our interviews with receivers, the ability of banks to detect financial distress on the part of firms to which they had lent varies considerably: those banks which relied mainly on information from the accounts were not able to detect financial problems until a relatively late stage. In our interviews with banks 'declining turnover where overdraft facilities are being used up to their limit' was most often said to be the major signal of financial distress. According to our interviews with banks, therefore, a firm's use of its overdraft facility does convey information to lenders about possible financial distress. This provides support for the hypothesis that an economy of scope between payments services and information collection is an important reason why the financial intermediaries which provide external finance are banks.

Neither in table 7.4 nor in our interviews was there any indication that bank representation on supervisory boards played a role in the detection of financial distress. In view of the findings discussed in earlier chapters concerning supervisory boards and bank representation on them, this is not surprising. As we have seen, supervisory boards generally have only limited information about the operations of the company and meet infrequently. Furthermore, bank representatives on supervisory boards are legally required to treat information obtained as confidential. Finally, only AGs and large GmbHs are required to have supervisory boards, and the evidence shows that bank loans are a very small source of investment finance for AGs: a substantial proportion of bank lending is made to firms which do not have supervisory boards, and hence there is no possibility of bank representation on such boards.

The variation in German banks' ability to detect financial distress noted in our interviews with receivers is confirmed by table 7.5, which shows the

Table 7.5. *Banks' ability to detect problem loans in time to avoid any losses*

Percentage of problem loans detected in time to avoid any losses	No. of banks responding	% of banks responding
>75 to 100	13	5.1
>50 to 75	77	30.0
>25 to 50	85	33.1
> 0 to 25	71	27.6
0	11	4.3
Total	257	100.1

Source: Drukarcyk *et al.* (1985), Table K–42, p. 125.

results of a question in the survey by Drukarcyk *et al.* (1985) which asked banks how many problem loans they could detect early enough to avoid any losses. Only a small elite of 5% of the 257 banks which replied were able to detect the vast majority of problem loans in time to avoid any losses, while another 30% recognised problem loans soon enough to avoid any losses more often than not. However, 65% of the banks were able to detect less than half of their problem loans early enough to avoid any losses. This evidence suggest that a substantial proportion of German banks cannot monitor the firms to which they make loans well enough to detect financial distress at an early stage.

An obvious question which arises from table 7.5 is what features characterise the small elite of banks which are able to recognise financial distress soon enough to avoid losses in most cases. Unfortunately, Drukarcyk *et al.* provide no information on this point. Conventional wisdom about the German system of finance for investment would be supported if this elite was comprised of banks with extensive supervisory board representation. However, given the absence of any evidence that representation on supervisory boards plays a role in detecting financial distress, it seems unlikely that such is the case.

German bank behaviour when firms are in financial distress or bankrupt

Tables 7.6 and 7.7 give some indication of the actions taken by German banks once financial distress has been detected. Table 7.6 shows the results of a question in the survey by Drukarcyk *et al.* (1985) which asked banks what courses of action they would take after becoming aware of a

Table 7.6. *Measures taken by German banks after financial distress has been detected*

Measures	No. of banks taking measure
Cancellation and calling-in of loans	213
Advice to and influence on management	181
Obtaining additional collateral	141
Threat of opening bankruptcy procedures	14
Securing collateral	10
Disclosure of assignments of assets	6
Forming a pool	3
Foreclosure proceedings	2
Total no. of responses	570
Total no. of banks responding	282

Source: Drukarcyk *et al.* (1985), Table K–44, p. 126.

severe financial crisis at a firm to which they had made loans. Table 7.7 summarises the responses of the receivers in the survey by Hesselmann and Stefan (1990) to a question asking what, in their view, were the measures taken by informed banks when an insolvency was threatening. The interpretation of this evidence is not straightforward. The banks' responses suggest that the cancellation and calling-in of loans is the most common response, being taken by 75.5% of the responding banks, while obtaining additional collateral is only the third most common response, behind advising and influencing management. In the receivers' view, however, obtaining additional collateral is the measure most frequently taken by banks, followed by withdrawal from the firm, which broadly corresponds to the cancellation and calling-in of loans. According to the receivers, banks would only infrequently attempt to influence management; this contrasts with the responses of the banks. Even taking account of the reorganisation recommendations measure in table 7.7, there is a striking difference between the banks and the receivers in the perceived importance of bank advice to and influence on management as a response to the detection of financial distress. A possible explanation for this difference is that the receivers only become involved in insolvencies at a relatively late stage in the crisis, and hence may not fully be aware of banks' true role in advising management and reorganising firms in financial distress, since successful reorganisations by the banks never reach the stage at which receivers become involved. Even if this explanation is accepted, the two most common measures adopted by banks according to table 7.6 seem somewhat contradictory. The widespread attempts to call

Table 7.7. *Measures taken by informed banks in cases of threatened insolvency, according to receivers, %*

Measure	Frequency according to receivers
Obtaining additional collateral	50
Withdrawal from firm	29
Influencing management	10
Reorganisation recommendations	9
Other	2

Source: Hesselmann and Stefan (1990).

in loans suggest that banks are not generally concerned with supporting firms in financial distress, but the fact that nearly two-thirds of the banks would attempt to advise and influence management can perhaps be seen as indicating that a significant proportion of banks are prepared to assist firms in financial distress to recover. A possible reconciliation of the contradiction is that banks try to cancel their loans in order to put pressure on the firm's management to respond to the financial crisis in a way the bank considers appropriate.

Whatever the explanation for the apparent contradiction between the two most common measures reported in it, table 7.6 shows that German banks do use the right they have under their general business conditions to withdraw loans from firms in financial distress. It therefore provides evidence in support of the argument in chapter 6 that long-term lending by banks to firms in Germany does not imply an unbreakable commitment of finance to a firm by a bank.[5]

The evidence from tables 7.6 and 7.7 that banks which detect financial distress sometimes respond by withdrawing from the firm was supported by the results of our interviews with banks. The ability of a bank which has recognised financial distress to withdraw from a firm implies that another bank has to step in, which can only be explained if banks' ability to detect financial distress varies considerably. According to our interviews, withdrawal by a bank after detection of financial distress is often the result of the failure of the firm's management to act in accordance with the bank's wishes after the crisis has become apparent. Such a failure of the firm to act as the bank would wish tends to be most pronounced for small firms, where it is often difficult to persuade the managing director, who is often the owner, to resign. The banks interviewed regarded this

[5] See pp. 135–136.

Table 7.8. *Results of problem loans reported by German banks, 1975, %*

Bankruptcy applied for but procedure not opened	14
Bankruptcy applied for and procedure opened	25
(includes 3.5% which were subsequently suspended due to lack of assets)	
Settlement in court	6
Reorganisation	23
Silent liquidation[a]	12
Unspecified	20

Note: [a] A silent liquidation occurs when a firm goes out of business but all creditors are paid off in full, so the legal framework for dealing with insolvency is not used.
Source: Gessner *et al.* (1978), Table III/4, p. 241.

problem as a good example of the limits of banks' ability to influence the operation of firms in financial distress. It illustrates the importance of recognising that many German firms – especially small ones – do not have supervisory boards, so that there is no possibility of banks being able to play a role in corporate governance via representation on these boards. For such firms, German banks – like banks in other countries – have no rights to determine operating decisions before default on a loan has actually occurred.

Some idea of the final outcome that resulted from the measures taken by banks when they detected financial distress is given by table 7.8, which is taken from Gessner *et al.* (1978) and is based on a written questionnaire completed by 122 banks referring to a total of 906 problem loans experienced in 1975. At least 35% of these problem loans were dealt with out of court, either as reorganisations or silent liquidations. A minimum of 23% of the problem loans were reorganised, and the actual proportion reorganised is likely to be higher, because of the 20% of the problem loans for which no outcome was specified. If it is assumed that the final results of the unspecified category are distributed among the five outcomes in proportion to the figures in the table, the proportion of reorganisations is estimated to be 28.75%. There was a high variance among the 122 banks whose responses are shown in table 7.8 in the proportion of problem loans which were dealt with through reorganisation: 10 of the banks succeeded in reorganising all their problem loans, while 60 banks did not reorganise any of their problem loans. Unfortunately Gessner *et al.* do not give any information about the characteristics of the 10 banks which reorganised all their problem loans. One reason for differences among banks in the proportion of problem loans that were reorganised is that, according to both Gessner *et al.*[6] and our interviews, only the three big banks and a few other large banks have special departments which deal with the financial and legal aspects of financial distress and insolvency. For most banks, problem loans are dealt with by the original loan officer, with some assistance from the bank's legal department. It seems reasonable to suppose that those banks with specialist departments are more likely to attempt reorganisations, and to complete them successfully, than the majority of banks, which are not in such a position. It may also be the case that the small minority of banks which are active reorganisers correspond to the small minority of banks in table 7.5 which were usually able to detect financial distress early enough to avoid any losses, but this is purely a conjecture.

The available evidence certainly does not support the view that the typical outcome for a German firm in financial distress is that it continues to operate after having been reorganised by its bank. Although a small number of banks do reorganise all their problem loans, overall it appears that roughly 70% of all firms in financial distress are not reorganised. Of course table 7.8 only shows the final outcome of problem loans; some ultimately unsuccessful attempts may have been made to reorganise some of the firms in financial distress, so the figures in table 7.8 may underestimate banks' willingness to attempt to reorganise firms in difficulty.

What considerations determine whether a bank attempts to reorganise a firm in financial distress? According to our interviews with banks, a precondition for any attempt at a reorganisation was the existence of a 'sound rescue concept'. The quality of the firm's management, and its market position, were seen as central elements of such a concept. The importance of the firm's management is reinforced by the findings of Hesselmann and Stefan, which show that, in the view of the receivers, lack of confidence by the bank in managerial capabilities was, together with lack of equity capital, one of the two most important reasons for failures of attempts to reorganise firms that were less than five years old. Banks must have confidence in the management of a firm for a reorganisation to be attempted: the importance of this factor suggests that banks do not take a direct part in managing a firm that is being reorganised.

Another consideration frequently mentioned in our interviews with banks as affecting the decision whether to reorganise a firm in financial distress was the effect on the bank's image in the eyes of customers and the public generally of liquidation or reorganisation of firms of different sizes. Such effects were stressed by all banks, not only those in the savings bank sector which, because they are owned by local and state governments, might be thought to be most subject to such influences. In general

---

[6] See Gessner *et. al.* (1978), pp. 238–239.

Table 7.9. *Indebtedness to banks of insolvent firms, 1975*

	One year before insolvency	At insolvency
Average no. of banks involved (based on 233 cases)	3.1	3.2
Average total of bank loans (DM million) (based on 202 cases)	3.5	3.9
% of bank loans covered by collateral	82.3	81.5

Source: Gessner *et al.* (1978), Table III/17, p. 254.

such image-effects are more important the larger the firm involved, but for savings banks and credit cooperatives, which operate in a relatively small local area, even small cases were seen as potentially affecting the bank's image, and thus, other things equal, having a positive effect on its willingness to reorganise rather than liquidate.

The discussion in chapter 6 showed that most bank loans to firms in Germany are secured by collateral, and table 7.9, which is taken from Gessner *et al.* (1978), gives some details about the extent to which collateral limits bank losses when a firm goes insolvent. The 122 banks which responded to the Gessner *et al.* survey gave a detailed account of a total of 275 insolvencies which had occurred in 1975, and table 7.9 is based on those insolvencies for which information was available on the characteristics listed in the first column. In the year before the firms became insolvent, the average total of bank loans to them increased by 11.4%, while the proportion of bank loans covered by collateral fell slightly. These figures show that banks were very well-secured in insolvencies, but in the year before insolvency banks on average increased their lending and were not able to collateralise these additional loans to quite the same extent as the loans made more than a year before bankruptcy. Even so, the figures in the table imply that 74.5% of the additional loans were secured. This suggests that banks are willing to support firms when financial distress is detected, and to extend further loans, somewhat less well-secured, in an attempt to avoid insolvency. Support for this view is provided by the receivers, who were of the opinion that banks were excessively generous in making loans to firms in the period before the actual insolvency; this emerged both in our interviews with receivers and in the survey by Hesselmann and Stefan.

The most striking feature of table 7.9, however, is that more than 80% of bank loans to insolvent firms are covered by collateral. According to Gessner *et al.*, a bank's average loss in the 275 insolvencies analysed is only 16%.[7] This average conceals a high variance: in 56% of the cases analysed banks did not lose anything, while in 10% banks lost everything. These figures are based on insolvencies of relatively small firms, and hence may underestimate the extent of bank losses: the insolvencies of larger firms seem to involve larger losses for banks (e.g. the settlement quotas of 40% for AEG and 25% for COOP, which imply substantial losses for banks). There was some evidence from our interviews with banks that the high proportion of secured loans reduced banks' incentives to attempt a reorganisation, since the loss to the bank if the firm became insolvent was small. This view is supported by the finding of Gessner *et al.* that the average loss in insolvency of those banks which had attempted a reorganisation was higher than that of the banks which had made no such attempt.[8] This finding suggests that banks are more inclined to attempt a reorganisation the more they stand to lose because a smaller proportion of their loans are secured by collateral. But although banks' well-secured position seems to reduce their incentives to attempt reorganisations, it also seems to reduce their incentives to force insolvency. There were several mentions in the interviews of court cases in which banks had been held liable for losses incurred by third-party creditors when banks had delayed applying for bankruptcy.[9]

The various considerations affecting banks' decisions whether to attempt to reorganise a firm in financial distress can explain the finding of Gessner *et al.* that reorganisation attempts are more likely to be made for large than for small firms. Of the insolvency cases for which the banks responding to the Gessner *et al.* survey provided a detailed account, 93 had seen attempts to avoid the formal insolvency procedures. Analysing these attempts by size of firm, Gessner *et al.* found that for firms with less than 10 employees reorganisation attempts had been made in 27% of the cases, while for firms with more than 500 employees such attempts had been made in 89% of the cases. There are several reasons for this difference. One is that image-effects are more pronounced for larger firms. A second is that it is easier to change the management of large firms, partly because senior management is less likely to have a major ownership stake in the firm, and partly because it is easier to find suitable replacements for the senior managers of a large firm than for the owner-manager of a small one. A third reason is that the accounts of smaller firms are usually less transparent than those of larger ones. Finally, to the extent that bank

---

[7] See Gessner *et al.* (1978), p. 243.

[8] See Gessner *et al.* (1978), Table III/26, p. 262.

[9] For example, *Zeitschrift für Wirtschaftsrecht und Insolvenzpraxis* (1985) refers to a case in which several banks were held liable for not applying for bankruptcy but rather improving their collateral position at the expense of other creditors, in this case workers.

loans to larger firms are less well secured than those to smaller firms, banks have a greater incentive to attempt reorganisations.

What actions do German banks typically take when an attempt is made to reorganise a firm in financial distress? As table 7.9 shows, insolvent firms have on average borrowed from three banks, reinforcing the conclusion of chapter 6 that it was rare for a firm to raise all its loan finance from a single bank. An attempt to reorganise a firm in financial distress therefore usually requires coordinated actions by several banks, and this is achieved by the establishment of a bank pool.[10] According to our interviews with banks, an essential condition for this to occur is that the bank with the largest involvement with the firm – usually the house bank (in the sense of the bank with the longest relationship with the firm) – must take an active role in coordinating the other banks. If the house bank does not act in this way, other banks hardly ever cooperate to attempt a reorganisation.[11] Such behaviour can be interpreted in terms of the reluctance of the bank with the largest involvement, or longest relationship, with a firm to take an active part in a reorganisation acting as a negative signal of its perception of the firm to the other banks. Even when the house bank acts as leader of the pool, it is usually necessary that all banks involved with the firm participate in the attempted reorganisation, since each individual bank usually makes its participation conditional on a unanimous agreement. However, it appears to be difficult for an individual bank to refuse to join a reorganisation pool which most other banks have agreed to, unless the bank has only a tiny stake in the firm in question.[12] Apart from the general pressure to join such a pool, which stems from the image-effects mentioned above, the banks supporting the reorganisation attempt can put pressure on a reluctant individual bank to participate in the pool. According to the interviews, the banks which have agreed to the reorganisation may put pressure on a reluctant bank by threatening not to participate themselves in a future reorganisation where the reluctant bank is more heavily involved. One bank even suggested in the interviews that a failure to join the reorganisation pool might have adverse consequences for that bank's refinance activities on the interbank market.

As we have seen, the existence of a 'sound rescue concept' appears to be a precondition for any attempt to reorganise the firm. The interviews suggest that, although the rescue concept is sometimes developed by the

---

[10] A pool of banks may also be formed simply to coordinate the realisation of collateral from a liquidated firm.

[11] See the 1988 example of PHB Weserhütte, which belonged to the Otto Wolff Konzern, where Deutsche Bank failed to take the initiative.

[12] See for example the AEG settlement in court, where two banks initially refused to join the pool but finally yielded to the pressure to do so.

bank itself, it is most often left to management consultancy firms. A development which seems to have occurred in the 1980s is that, however the rescue concept is developed, a management consultancy firm takes responsibility for the validity of the rescue concept, because of the court cases, already mentioned, which have held banks liable for damaging other creditors by delaying insolvency. As a reorganisation attempt which failed would potentially fall into the category of an insolvency which had been delayed to the detriment of other creditors, rescues now require a 'neutral third party' to certify that the behaviour of the bank is 'correct'.

The interviews made it very clear that, in contrast to Japanese banks,[13] German banks do not in general get directly involved in the reorganisation of a firm in financial distress at the level of day-to-day management, and do not possess any personnel who are specialists at turning unprofitable firms around. The reason for this, besides a strong convention that industrial and bank management are distinct, is that a direct involvement of the bank in the reorganisation would inevitably raise liability questions for the bank if the reorganisation failed, for the reasons discussed in the previous paragraph. Even the specialist departments for handling problem loans, possessed by a small number of banks, have expertise only in the financial and legal aspects of such loans, and their role in developing a rescue concept is restricted to these features of a reorganisation. The banks do, of course, give advice to the management in the course of a reorganisation and, as we have seen, if the management is not willing to act in the way the banks consider appropriate, a reorganisation attempt is unlikely to occur. According to the interviews, an important function of the banks is to use their contacts to bring in suitable new management. Somewhat less common is the use of bank contacts to facilitate a merger with another firm as a means of resolving the crisis. But although the giving of advice to management, and attempting to influence it, is an important part of German banks' activities in reorganisations, direct management of the reorganising firm by the bank is not.

A final issue concerns German banks' holdings of equity in financially distressed firms. As the discussion on p. 159 pointed out, decisions by suppliers of debt about the reorganisation or liquidation of a firm are likely to be inefficient because no account is taken of returns to equity holders. This problem can be mitigated if suppliers of debt also hold equity, though it will only be fully eliminated if all the firm's equity is held by suppliers of debt. Chapter 3 showed that the amount of equity supplied to firms by German banks was very small relative to the amount of loan finance supplied,[14] so that typically banks will not have an equity holding

[13] See Corbett (1987).
[14] See p. 64.

in a firm suffering financial distress. It is, however, possible for banks to transform loans to firms in financial distress into equity, and thereby improve their incentives to take efficient decisions about the firm's operation. However, according to the interviews, this option is used only rarely, because it considerably worsens the bank's position in the event of the reorganisation failing. The legal position is that if a bank has an equity holding in a firm, even the claims arising from that bank's loans to the firm are treated as ranking behind the claims of all other creditors if the firm becomes insolvent. Despite this, banks do occasionally take equity stakes as part of a reorganisation attempt, as happened in the 1980s in the cases of AEG, Hapag-Lloyd, and Klöckner. However, it is not a common occurrence.[15]

Conclusion

The evidence on German bank behaviour when firms are in financial distress does not support the view that banks are able to reduce the costs of financial distress and bankruptcy by close monitoring and control of the actions of managers of firms in financial difficulty. The ability of banks to detect financial distress varies considerably: although a small number of banks regard themselves as able to identify problem loans early enough to avoid all losses in most cases, the majority of banks appear to be able to do so in less than half the cases. Given the concentration of bank supervisory board representation in the hands of a relatively small number of banks, it might be argued that the important characteristic of this small number of banks who detect financial distress early is representation on supervisory boards but, according to our interviews with banks, supervisory board representation did not help to identify problem loans, a conclusion which is supported by our findings in earlier chapters concerning the role of such representation in German bank lending behaviour.

There is thus no evidence of a widespread ability of German banks to detect financial distress at an early stage. There is also no evidence that banks in general take a direct part in managing a firm in financial distress. As we have seen, reorganisations are usually attempted before the firm in question has become insolvent. Consequently, banks have no formal rights to control the operations of the firm in most reorganisations. There

---

[15] According to the Bundesverband deutscher Banken (1989), in the period 31 December 1986 to 31 August 1989, for the ten largest commercial banks as a whole, there were only five cases in which an equity holding of more than 10% was acquired in a firm as part of a reorganisation. In only one of these cases did the holding acquired amount to more than 50% of the equity.

was evidence that banks were often unable to persuade the existing management to act as the bank would wish – particularly in the case of smaller firms where the owner-manager could not be induced to resign – with the consequence that the bank would not attempt a reorganisation. A necessary condition for banks to attempt a reorganisation appears to be that they must be convinced of the quality of management of the firm. What this suggests is that German banks are willing to attempt reorganisations if they have confidence in the management of the firm, and particularly in their own ability to influence the management. The importance of the management's receptiveness to the bank's views, however, underlines the fact that in most reorganisations the banks have no formal rights to manage the firm's operations.

There is, in addition, no evidence that German banks send managers to work with firms in financial distress which are attempting to reorganise. The major role of banks in a reorganisation in Germany is to coordinate the financial side of the reorganisation attempt, such as the rescheduling of interest and principal payments, or the reduction of interest charges and debts. A small number of large banks have specialist departments for dealing with the financial and legal aspects of bankruptcy and financial distress, but these departments do not contain specialists at managing firms in financial difficulty.

There is also some evidence which suggests that banks' financial incentives to attempt reorganisations may be weak. German banks' loans to firms are very well-secured, and the losses suffered by banks when firms become insolvent are generally quite small, although they tend to be larger for larger firms. As a result, the gains to banks from attempting a reorganisation rather than liquidating a firm in financial distress are limited. In addition, banks do not often have equity stakes in financially troubled firms, so they do not usually share in the upside return to a successful reorganisation.

The evidence presented in this chapter provides no general support for the view that bank representation on supervisory boards enables the costs of bankruptcy and financial distress to be reduced, by enabling banks to detect financial distress early and to take an active role in the management of a firm which is being reorganised. It is possible, however, that bank supervisory board representation has some limited positive effect on the likelihood of reorganisation, not because it enables early detection of financial distress by banks, nor because it gives banks influence on the operational management of the firm, but because the image-effects which increase a bank's willingness to attempt a reorganisation are enhanced by supervisory board representation. As has been seen, reorganisation attempts are more common for larger firms than smaller ones, partly as a result of such image-effects and partly because it is easier to replace the management of large firms. Large German firms will typically have supervisory boards whose function is to appoint and dismiss the management board. This raises the question of whether representation on supervisory boards enables banks to have a decisive influence on the replacement of managers of large firms. The general question of the role German banks play in monitoring the management of AGs is examined in chapters 8 and 9.

8 The ownership structure of large German firms, and its implications for German banks' corporate control role

Introduction

An important component of the view that German banks contribute to good economic performance in Germany concerns the role that banks are supposed to play in corporate governance. German banks are able to exercise proxy votes at the shareholders' meetings of AGs on behalf of shareholders who have deposited their shares with the banks for safe-keeping. The significant control of equity voting rights that banks have as a consequence of their proxy voting power is seen as giving them the ability to place bank representatives on the supervisory boards of AGs. Since the supervisory board is the body which appoints and dismisses the management board of an AG, the combination of bank control of equity voting rights via proxy votes and supervisory board representation is claimed to be an efficient mechanism of ensuring that the managements of companies with widely-dispersed share ownership are monitored and faced with incentives to perform well. In particular, delegating the exercise of equity's control rights to banks in this manner is regarded as being superior to the hostile takeover mechanism, on which the UK and USA have to depend in order to monitor and control the managements of widely-held companies.

What role German banks actually play as delegated exercisers of equity's control rights is the subject of this and the following chapter. In this chapter the general background for the analysis of banks' corporate control function is set out. The problem of individual suppliers of equity finance not having incentives to monitor and control managerial behaviour is one which arises primarily for large firms. The second section discusses the ownership and control of large German firms. It begins with an analysis of the structure of share ownership in Germany, which shows that the single most important shareholder group is non-financial enterprises. The evidence on share ownership patterns among large listed AGs

178

is then examined, and compared with the evidence on the ownership of public limited companies in the UK. There appear to be many fewer companies in Germany which do not have a shareholder owning 25% or more of the voting capital than there are in the UK. If a shareholder with an ownership stake of at least 25% is regarded as having adequate incentives to monitor and control managers, which is a reasonable supposition, it would seem that there is very little scope for problems arising from lack of managerial monitoring to occur in Germany. However, the widespread ownership of shares by non-financial enterprises in Germany means that care is required before this conclusion is accepted. This section concludes with some evidence showing that, because many of the holders of stakes of 25% or more in large German firms are other large companies with widely-dispersed share ownership, there is more scope for corporate control problems to arise in Germany than is apparent from the simple share ownership figures.

As has been noted, one mechanism which may restrict the extent to which the managers of large, widely-held firms pursue their interests at shareholders' expense is the threat of a hostile takeover in an active market for corporate control. The effectiveness of this mechanism for disciplining inefficient managements in practice is open to some doubt, as was noted in chapter 2. In Germany, however, hostile takeovers are almost completely unknown, so that this mechanism for inducing managers to run AGs in the interests of owners does not operate. The reasons for the rarity of hostile takeovers in Germany are examined in the third section.

The fourth section draws a brief conclusion, which considers the implications of the analysis of the chapter for banks' role as delegated exercisers of equity's control rights. Evidence on German banks' performance of this role is set out in detail in chapter 9.

The ownership and control of large German firms

The structure of share ownership in Germany

We begin the analysis of the ownership and control of AGs with a discussion of the evidence on the aggregate ownership of shares by different types of shareholder. As was noted in chapter 4, AGs and KGaAs are the only two legal forms of enterprise in Germany which can issue shares that are legal evidence of ownership. The best available estimates of the ownership of shares issued by AGs (and KGaAs) are those obtained from the statistics on securities deposits collected by the Deutsche Bundesbank, rather than those obtained from the capital

Table 8.1. *Ownership of shares issued by German enterprises (excluding insurance enterprises), 1984 and 1988, %*

	1984	1988
Private individuals	18.8	19.7
Non-financial enterprises	36.1	39.1
Banks	7.6	8.1
Investment funds	2.7	3.5
Insurance enterprises	3.1	2.7
Government	10.2	7.0
Foreigners	21.4	20.0
Total	99.9	100.1

Source: Die Entwicklung der Wertpapierdepots im Jahre 1988, Supplement to *Statistical Supplements to the Monthly Report of the Deutsche Bundesbank*, Series 1, July 1989, p. 3.

finance account of the Bundesbank. The latter are often quoted as estimates of the ownership of shares in German AGs (see, for example, Deutsche Bundesbank, 1984a), but they are in fact estimates of the ownership of assets in the form of shares. If Germans own shares issued by foreign companies, the ownership of assets in the form of shares is a different concept from the ownership of shares in German AGs. The share ownership figures derived from the capital finance account of the Bundesbank actually show the ownership of an aggregate consisting of the sum of the shares issued by German AGs and holdings by Germans of foreign shares. By contrast, the statistics on securities deposits give the distribution of ownership of shares issued by German enterprises, excluding those issued by insurance enterprises.[1] These are the share ownership figures we want.

Table 8.1 shows the estimated distribution of ownership in 1984 and 1988 of shares issued by German enterprises, according to the statistics on securities deposits. These estimates are based on the nominal values of shares.[2] German non-financial enterprises were the shareholder group with the largest holding of shares in German enterprises in both 1984 and 1988. Foreigners and private individuals were the shareholder groups

[1] According to the capital finance account of the Deutsche Bundesbank, shares issued by insurance enterprises (including private private pension funds) were 1.2% of all German enterprises' outstanding shares in 1960, and 3.8% in 1989 (Deutsche Bundesbank, 1990), so this exclusion is not significant.

[2] A share must have a nominal value of at least DM 50: larger nominal values must all be in multiples of DM 100. The vast majority of German companies have shares with a DM 50 nominal value.

with the next largest holdings. The shareholdings of the various types of financial enterprises, and of the government, were relatively small. The securities managed by investment funds have to be deposited with a bank, and investment funds are usually owned by the banks with which they have deposited shares. Hence bank ownership of shares is more appropriately estimated by adding the figures for investment fund share ownership in table 8.1 to those for bank share ownership, thus obtaining estimates of 10.3% in 1984 and 11.6% in 1988. Even with this adjustment, however, banks as a whole do not own a particularly large proportion of shares in German enterprises.

The statistics on securities deposits do not provide any estimates of the ownership of shares in German enterprises before 1984. The only source for such estimates is the capital finance account of the Deutsche Bundesbank which, as has been noted, provides data on the ownership of assets in the form of shares rather than the ownership of shares in German enterprises. Furthermore, the capital finance account values shares at their price on issue, i.e. at nominal value plus issue premium, rather than at nominal value as in the securities deposit statistics. Table 8.2 shows the estimates of the structure of share ownership in Germany derived from this source for 1960, 1970 and, for comparison with the estimates obtained from the statistics on securities deposits, 1988. Comparing the figures for 1988 in tables 8.1 and 8.2 it can be seen that the share ownership estimates for non-financial enterprises, insurance enterprises, and households derived from the capital finance account are larger than those derived from the securities deposit statistics, and correspondingly smaller for government and foreigners. The quite substantial differences between the two sets of estimates for 1988 are not surprising. Shares are valued on a different basis in the two sets of estimates, although it is not clear how this difference is likely to influence the estimates. In 1988 only 60.7% of total assets arising from shares in Germany were shares issued by German firms: the other 39.3% consisted of foreign shares owned by Germans. Even if the different valuation basis is ignored, the large difference between assets arising from shares in Germany and shares issued by German firms is likely to result in significant differences in share ownership estimates derived from these two concepts. In 1960, however, 93.6% of total assets arising from shares in Germany comprised shares issued by German firms, and only 6.4% were foreign shares owned by Germans. Thus, if the different valuation basis is ignored, the 1960 figures in table 8.2 can be regarded as reasonably comparable to those in table 8.1. Over the period 1960–1988 it would appear, therefore, that the importance of private individuals and government as holders of shares in German enterprises has decreased, while that of foreigners, banks, and

Table 8.2. *Ownership of assets arising from shares in Germany, 1960, 1970 and 1988, %*

	1960	1970	1988
Households	28.1	29.8	21.1
Non-financial enterprises	35.7	36.9	43.0
Banks	7.0	7.6	10.4
Insurance enterprises [a]	3.6	4.0	8.8
Government	13.6	9.3	4.6
Foreigners	12.0	12.4	12.1
Total	100.0	100.0	100.0

Note: [a] Including private pension funds and building and loan associations.
Source: Deutsche Bundesbank (1990).

non-financial enterprises has increased. Non-financial enterprises were, however, the largest shareholder group in 1960 as well as in the 1980s, so this feature of the structure of share ownership in German enterprises has been constant over the period as a whole.

The structure of share ownership in Germany is very different from that in the UK, where non-financial enterprises have consistently had relatively small holdings of shares. Over the period 1950–1989 the main changes in UK share ownership have been a fall in holdings by individuals and a rise in holdings by non-bank financial enterprises (pension funds, insurance companies, unit trusts, etc.). At the end of 1986 the ownership of total ordinary and preference shares (in nominal values) by sector in the UK was as follows: personal sector 26.2%; industrial and commercial companies 10.5%; banks 4.8%; other financial institutions 53.3%; and government (including public corporations) 5.2% (*UK National Accounts*, 1988). Financial institutions as a whole own a much larger proportion of shares in the UK than in Germany, although the fraction of shares owned by banks alone is smaller in the UK than in Germany.

The ownership of large AGs

The agency problems which lead to insufficient monitoring and control of managers by suppliers of equity finance are most likely to occur in large AGs, as it is these companies which are most likely to have dispersed share ownership. In this subsection we discuss the available evidence on the ownership of large AGs in order to assess how important such agency problems have been in Germany.

Typically, even large AGs have at least one shareholder owning a

Table 8.3. *Listed AGs by holding of largest shareholder, 1963–1983, %*

Share of largest shareholder %	No. of AGs			Nominal value of equity capital of AGs			Market value of equity capital of AGs		
	1963	1973	1983	1963	1973	1983	1963	1973	1983
≥ 75	22.1	32.3	38.9	13.6	17.4	17.7	13.1	24.3	17.9
≥ 50 and < 75	33.6	31.1	26.6	26.0	21.2	20.3	22.7	19.3	16.9
≥ 25 and < 50	29.1	29.3	22.9	21.6	28.7	25.1	24.7	28.5	32.2
≥ 1 and < 25	3.2	2.3	5.0	9.3	9.5	15.4	11.2	9.2	16.5
< 1	12.0	5.0	6.6	29.5	23.3	21.5	28.3	18.7	16.6
Total	100.0	100.0	100.0	100.0	100.1	100.0	100.0	100.0	100.1

Source: Iber (1985), Table 3, p. 1111.

significant fraction of the total equity. A study by Iber (1985) shows this very clearly. Iber examined the structure of shareholdings in a sample of large listed AGs for each of the years 1963, 1973, and 1983. These samples comprised all domestic AGs above a certain size listed on the German stock market in either the official market or the regulated free market.[3] In 1963 the sample consisted of all listed AGs with a nominal share capital of DM 4.75 million or more; in 1973 the sample was all listed AGs with a nominal share capital of DM 6 million or more; and in 1983 the size requirement was a nominal share capital of DM 10 million or more. The size criterion was intended to be equivalent in all the three years after allowing for inflation. There were 375 AGs in the 1963 sample, 341 in the 1973 sample, and 301 in the 1983 sample. In each of the three years the sample comprised over 95% of the nominal capital of all listed AGs in that year.

Table 8.3 shows the distribution of these three samples of listed AGs according to the share of the voting capital held by the largest shareholder in each AG. The proportion of those AGs in which a single shareholder had at least half of the voting capital increased from 55.7% in 1963 to 65.5% in 1983. Over the same period, the proportion of widely-held AGs in the samples, defined as those with no single shareholder having 1% of the voting capital, fell from 12.0% to 6.6%. The figures for the distribution of the total value of equity capital of these samples of AGs by the holding of the largest shareholder are broadly similar whether nominal or market value of equity capital is used. The AGs in which there was a majority shareholder accounted for 39.6% of the nominal equity capital

[3] The regulated free market is the secondary tier of the German stock market.

of the sample in 1963 (35.8% in terms of market value), and 38.0% in 1983 (34.8% in terms of market value). As would be expected, therefore, the AGs which had a majority shareholder tended to be the smaller ones in the sample. The widely-held AGs accounted for 29.5% of the nominal equity capital of the sample in 1963 (28.3% in terms of market value), and 21.5% in 1983 (16.6% in terms of market value). Thus the widely-held AGs tended to be the larger ones in the sample.

According to Iber's data, therefore, the proportion of large AGs which had a majority owner increased over the period 1963–1983, although in terms of the total value of equity capital the significance of AGs with a majority shareholder did not change. The proportion of large AGs which were widely-held fell over this period, both in terms of numbers and total value of equity capital.

The structure of share ownership in large listed AGs in Germany is very different from that in public limited companies in the UK. Table 8.4 shows the distribution of the Leech and Leahy (1991) sample of 470 UK listed companies in 1983–5 by the size of holding of the largest share-holder. This sample was selected on the basis of availability of sufficiently detailed ownership data. It includes 325 companies from *The Times* 1000 largest industrial companies. Both Iber's and Leech and Leahy's samples consist of listed companies, but the AGs in Iber's samples were selected to be above a certain size, while Leech and Leahy did not use size as a criterion for selecting their sample. On average, therefore, the UK public limited companies in the Leech and Leahy sample are smaller than the AGs in Iber's sample. This feature of the UK sample is likely to impart an upward bias to the proportion of companies with a majority shareholder when comparisons are made with the German sample. However, even taking no account of this possible bias, the proportion of UK public limited companies with a majority shareholder is far smaller than is the case for AGs in Germany. 65% of Iber's 1983 sample had a single shareholder with 50% or more of the voting capital, while only 5.3% of Leech and Leahy's 1983–5 sample had a single shareholder with more than 50%. The difference is equally striking if the proportion of com-panies in which the largest shareholder had more than 20% is compared. 88.4% of Iber's 1983 sample had a single shareholder with 25% or more of the voting capital, while only 34.0% of Leech and Leahy's sample had a single shareholder with more than 20%. 39.3% of the UK public limited companies had a largest single shareholder owning 10% or less of the share capital. By contrast, only 11.6% of Iber's 1983 sample had a largest shareholder owning less than 25% of the share capital.

A less detailed comparison of share ownership in Germany and the UK, but one based on companies of comparable size, is reported by Franks

Table 8.4. *Listed UK PLCs by holding of largest shareholder, 1983–1985*

Share of largest shareholder %	No.	%
> 50	25	5.3
20–50	135	28.7
10–20	125	26.6
5–10	144	30.6
< 5	41	8.7
Total	470	99.9

Source: Leech and Leahy (1991), Table 2, p. 1421.

Table 8.5. *Listed AGs owned by a single majority[a] shareholder, by type of majority owner, 1963–1983, %*

Type of majority shareholder	No. of AGs			Nominal value of equity capital of AGs			Market value of equity capital of AGs		
	1963	1973	1983	1963	1973	1983	1963	1973	1983
Families[b]	26.7	23.8	22.6	15.0	8.9	6.9	10.2	7.6	6.4
Non-financial enterprises	6.9	11.1	11.3	5.5	7.9	7.1	3.0	7.2	5.3
Government	8.0	8.5	9.3	10.3	11.3	12.9	11.4	8.7	8.9
Foreigners	7.7	9.7	11.3	6.6	7.5	7.5	9.1	14.5	9.2
Banks	4.3	8.5	8.0	1.6	2.3	2.5	1.2	4.5	3.3
Insurance enterprises	1.6	0.9	1.7	0.3	0.2	0.5	0.4	0.3	1.1
Other[c]	0.5	0.9	1.3	0.3	0.5	0.6	0.5	0.8	0.6
Total	55.7	63.4	65.5	39.6	38.6	38.0	35.8	43.6	34.8

Notes: [a] Including direct and indirect holdings.
[b] Holdings of individuals, families and foundations.
[c] Holding companies in the possession of various types of shareholder.
Source: Iber (1985), Table 4, p. 1113.

and Mayer (1992). They found that nearly 90% of the largest 200 companies in Germany at the end of the 1980s had at least one shareholder with an ownership stake of at least 25% of the share capital. In the UK, however, two-thirds of the largest 200 companies had no single shareholder with a holding of more than 10% of the share capital. These figures reinforce the conclusion that emerges from comparing the Iber and Leech and Leahy studies.

Iber's study also gives details of the majority shareholders in the AGs in his samples, and these are shown in table 8.5. In all three years, the most important type of majority shareholder, in terms of the proportion of the number of large listed AGs, was families. However, in terms of the proportion of the total value of AGs in the sample, government and foreigners were the most important types of majority shareholder in 1973 and 1983. In terms of the proportion of all the large listed AGs, the significance of non-financial enterprises and banks as majority share-holders increased over the period. But even in 1983 banks were the majority shareholders for only 8.0% of the AGs in the sample, and these tended to be among the smaller majority-owned AGs, accounting for only 2.5% of the total nominal value of equity capital in the sample (3.3% in terms of market value). Non-financial enterprises were the majority share-holders in 11.3% of the AGs in the 1983 sample, and these too tended to be the smaller majority-owned ones, accounting for 7.1% of the nominal value of equity capital of the sample (5.3% in terms of market value). At first sight, the relatively small number of majority shareholders in the AGs in Iber's samples which were non-financial enterprises appears to be inconsistent with the evidence on pp. 180–182 that non-financial enter-prises are the largest shareholder group in Germany. The reconciliation of this apparent inconsistency involves noting that unlisted AGs are approximately equal in importance within the German economy to listed AGs,[4] and that many non-financial enterprise shareholdings take the form of majority holdings in unlisted AGs. Furthermore, non-financial enterprises also have considerable holdings of less than 50% but greater than 25% of the share capital in large listed AGs.

In many circumstances, large minority shareholders are also in a posi-tion to exert a substantial influence on the outcome of votes at the general meeting of shareholders in a corporation. This is especially the case if the holdings of other shareholders are widely dispersed.[5] In Germany a shareholding of more than 25% enables the holder to block major decisions by an AG, such as changes in the articles of association, increases in share capital, and mergers. Large minority shareholders therefore also have incentives to collect information about managerial performance and to monitor management closely. Iber's study shows that only a very small proportion of the largest listed AGs in his samples did not have a shareholder with a holding of 25% or more of the voting capital. There were 57 such AGs in the 1963 sample, 25 in the 1973 sample, and 35 in the 1983 sample. As the figures for the value of equity

---

[4] See p. 87.
[5] See Cubbin and Leech (1983) for an analysis of this point in terms of a probabilistic shareholder-voting model.

capital in table 8.3 show, these AGs tended to be the larger ones in the sample. If there is only a very small number of the largest listed AGs with no shareholder having 25% or more of the voting capital, as Iber's study shows, it seems reasonable to suppose that this conclusion continues to hold when account is taken of smaller AGs. Some evidence to back up this supposition is provided by the study of Kurth (1987). Kurth examined share ownership data for all 711 AGs with shares traded on any of the three tiers of the German stock market (official market, regulated free market, and unregulated market) in the mid 1980s, and found that fewer than 30 of these AGs had no single shareholder with 25% or more of the voting capital.

The general conclusion from this analysis of the structure of shareholdings in large AGs is that, by comparison with public limited companies in the UK, very few large companies in Germany do not have a shareholder with a large enough holding to provide adequate incentives to monitor management. It would therefore appear that the problem of lack of monitoring of managers caused by wide dispersion of shareholding is of rather limited significance in Germany. However, before concluding that issues of corporate control are relatively unimportant in Germany, it is necessary to take account of the fact that, as we have seen, non-financial enterprises are the largest single group of owners of shares in German AGs. Although non-financial enterprises had only a relatively small number of majority holdings among the largest listed AGs studied by Iber, they would have had holdings of 25% or more in many more cases. Among AGs as a whole, non-financial enterprises have a large number of majority holdings. This is particularly true for the very largest AGs, which are often widely-held, and have extensive majority holdings in other AGs (and GmbHs). It is not obvious that the existence of a large shareholder – one with a holding of 25% or more – will result in sufficient monitoring of the management of the AG to ensure that it acts in the interests of the suppliers of equity finance when the large shareholder in question is another AG with widely-dispersed share ownership. In such a case it cannot be assumed that the managers of the latter AG will necessarily use the large shareholding in the former AG in the interests of suppliers of equity, since these managers may themselves not be subject to monitoring and control. The implications for corporate control issues of widespread shareholdings by non-financial enterprises are examined in the next subsection.

The control of large enterprises

A study by Schreyögg and Steinmann (1981) shows how the extensive holdings of shares by non-financial enterprises in Germany makes it

Table 8.6. *Control classification of largest 300 German firms, 1972*

	Classification in terms of direct ownership[a]		Classification in terms of ultimate ownership[a]	
	% of no. of firms in sample	% of total turnover of sample	% of no. of firms in sample	% of total turnover in sample
Owner-control[a]	89.7	75.1	49.7	35.4
Manager-control[a]	10.3	24.9	50.3 (13.0)[b]	64.6 (15.7)[b]

Notes: [a] See text for definitions of direct and ultimate ownership, and owner- and manager-control.
[b] Bracketed figures show the percentages of the firms in the sample, and of the total turnover of the sample, which are government-owned firms and hence classified as manager-controlled.
Source: Schreyögg and Steinmann (1981), Tables 2, 3 and 5, pp. 544, 546.

necessary to be careful before concluding that ownership patterns in large firms are such that corporate control issues are relatively insignificant. Schreyögg and Steinmann analysed the structure of ownership and control in the 300 largest German industrial enterprises in 1972, irrespective of legal form, taking into account the implications of the ownership of many firms by other firms. The sample studied by Schreyögg and Steinmann comprised firms of all legal forms, not just AGs, although many were AGs. The main conclusion of the study concerns the implications of non-financial enterprises having substantial ownership stakes in other firms, and is applicable to large AGs as well as to large enterprises in general.

In the first stage of their analysis, Schreyögg and Steinmann classified the 300 enterprises as either owner- or manager-controlled simply on the basis of their direct ownership, without taking any account of whether the owners were other enterprises. Enterprises were categorised as manager-controlled if no single owner had more than 1% of the voting rights or, where a single owner or owners had more than 1% of the voting rights, if the sum of the holdings of such owners was less than 25%. Large cooperatives, trade-union-owned firms, and government-owned firms were included in the manager-controlled category. Enterprises not categorised as manager-controlled were classified as being subject to one of three forms of owner-control. The results of this classification are shown in the first two columns of table 8.6, from which it can be seen that about 90% of the firms in the sample, accounting for about 75% of total turnover of the sample, were owner-controlled. This conclusion is broadly what would be expected on the basis of Iber's study. Only a small proportion of large enterprises were not owner-controlled when the categorisation of such enterprises into owner- and manager-controlled was based on their direct ownership. The small proportion of enterprises which were manager-controlled in terms of their direct ownership tended to be the largest firms in the sample, as is shown by the percentage of total turnover they accounted for.

In the second stage of their analysis, Schreyögg and Steinmann investigated the ultimate ownership pattern of the firms in their sample. This involved taking account of the fact that many holders of large ownership stakes in firms were other enterprises which were manager-controlled. Firms were reclassified as manager- rather than owner-controlled in this second stage of the analysis if the conditions for being owner-controlled were no longer met once account had been taken of the significant ownership stakes in firms held by manager-controlled enterprises. Since there may be several layers of ownership by enterprises, a number of steps may be required to establish the ultimate ownership pattern of firms. Suppose, for example, that 75% of firm A is owned by firm B, with the remaining 25% ownership being widely-dispersed. Firm B, in turn, is 50% owned by firm C, with the other 50% being widely-dispersed. Firm C is a widely-held company, with all 100% of its capital dispersed among individual shareholders. In terms of direct ownership, firms A and B would be classified as owner-controlled, while firm C would be manager-controlled. In terms of ultimate ownership, however, all three firms would be classified as manager-controlled. The results of the second stage of Schreyögg and Steinmann's analysis are shown in the third and fourth columns of table 8.6. About 50% of the firms in the sample, accounting for about 65% of the total turnover of the sample, were manager-controlled when classification was carried out on the basis of ultimate ownership.

The main conclusion which emerges from Schreyögg and Steinmann's analysis in particular, and from this section in general, is that the importance of non-financial enterprises as shareholders in Germany means that care is required when share ownership data are used to draw inferences about the significance of corporate control problems in Germany. There is only a relatively small number of firms which have a widely-dispersed share ownership, and it might be argued that the problems of inadequate monitoring and control of management by shareholders can only possibly be serious for this small group of firms. But these firms are large ones, and they have large ownership stakes in substantial numbers of other German firms. Any inadequacies in the monitoring and control of the managements of this relatively small number of firms have potentially very important consequences for the monitoring and control of the managements of a much larger number of German firms, because of the pattern of holdings of shares by non-financial German enterprises in other German non-financial enterprises.

Why are hostile takeovers so rare in Germany?

The preceding section showed that the pattern of share ownership in Germany is such that there is only a relatively small number of large firms with widely-dispersed share ownership. But the widespread holdings of substantial ownership stakes in other firms by this relatively small group of firms means that we cannot argue that problems resulting from inadequate monitoring and control of managers by shareholders are unimportant solely on the basis of share ownership patterns. One mechanism which, it is argued, ensures that the managers of large, widely-held firms restrict the extent to which they pursue their interests at shareholders' expense is the threat of a hostile takeover in an active market for corporate control. As discussed in chapter 2, the theory underlying the claim that hostile takeovers act as a mechanism for ensuring that managers act in shareholders' interests is based on the view that any failure of the existing management of a firm to maximise profits will be reflected in the firm's share price. Hence a takeover raider can become the majority owner of the firm by purchasing shares at a price below the value that the firm can achieve when profit-maximising policies are adopted. The takeover raider can ensure that such policies are implemented, and thus obtain a capital gain from the resulting appreciation of the firm's share price, by using its position as majority owner to change the firm's management. Whether hostile takeovers do function in this way in practice is open to some doubt, as was noted in chapter 2. In Germany, however, hostile takeovers are almost completely unknown, so that this mechanism for inducing managers to run AGs in the interests of owners does not operate. The reasons for the rarity of hostile takeovers in Germany are examined in this section.

If hostile takeovers are to be an effective mechanism for disciplining managements it must be possible for a takeover raider to change existing management relatively easily once the raider has become the majority owner. One explanation that has been advanced for the absence of hostile takeovers in Germany relates to various features of the legal framework surrounding the appointment and dismissal of the management of AGs; it is claimed that these legal features prevent this condition for hostile takeovers to function from being met. The management board of an AG is appointed by the supervisory board, which comprises both shareholder and employee representatives. It is argued that employee representatives will tend to support the existing management against a takeover raider, thus preventing the raider being able to dismiss the existing management. But, if they wish to, shareholder representatives acting in concert can always determine supervisory board decisions. Shareholder representatives account for two-thirds of the supervisory board members of AGs with 2,000 or fewer employees.[6] For AGs with more than 2,000 employees the shareholder representatives comprise only half the supervisory board members, but the chairman, who is always a shareholder representative, has a casting vote in situations of stalemate. If a takeover raider can gain control of all the shareholder representatives on the supervisory board it can, therefore, gain control of the supervisory board. Unless the existing supervisory board members (the ones appointed by shareholders before the raider appeared) cooperate, however, a 75% majority at a shareholders' meeting is required to replace them before their term of appointment (usually five years) expires.[7] A takeover raider can therefore gain control of the shareholder representatives on the supervisory board, and hence the supervisory board, by securing 75% of the shares of an AG. In practice this requirement for a raider to gain control is no more onerous than is the case in the UK, where the City Code on Takeovers and Mergers strongly discourages takeover bids for more than 30% but less than 100% of a company's voting shares, and permits such partial bids to be made only with the consent of the Panel on Takeovers and Mergers. Once a raider has control of the supervisory board, the management board can be replaced before its term of appointment expires (again usually five years) by a simple majority decision of the supervisory board, provided that there is an 'important reason'.[8] Lack of confidence by the new owner can constitute such a reason.

One feature of German institutional arrangements which, by comparison with the corresponding UK arrangements, makes hostile takeovers easier is that a shareholder in Germany is only required to disclose a holding of greater than 25% of an AG's shares, in contrast to the UK where a much smaller holding – originally more than 5%, now more than 3% – must be disclosed. A takeover raider in Germany can therefore

---

[6] Until 1976, shareholder representatives accounted for two-thirds of the supervisory board membership of all AGs.

[7] See Section 103 of the Aktiengesetz. However Otto (1991) claims that the articles of association of most AGs have been modified to allow a simple majority to be sufficient.

[8] Section 84(3) of the Aktiengesetz states that the supervisory board can reverse the appointment of members of the management board if there is an important reason. Such reasons are, in particular, a serious neglect of duty; inability to conduct business in an orderly manner; or the withdrawal of confidence by the general shareholders' meeting, unless the reasons for this withdrawal of confidence are obviously not objective.

accumulate a much larger stake in an AG before having to disclose it than would be the case in the UK.

The legal framework for the appointment and dismissal of the management board of an AG does not, therefore, prevent a hostile takeover raider changing the management of an AG, provided that the raider holds 75% of the voting shares in the AG. A major reason for the absence of hostile takeovers in Germany, however, is that it is not easy for a raider to obtain a 75% majority. As we saw in the previous section, most AGs have a large shareholder who owns 25% or more of the shares. In such cases a raider cannot gain effective control without purchasing the holding of the large shareholder, both because of the need to have a 75% majority at the shareholders' meeting in order to replace the supervisory board, and because a shareholder with a holding of more than 25% can block merger decisions. The raider will not necessarily be able to buy the large shareholder's holding at a price low enough to make the takeover worthwhile. If the large shareholder is another AG, then the other AG may value the shareholding above the market price of the shares for strategic or other reasons, while if the large shareholder is a family or individual then it is likely that holding such a substantial fraction of the AG's shares creates strong enough incentives to monitor the existing management sufficiently closely that there are very limited departures from profit-maximisation, and so very limited gains available to a takeover raider.

The pattern of share ownership therefore seems to restrict the number of AGs for which a successful takeover raid is possible to the relatively small number that have no single shareholder with a holding of 25% or more. The study by Iber (1985), discussed in the previous section, showed that there were 57 such AGs in 1963 and 35 in 1983. Some of these possible subjects of a hostile takeover bid, however, have restrictions in their articles of association on the number of votes that can be exercised by any single shareholder, irrespective of the number of voting shares held by such a shareholder. Baums (1990) found that 23 AGs had voting restrictions in 1989, usually limiting the voting rights of any one shareholder to 5 or 10% of the nominal equity capital. Eleven of these 23 were widely-held companies with no single shareholder owning more than 1% of the equity capital.[9] These voting restrictions act as a further impediment to the mounting of hostile takeover bids in Germany, but they do not prevent such bids altogether. It is possible for a group of non-related shareholders to pool their votes in order to avoid the voting restrictions because, in

[9] According to *Wer gehört zu wem* (Who belongs to whom), a guide to capital links among German companies, published by Commerzbank, these eleven were: BASF, Bayer, Continental, Deutsche Babcock, Deutsche Bank, Hoesch, IWKA, Mannesmann, SABO, Schering, VEBA.

contrast to the UK, there are no limitations on the activities of share-holders working in concert. This tactic was used in the acquisition of a 40% stake in Feldmühle Nobel AG by VEBA AG,[10] in the attempted takeover of Continental AG by Pirelli, and in the takeover of Hoesch AG by Friedrich Krupp GmbH in 1991/2.

Is the role of the German banks a major part of the explanation for the very small number of hostile takeover bids in Germany? In so far as banks hold shares in AGs they can, of course, influence the outcome of a hostile bid through their decision of whether to sell but, as we have seen, their shareholdings are not a large enough proportion of total shares for them to be able to inhibit hostile takeovers simply by refusing to sell their own holdings. A more important source of banks' influence stems from their exercise of proxy voting rights on behalf of shares that are deposited with them by shareholders. According to Baums (1990) the introduction of restrictions on the voting rights of any single shareholder in German AGs has always been initiated by the existing management, but has been supported by the banks, which have used their control of proxy votes to achieve the 75% majority required at the shareholders' general meeting in order to change the articles of association to limit voting rights. Such voting restrictions do not affect the dominant voting position of the banks themselves, since this is based on the exercise of proxy voting rights for shares which the banks do not themselves own. One consequence of the implementation of voting restrictions, of course, is the strengthening of banks' voting power at subsequent shareholder general meetings.

It would be incorrect, however, to view the role of banks as being any more than a contributory factor in the explanation of the very small number of hostile takeover bids in Germany. The support of the banks is necessary for the introduction of voting restrictions, since banks' proxy voting rights enable them to determine the outcome of votes about changes to the articles of association at the shareholders' general meeting. But although voting restrictions make hostile takeover bids difficult to mount, they do not prevent such bids occurring, as we have seen. The unimportance of hostile takeovers in Germany is due to more funda-mental reasons. The hostile takeover mechanism can only apply to listed companies, of which there is only a small number in Germany. The vast majority of large listed AGs have a shareholder who owns 25% or more of the shares, so that it is very difficult for a takeover raider to acquire the 75% of an AG's shares necessary to gain control. The banks contribute to these difficulties via their own holdings of shares and exercise of proxy voting rights, but it is clear that the main reason why hostile takeovers are

[10] See Franks and Mayer (1990) for details.

so rare in Germany is that there are only a very small number of AGs for which it would be possible to mount a successful takeover bid.

Conclusion

The vast majority of German AGs have a single shareholder who owns 25% or more of the voting capital. In this respect the structure of share ownership in Germany is markedly different from that in the UK. The available evidence, which has been discussed in this chapter, does not permit precise comparisons to be made, but there is no question that far more German than UK companies have a large shareholder with an equity stake which permits effective control of the firm, as was shown by the comparison of Iber's 1983 German data with the UK data reported by Leech and Leahy. This feature of share ownership patterns in German AGs is the major reason for the unimportance of hostile takeover bids as a mechanism of corporate control in Germany. An ownership of 25% or more in a German AG gives the holder rights to block various decisions at the shareholders' general meeting, and is likely in most cases to give the holder effective control of votes at this meeting. Such a large shareholder will certainly have incentives to incur the costs involved in monitoring the performance of the firm's management. It may, therefore, be the case that the agency problems which result from a lack of monitoring and control of managers by suppliers of equity finance are much less serious in Germany than in the UK because of the structure of share ownership in Germany.

Before this conclusion is accepted, however, the implications of the importance of non-financial enterprises as shareholders in Germany must be considered. As this chapter has shown, non-financial enterprises are the largest shareholding group in Germany, and in many cases the large shareholder in a German company is another German company which has a widely-dispersed share ownership, and hence may be controlled by a management that is not subject to monitoring by shareholders. In such circumstances it is not obvious that the agency problems resulting from inadequate monitoring and control of managers by shareholders are unimportant. The issues here are complicated ones. On the one hand it can be argued that there is no reason why the management of a large AG with a widely-dispersed share ownership should use their ability to monitor and control the behaviour of the managers of another company in which the AG has a large shareholding to impose cost-minimising discipline on the managers of the other company. If the management of the former AG are not subject to any monitoring and control to make them act in the interests of the suppliers of equity finance, then their incentives to act in such a way that the managers of the latter company run it so as to maximise the return to shareholders are not clear. Against this, however, it can be argued that the management of an AG with a large shareholding in another company will wish to ensure that the managers of the latter company run it efficiently, even if there is no pressure on that AG's management to act in shareholders' interests. From the viewpoint of the AG's management, the more efficiently the managers of the latter company manage it, the greater are the returns available to the AG's management for the pursuit of its own interests. Which of these two views is correct is a question that can be settled only on the basis of empirical evidence.

Chapter 9 addresses this question, in the context of a general assessment of the role of German banks in corporate governance and control in Germany. As we have seen, there has been only a small number of large widely-held AGs for much of the post-war period, but these firms have had large ownership stakes in many other German firms. If German banks have used proxy voting rights to act as delegated exercisers of equity's control rights for these firms, their contribution to good German economic performance may have been substantial, despite the small number of such large widely-held AGs. Banks' exercise of a corporate control function which induced the management of these AGs to act in shareholders' interests might have a substantial impact because of the extensive shareholdings of these large AGs in other companies. If bank monitoring and control of the managements of these AGs made them use their large shareholdings in other companies to ensure that these other firms were efficiently operated, the effects of this bank monitoring would clearly spread throughout the German economy. Even if the management of large widely-held AGs used their shareholdings in other companies to impose profit-maximising discipline on the managers of these other companies only in order to have more funds with which to pursue their own interests, the banks' corporate control function may be substantial if it limits the extent to which these funds are dissipated. The evidence on German banks' corporate control activities is examined in chapter 9.

9   Do German banks act as delegated exercisers of equity's control rights?

Introduction

There is a great deal of evidence available which is superficially consistent with the view that German banks act as delegated exercisers of equity's control rights. The banks, especially the three big banks, have control of a substantial proportion of the equity voting rights at the general meeting of shareholders in large AGs, mainly derived from the proxy votes they exercise rather than from their own holdings of shares. Gottschalk (1988), for example, analysed the votes cast at the shareholders' meetings of those 32 AGs among the largest 100 enterprises in 1984 which had more than 50% of their share capital either widely dispersed or owned by banks. All banks together had a majority of the votes cast in 31 of the 32 cases, and in 22 cases controlled more than 75% of the votes cast. The three big banks had a majority of the votes cast in 15 cases, and in a further 10 cases the big banks controlled between 25% and 50% of the votes cast. Banks are also represented on the supervisory boards of many large AGs, and again this representation is concentrated among the three big banks. The Monopolkommission (1980) found that in 1978 bank representatives occupied 145 seats on the supervisory boards of the largest 100 AGs. Bank representatives accounted for 9.8% of all supervisory board members, and 19.6% of shareholder representatives on supervisory boards. There were 20 supervisory board chairmen, and 6 deputy chairmen, among these 145 bank representatives. Banks as a whole were represented on the supervisory boards of 61 of the top 100 AGs. The three big banks accounted for 94 of the 145 bank representatives, and were represented on the supervisory boards of the following numbers of AGs: Deutsche Bank 38, Dresdner Bank 23, and Commerzbank 14.

The evidence that German banks control substantial equity voting rights in many AGs, and are represented on the supervisory boards of many AGs, is not, however, sufficient on its own to establish that banks act as delegated exercisers of equity's control rights. The argument that banks behave in this way sees the proxy vote system as enabling banks to act as voting agents on behalf of individual shareholders at shareholders' meetings. Concentrating the votes of small shareholders in the hands of banks is seen as giving the banks the power to influence the outcome of votes at these meetings, in particular the election of shareholder representatives to the supervisory board, the body which appoints and dismisses the board of managers of an AG. Banks are thus seen as being in a position where by using proxy voting rights to place bank representatives on the supervisory board, they can significantly influence the appointment and dismissal of managers, and hence as having incentives to monitor the performance of managers. If the argument that banks act as delegated exercisers of equity's control rights is correct, there should be a positive relationship between the degree of bank control of equity voting rights due to proxy votes and bank representation on supervisory boards. The existence of such a relationship is not, however, obvious, since banks may be represented on the supervisory boards of AGs for reasons other than the delegated exercise of equity's control rights. German banks themselves argue that their representation on supervisory boards reflects their ability to perform a consultancy function, assisting the management board rather than controlling it on behalf of shareholders.[1]

The second section of this chapter discusses the evidence from the Monopolkommission study on bank control of equity voting rights and supervisory board representation among the largest 100 AGs in 1974. This study provides by far the most comprehensive information available on banks' ability to act as delegated exercisers of equity's control rights by means of proxy votes and representation on supervisory boards, and the evidence from it is therefore worth analysing in detail. The results suggest that although banks, and in particular the big banks, have both substantial control of equity voting rights from proxy votes and extensive supervisory board representation, proxy voting power is, at best, weakly associated with the degree of bank representation on the supervisory board. This finding is not consistent with the view that German banks act as delegated exercisers of equity's control rights.

The third and fourth sections discuss further aspects of the argument that German banks act as delegated exercisers of equity's control rights. The third section examines the evidence on whether bank representatives

---

[1] Ellen Schneider-Lenné, a member of the board of managing directors of Deutsche Bank, states that 'the emphasis of the supervisory board's work has shifted more and more towards advising and counselling the board of managing directors ... "Consultancy" of this nature presupposes expert knowledge and a comprehensive view – both endowments which people seem to think bankers possess to an eminent degree' (Schneider-Lenné, 1992, p. 20).

are able to determine supervisory board decision-making, and whether the supervisory board is able to monitor and control the management board closely. The fourth section discusses whether banks have appropriate incentives to use their proxy voting rights in the interests of the suppliers of equity finance. The conclusion of both sections is that, in addition to the lack of a strong relationship between bank proxy voting power and supervisory board representation, there are also a number of problems with the argument that German banks play a corporate control role.

In view of the questions raised by these sections about the view that banks act as delegated exercisers of equity's control rights, the fifth section briefly considers an alternative explanation of bank representation on the supervisory boards of AGs. According to this alternative view, such representation is most appropriately regarded as part of a system which promotes the maintenance of commercial relationships that are efficient in the absence of self-interested opportunism, rather than as a system which minimises the agency costs of the separation of ownership from control by disciplining management.

In the end, empirical evidence which relates the performance of AGs to the degree of bank control of equity voting rights and bank supervisory board representation is required to assess whether German banks act as corporate controllers. The sixth section considers the influential empirical study of Cable (1985) in the light of the questions that have been raised by earlier sections about the view that banks behave in this way. It is argued that Cable's results do not in fact provide very much support for this view, contrary to his interpretation of them.

The seventh section draws a brief conclusion.

Bank control of equity voting rights and supervisory board representation among the 100 largest AGs in 1974

The most detailed information available about bank control of equity voting rights and supervisory board representation is contained in a study of the largest 100 AGs (in terms of turnover) in 1974 by the German Monopoly Commission (Monopolkommission, 1978). These 100 largest AGs accounted for most of the turnover of the entire AG sector. Figures for the proportion of all AGs' turnover attributable to the largest 100 were unavailable, but the largest 50 AGs accounted for about 75% of the turnover of all AGs. The extent of bank control of equity voting rights was investigated by examining the lists of shareholders actually present at the general meeting of shareholders of these AGs in 1975: the votes controlled by banks were calculated as a proportion of the total equity votes represented at these meetings.

Table 9.1. *Bank control of equity voting rights in 56 cases where combined vote exceeded 5%, 1975*

Rank class of AGs by turnover (1)	No of AGs with combined bank vote > 5% (2)	Average % of bank vote in AGs in (2)[a]		
		From own shareholdings (3)	From proxy votes (4)	Combined votes (5)
1–10	8	3.56	63.48	67.03
11–25	6	6.10	48.19	54.29
26–50	14	14.65	25.03	39.68
51–100	28	13.52	29.01	42.53
1–100	56	7.28	49.45	56.73

Note: [a] Averages are weighted averages with weights given by nominal capital of AGs.
Source: Monopolkommission (1978), p. 295.

There were 56 AGs for which the combined vote of all banks – the sum of their own holdings of shares and the proxy votes they exercised – amounted to more than 5% of the total share capital represented at the shareholders' meeting. Table 9.1 shows the relative importance of banks' own holdings of shares and proxy votes in these 56 AGs. On average, banks' control of equity voting rights was mainly derived from proxy votes. The relative importance of proxy votes was most marked for the largest AGs, in which the banks, on average, controlled a majority of the votes cast. To the extent that the largest AGs tended to be the ones with widely-dispersed share ownership, the tendency for both bank control of voting rights and the importance of proxy votes relative to banks' own holdings of shares to decrease as the size of AGs decreases is what would be expected.

The 44 AGs for which the combined vote of all banks was 5% or less of the share capital represented were all AGs with some form of dominant shareholder.[2] However, there were a number of cases in which banks controlled a substantial proportion of equity voting rights in an AG

---

[2] These 44 cases comprised:

Subsidiaries of foreign firms	18
Subsidiaries of domestic firms	11
Corporations where families or private foundations held the majority of the shares	9
Government-owned corporations	6

despite there being a non-bank shareholder with more than 25% of the share capital. Bank control of voting rights as a result of proxy votes was not restricted to AGs lacking a large shareholder (one with more than 25% of the equity). As it is possible for more than 25% of an AG's shares to be owned by a single shareholder while 50% or more of its shares are widely-dispersed, this is perhaps not surprising. It does, however, mean that banks' proxy voting power was in some cases a supplement to, rather than a substitute for, the existence of a large shareholder with incentives to monitor and control management.

Banks were represented on the supervisory boards of 75 of the largest 100 AGs in 1974. The 25 AGs which had no bank representatives on their supervisory boards were distributed between subsidiaries of foreign firms (11), family-owned AGs (8), and AGs owned by other domestic non-banks (6). The existence of bank control of more than 5% of the equity voting rights was neither a necessary nor a sufficient condition for bank representation on the supervisory board. The Monopolkommission found that there were five cases in which banks controlled more than 10% and less than 25% of the votes at an AG's shareholder meeting but were not represented on the supervisory board. All of these five AGs had a majority shareholder. Bank control of more than 5% of the equity votes was thus not sufficient for bank supervisory board representation. There were 24 cases in which banks were represented on the supervisory board despite having less than 5% of the votes at the shareholders' meeting. Banks were represented on the supervisory boards of 75 AGs, but had more than 5% of the votes in only 56 and, as we have seen, in five cases banks were not on the supervisory board despite having between 10 and 25% of the votes. Bank control of more than 5% of the equity votes was therefore not necessary for bank supervisory board representation.

One possible explanation for banks being represented on the supervisory board of an AG in which banks controlled less than 5% of the equity votes is that another AG had a large shareholding in the first AG, and banks controlled a significant fraction of the equity voting rights in this other AG. If this were the case, banks might be represented on the supervisory board of the first AG because of their control of votes in the other AG, which was a major shareholder in the first AG. The evidence suggests that this explanation for bank representation on the supervisory boards of AGs in which they controlled less than 5% of the votes cannot be the only one. There were 18 AGs that were subsidiaries of foreign firms in which banks had less than 5% of the votes, but only 11 in which they were not represented on the supervisory board. Clearly 7 German subsidiaries of foreign firms had German banks represented on their supervisory board, the reason for which could not be that the banks controlled a significant fraction of the equity votes in the foreign parent company. Similarly there were six government-owned AGs in which banks had less than 5% of the votes, but all of these had bank representation on their supervisory boards. The representation of German banks on the supervisory boards of AGs is not therefore solely due to bank control of equity voting rights, direct or indirect.

A total of 179 seats were occupied by banks on the supervisory boards of those 75 among the largest 100 AGs on which banks were represented. Bank representatives therefore accounted for 14.9% of the total of 1203 members of the supervisory boards of the largest 100 AGs in 1974. In 1974, employee representatives occupied one-third of the supervisory board seats of all AGs, so bank representatives accounted for 22.4% of shareholder seats on the supervisory boards of the largest 100 AGs. These proportions are based on all the largest 100 AGs, but since banks were represented on the supervisory boards of only 75 AGs, the figures underestimate the importance of bank representatives on those supervisory boards on which banks have seats. On average, banks had 2.4 seats on each of the 75 AGs among the largest 100 on which they were represented. The average size of supervisory boards among the largest 100 AGs was 12.0, so on average bank representatives accounted for 20% of the supervisory board members for those AGs among the largest 100 on which banks had seats.

Table 9.2 gives a detailed analysis of bank control of equity voting rights and supervisory board representation for the 41 AGs among the largest 100 in which the combined vote of all banks was greater than 25%. These 41 AGs included all the widely-held companies among the largest 100, and they had a total of 114 bank representatives on their supervisory boards, 63.7% of all bank supervisory board seats among the largest 100.

A number of points emerge from table 9.2 which are relevant for assessing the argument that the proxy voting power of banks enables them to act as delegated exercisers of equity's control rights for companies with sufficiently dispersed share ownership that no single shareholder has incentives to monitor management. The Monopolkommission Report gave details of the share ownership in 1977 of roughly the largest 70 of the 100 AGs. Since the bank voting data refers to the 1975 shareholders' meeting, the share ownership figures are not strictly comparable, but it is unlikely that any serious errors will result from using 1977 data for share ownership with 1975 data for bank voting. Table 9.2 shows that there were seven AGs among the largest 100 which unambiguously fell into the category of having a widely-dispersed share ownership – BASF, Siemens, Hoechst, Bayer, AEG, Mannesmann and Linde. In each of these AGs, banks as a whole controlled over 70% of the votes

Table 9.2. Bank control of equity voting rights and supervisory board seats in the 41 AGs among the largest 100 in 1974 for which the combined bank vote exceeded 25%

Name of AG	Rank in largest 100	* indicates non-bank shareholder with >25% of total shares	% of total shares widely dispersed	Deutsche Bank			
				Own votes	Proxy votes	Combined votes	SB seats (c = chairman)
Thyssen	1	*	≈56	0	10.0	10.0	1
VEBA	2	*	≈56	0	6.9	6.9	1
BASF	3		94.7	0	26.9	26.7	1
Volkswagenwerk	4		60	0	4.1	4.1	1
Daimler-Benz	5		<25	30.6	4.0	34.6	2(c)
Siemens	6		89	0	19.4	19.4	2
Hoechst	7		100	0	19.4	19.4	0
Bayer	9		>80	0	23.5	23.5	1
AEG	11		>80	0	23.4	23.4	1
Mannesmann	13		100	0	26.7	26.7	1(c)
Metallgesellschaft	19	*	<35	0	0	0	2
Karstadt	24		0	25.3	2.6	27.9	2(c)
Kaufhof	26		<25	0	0.7	0.7	1
Degussa	28		>50	0	14.0	14.0	0
Klöckner-Humboldt-Deutz	31	*	<50	0	40.0	40.0	1(c)
Klöckner-Werke	33	*	>50	0	19.0	19.0	1
Brown, Boveri & Cie	34	*	<44	0	6.1	6.1	1
Preussag	38		≈60	0	9.4	9.4	1
Deutsche Babcock	39	*	>50	0	12.5	12.5	0
BayWa	41	*	0	0	0	0	0

Philipp Holzmann	48		<50	39.3	9.1	48.4	1(c)
Hochtief	51	*	<25	0	1.4	1.4	0
Neckermann Versand	52		<50	0	5.8	5.8	0
Hapag-Lloyd	57		<25	25.9	8.0	33.9	2(c)
Papierwerke Waldhof-Aschaffenburg	58	NA	NA	0	2.4	2.4	1
Continental Gummi-Werke	59		>50	0	12.1	12.1	1(c)
Rütgerswerke	62	NA	NA	0	38.4	38.4	1
Schering	64		>50	0	19.9	19.9	1
Strabag Bau	68		<50	0	2.7	2.7	1
Linde	70		≈90	0	17.8	17.8	0
Dortmunder Union	76	NA	NA	0	4.3	4.3	0
Andreae-Noris Zahn	78	NA	NA	0	4.3	4.3	0
Bilfinger + Berger Bau	79		<35	0	5.8	5.8	0
Hamburgische Electricitäts-Werke	80	NA	NA	0	2.9	2.9	0
Beton-und Monierbau	83	NA	NA	0	17.3	17.3	0
Kali-Chemie	84	NA	NA	0	76.7	76.7	1(c)
Beiersdorf	91	NA	NA	0	2.4	2.4	0
Flachglas	93	NA	NA	0	14.9	14.9	1(c)
Portland-Zementwerke	95	NA	NA	0	12.4	12.4	1(c)
Triumph International	96	NA	NA	0	0.1	0.1	1
Bergman-Electricitäts-Werke	98	NA	NA	36.7	0.2	36.9	1(c)

Table 9.2. (cont.)

	Dresdner Bank				Commerzbank				All banks			
	Own votes	Proxy votes	Combined votes	SB Seats (c = chairman)	Own votes	Proxy votes	Combined votes	SB Seats (c = chairman)	Own votes	Proxy votes	Combined votes	SB Seats (c = chairman)
Thyssen	0	6.3	6.3	1	0	4.1	4.1	1	0.01	45.3	45.3	5
VEBA	0	6.8	6.8	1	0	3.6	3.6	0	0.2	37.8	40.0	4
BASF	0	15.3	15.3	0	0	7.1	7.1	0	0.1	87.1	87.2	1
Volkswagenwerk	0	1.4	1.4	0	0	2.8	2.8	0	0.1	25.1	25.2	4
Daimler-Benz	0	17.2	17.2	1	0	1.1	1.1	1	30.7	26.3	56.9	4(c)
Siemens	0	10.2	10.2	1	0	5.1	5.1	0	0.9	80.1	81.0	4
Hoechst	0	22.9	22.9	0	0	8.2	8.2	1	0.4	88.2	88.6	1
Bayer	0	13.5	13.5	0	0.4	7.3	7.7	1	0.6	78.5	79.1	2
AEG	0	19.8	19.8	1	0	6.6	6.6	1	0.1	89.2	89.3	5
Mannesmann	0	13.2	13.2	0	0.3	6.8	7.1	0	0.4	76.6	77.0	3(c)
Metallgesellschaft	26.1	15.0	41.1	2(c)	0	0.5	0.5	0	26.3	43.9	70.2	4(c)
Karstadt	0	2.2	2.2	1	31.8	1.6	33.4	2	57.2	11.1	68.3	7(c)
Kaufhof	34.2	3.7	37.9	1	35.9	3.7	39.6	1(c)	70.2	16.8	87.0	3(c)
Degussa	0	6.8	6.8	1	0	5.4	5.4	0	0.4	47.3	47.7	1
Klöckner-Humboldt-Deutz	0	5.2	5.2	1	0	3.6	3.6	1	0.1	86.5	86.6	4(c)
Klöckner-Werke	0	0.3	0.3	1	0	7.6	7.6	0	0	60.3	60.3	1
Brown, Boveri & Cie	0	5.7	5.7	0	0	2.0	2.0	1	0.8	28.6	29.4	2
Preussag	0	6.3	6.3	0	0	4.4	4.4	1	50.2	45.4	95.6	4(c)
Deutsche Babcock	0	6.6	6.6	0	0	4.1	4.1	0	16.2	62.1	78.3	2(c)
BayWa	0	0	0	0	0	0	0	0	66.2	14.1	80.3	2(c)
Philipp Holzmann	0	1.9	1.9	0	0	1.3	1.3	0	40.1	20.2	60.3	2(c)
Hochtief	0	0.7	0.7	0	31.4	0.8	32.2	2	33.2	4.6	37.8	6
Neckermann Versand	0	13.8	13.8	0	0	0	0	0	0.1	83.0	83.1	3
Hapag-Lloyd	25.9	7.0	7.0	1	0	0.4	0.4	0	51.8	17.9	69.7	3(c)

Papierwerke Waldhof-Aschaffenburg	0	1.4	1.4	0	0	0.4	0.4	0	60.0	8.8	68.8	3(c)
Continental Gummi-Werke	0	10.3	10.3	0	0	5.2	5.2	0	0	44.8	44.8	1(c)
Rütgerswerke	0	4.4	4.4	0	0	3.6	3.6	1	0.1	53.5	53.6	2
Schering	0	12.3	12.3	0	0	11.7	11.7	0	0.3	81.0	81.3	2(c)
Strabag Bau	0	0.6	0.6	0	0	0.8	0.8	0	33.8	31.4	65.2	4(c)
Linde	0	11.8	11.8	0	0	4.4	4.4	0	0.2	72.3	72.5	1
Dortmunder Union	33.4	2.4	35.8	2	0	3.0	3.0	0	80.1	15.8	96.9	6(c)
Andreae-Noris Zahn	0	3.9	3.9	0	0	0.8	0.8	0	53.0	37.1	90.1	2(c)
Bilfinger + Berger Bau	74.4	7.4	81.8	2(c)	0	2.4	2.4	0	74.4	22.3	96.7	2(c)
Hamburgische Electricitäts-Werke	0	1.9	1.9	0	0	2.8	2.8	1	12.0	14.9	26.9	2
Beton-und Monierbau	0	3.2	3.2	0	0	37.4	37.4	1	23.5	71.7	95.2	2
Kali-Chemie	0	1.9	1.9	0	0	3.8	3.8	0	0	89.5	89.5	1(c)
Beiersdorf	0	1.0	1.0	0	0	1.6	1.6	0	0.02	42.5	42.5	1
Flachglas	0	0.2	0.2	0	0	4.2	4.2	0	0	25.1	25.1	1(c)
Portland-Zementwerke	33.8	3.9	37.8	1	0	1.5	1.5	0	35.3	25.6	60.9	4(c)
Triumph International	0	0.1	0.1	0	0	0	0	0	8.9	22.7	31.6	1
Bergman-Electricitäts-Werke	0	0	0	0	0	0	0	0	62.5	0.6	63.1	2(c)

Source: Monopolkommission (1978), Table IV.7.

at the 1975 shareholder meeting. But this dominant position in terms of equity voting rights was not systematically reflected in the number of bank representatives on the supervisory board, the body with the legal responsibility for controlling the management of an AG. Although there were five bank representatives on the supervisory board of AEG, four on that of Siemens, and three on that of Mannesmann, there were only two on Bayer's supervisory board, and just one each on those of BASF, Hoechst and Linde. Bank control of equity voting rights in widely-held AGs due to proxy votes did not necessarily result in a substantial bank presence on the body which appoints and dismisses the management of these AGs.

The absence of a clear relationship between bank proxy voting power and bank supervisory board representation suggested by the figures for these widely-held AGs is confirmed by a simple regression analysis. The Monopolkommission report gave details of the votes controlled by all banks due to both their own shareholdings and to proxy votes, together with the total number of bank representatives on the supervisory board, for the 56 AGs in which the combined votes of all banks exceeded 5%. Five of these 56 AGs had no bank representatives on their supervisory board. A regression of the total number of bank supervisory board seats on the proportion of votes controlled by all banks due to own shareholdings and to proxy votes yielded the following results (t-ratios are shown in brackets):

Bank supervisory = 1.68 + 0.0289 Bank own + 0.008 Bank proxy
board seats   (3.82)   (3.12)   votes   (0.97) votes

$R^2 = 0.156$ $\bar{R}^2 = 0.124$ No. of observations = 56

This regression equation suggests that there is a relationship between the number of bank supervisory board representatives and banks' own shareholdings in AGs, but the estimated coefficient of the bank proxy votes variable is not significantly different from zero. These results cast considerable doubt on the view that German banks use their proxy voting rights to act as delegated exercisers of equity's control rights. If the banks were to behave in this manner, the natural way for them to exercise the rights to appoint and dismiss management would be by using their proxy votes to ensure significant bank representation on supervisory boards. There is, however, no evidence of a relationship between banks' proxy voting power and their supervisory board representation for the 56 AGs in which the combined votes of all banks exceeded 5%. This conclusion is reinforced when it is recalled that there were a further 24 AGs among the largest 100 in 1974 which had bank representatives on their supervisory boards despite the combined votes of all banks having been less than 5%.

Table 9.3. *Bank representation on supervisory boards of the largest 100 AGs in 1974, by bank and type of seat*

	Chairman	Deputy Chairman	Simple membership	Total
Big banks	21	19	62	102
of which:				
Deutsche Bank	18	11	26	55
Dresdner Bank	2	6	18	26
Commerzbank	1	2	18	21
All other banks	10	16	51	77
of which:				
Regional and other commercial banks, and private bankers	8	15	34	57
Savings bank sector	1	1	5	17
Credit cooperative sector	1	–	2	3
Total	31	35	113	179

Source: Monopolkommission (1978), pp. 301, 303, 304, 305.

In view of the evidence presented in chapter 5, which showed that proxy votes and bank supervisory board seats were concentrated in the hands of the three big banks, it may, however, be the case that the delegated exercise of equity's control rights is performed mainly by these banks, rather than by all banks. Certainly bank representation on the supervisory boards of the largest 100 AGs in 1974 was dominated by the three big banks, as table 9.3 shows. The three big banks accounted for 67.7% of the supervisory board chairmen who were bank representatives, and 57.0% of all bank supervisory board representatives. Most of the remaining bank supervisory board representatives were from the commercial bank sector: the savings bank sector provided only 9.5% of all supervisory board representatives, and the credit cooperative sector a mere 1.7%. Among the three big banks, Deutsche Bank was dominant, accounting for 58.1% of all chairmen who were bank representatives, and 30.7% of all bank supervisory board representatives. The 55 seats held by Deutsche Bank gave rise to representation on the supervisory boards of 48 AGs. The big banks as a group were represented on the supervisory boards of 56 AGs, outnumbering all the other commercial banks (represented on the supervisory boards of 37 AGs), the savings bank sector (14), and the credit cooperative sector (2). It is therefore important to analyse the relationship between proxy voting power and supervisory board representation for the three big banks.

Of the 114 bank representatives on the supervisory boards of the 41 AGs shown in table 9.2, 66 came from the three big banks – 33 from Deutsche Bank, 17 from Dresdner Bank and 16 from Commerzbank. The big banks thus accounted for 57.9% of all bank representatives on the supervisory boards of these AGs, a slightly higher proportion than the big banks' share of the combined votes of all banks, which was 53.4%.[3] Deutsche Bank alone accounted for 28.9% of all bank supervisory board representatives among these 41 AGs, while its share of the combined votes of all banks was 25.1%. The big banks' dominance of bank supervisory board representation thus appears broadly to reflect their share of the total equity voting rights of banks. However, the fact that 11 of the 22 supervisory board chairmen among these AGs who were bankers came from Deutsche Bank is not easy to explain solely in terms of Deutsche Bank's control of voting rights, which were only one-quarter of the total votes controlled by banks.

The Monopolkommission report gave details of the big banks' control of votes due to their own shareholdings and proxy votes, as well as their supervisory board representation, for those 51 AGs in which both the combined vote of all banks exceeded 5% and banks were represented on the supervisory board. The big banks as a group were represented on the supervisory boards of 41 of these 51 AGs, holding a total of 76 seats. A regression of the number of big bank supervisory board seats on the proportion of votes controlled by the big banks due to their own shareholdings and proxy votes for these 51 AGs produced the following equation (t-ratios in brackets):

Big bank supervisory = 0.846 + 0.0332 Big bank + 0.016 Big bank
board seats   (3.53)   (4.44) own votes   (2.02) proxy votes

$R^2 = 0.301$ $\bar{R}^2 = 0.272$ No. of observations = 51

This regression equation shows evidence of a closer association between supervisory board representation and control of equity voting rights for the big banks than for all banks together. The estimated coefficient of the proxy vote variable in this equation is significantly different from zero at the 5% level, in contrast to the corresponding coefficient in the equation estimated for all banks. However, even for the big banks, the evidence suggests that there is a stronger relationship between supervisory board seats and votes due to own shareholdings than there is between supervisory board seats and proxy votes. The conclusion that the relationship

[3] This figure is the unweighted average of the big banks' combined vote as a proportion of the unweighted average of all banks' combined votes. The corresponding figures for own votes and proxy votes are 54.5% and 52.9% respectively.

between the big banks' supervisory board seats and their control of proxy votes is not particularly strong is reinforced when it is borne in mind that the big banks were represented on the supervisory boards of a further 15 AGs, in which the combined votes of all banks were less than 5%, in addition to those included in the above regression equation. The big banks held 26 seats on the supervisory boards of these 15 AGs, or 1.73 per AG on average, which is only a little smaller than the average of 1.85 seats per AG held by the big banks in the 41 AGs on which they were represented among the 51 for which data on their control of voting rights was available. It is likely that sample selection bias in the above regression is exaggerating the strength of the true relationship between big bank supervisory board representation and control of equity voting rights.

Tables 9.2 and 9.3 have shown the dominant position of Deutsche Bank in terms of bank representation on the supervisory boards of the largest 100 AGs in 1974. This dominance cannot, however, be explained in terms of Deutsche Bank's control of proxy votes, as the following regression equation shows (t-ratios in brackets).

Deutsche Bank = 0.614   + 0.0266 Deutsche Bank + 0.008 Deutsche Bank
board super-   (5.35)   (3.00)   own votes   (1.02) proxy votes
visory seats

$R^2 = 0.168$ $\bar{R}^2 = 0.133$ No. of observations = 51

This equation was estimated on data for the same 51 AGs as were used for the big bank regression equation. The estimated coefficient on Deutsche Bank's proxy votes is not significantly different from zero at conventional levels, suggesting that Deutsche Bank's dominant position in terms of bank supervisory board representation does not arise from its use of proxy votes to act as a delegated exerciser of equity control rights.

The evidence examined in this section concerning the relationship between bank control of equity voting rights and bank supervisory board representation gives little support to the view that banks use their proxy voting power to act as delegated exercisers of equity's control rights by placing bank representatives on the supervisory boards of AGs. The regression analysis of the relationship between bank supervisory board seats and control of equity voting rights for those AGs where data was available showed that there was a consistent relationship between bank supervisory board representation and banks' own holdings of shares, as would be expected. However evidence of a consistent and strong relationship between bank supervisory board seats and banks' proxy voting power, as is required by the view that banks act as delegated exercisers of equity's control rights, was not found. Only the regression equation for the big banks taken together yielded a statistically significant estimated coefficient for proxy votes. When account is taken of the likely sample selection bias resulting from the fact that AGs which had bank representatives on their supervisory boards despite the combined vote of all banks at their shareholder meeting being less than 5% could not be included in the regression analysis, the relationship between bank supervisory board representation and control of votes appears even weaker. It is, of course, possible to argue that banks use their proxy votes to elect to the supervisory boards of AGs non-bankers who still monitor and control management in the interests of banks (and ultimately the suppliers of equity finance), but this seems to involve carrying the delegation of equity's control rights to exaggerated lengths.

Bank representation on supervisory boards and corporate control

The supervisory board is the body which, because of its right to appoint and dismiss members of the management board, formally controls the managers of an AG. In this section we continue the analysis of the argument that German banks act as delegated exercisers of equity's control rights by examining the evidence on the numerical importance of bank representatives on supervisory boards, and on the extent to which managers are in practice controlled by supervisory boards.

The evidence discussed in the previous section showed that, on average, bank representatives accounted for 20% of the total supervisory board membership of the 75 AGs among the largest 100 on which banks had seats. Even if all bank representatives acted in concert, therefore, they were not sufficiently numerous to determine the decisions of the supervisory board on their own, although they were obviously in an influential position. Banks' role as delegated exercisers of equity's control rights is potentially most important for the small number of AGs with a widely-dispersed share ownership, but table 9.2 shows that, while the number of bank representatives on the supervisory boards of AEG, Siemens and Mannesmann was relatively large, Bayer had only two bank representatives, and BASF, Hoechst and Linde only one each. The chairman of the supervisory board is its most important member in terms of managerial control, as he is usually informed and consulted by the management at least once a month. Table 9.2 shows, however, that only one of the group of large, widely-held AGs (Mannesmann) had a bank representative as its supervisory board chairman.

The study of Gerum, Steinmann and Fees (1988) confirms that bank representation on supervisory boards is not great enough numerically to enable bank representatives to control decision-making, even if they all act together. This study analysed the composition of the supervisory

Table 9.4. *Shareholder representatives on supervisory boards of AGs with more than 2,000 employees, 1979*

Type of shareholder representative	% of total shareholder seats
Domestic non-banks	39.7
of which:	
a) holding more than 50% of equity	13.1
b) holding up to 50% of equity	8.1
c) holding no equity	18.5
Domestic banks	16.4
of which:	
a) holding more than 50% of equity	0.7
b) holding up to 50% of equity	4.4
c) holding no equity	11.3
Foreign firms	5.9
Government	13.2
of which:	
a) holding some equity	11.7
b) holding no equity	1.5
Private shareholders	5.7
Small shareholder associations	1.5
Former top executives	4.2
Consultants	13.5
Total	100.1

Source: Gerum, Steinmann and Fees (1988), Table D–3, p.48.

boards of all the 281 AGs which had more than 2,000 employees in 1979 (i.e. all AGs for which half the supervisory board members were employee representatives). Table 9.4 shows the importance of different types of shareholder representatives on these boards. Banks' representatives accounted for 16.4% of shareholder seats on average, or 8.2% of the total membership of these supervisory boards, bearing in mind that shareholder representatives comprised only half the supervisory board for these AGs. One point in particular worth noting from table 9.4 is that 18.5% of the shareholder seats were occupied by representatives of domestic non-banks with no equity holding in the AG, more than there were from all domestic banks (16.4%) and, *a fortiori*, from domestic banks holding no equity (11.3%). Again this emphasises that representation on supervisory boards cannot straightforwardly be explained by proxy voting power.

Table 9.5 shows the distribution of supervisory board chairmen by type

Table 9.5. *Type of shareholder representative acting as chairman of supervisory board of AGs with more than 2,000 employees, 1979*

Type of shareholder representative	% of total chairmen
Domestic non-banks	37.4
Domestic banks	19.2
Foreign firms	7.5
Government	9.7
Private shareholders	8.2
Former top executives	7.1
Consultants	11.0
Total	100.1

Source: Gerum, Steinmann and Fees (1988), p.54.

of shareholder representative for the 281 AGs in the sample. This is similar to the corresponding distribution of all shareholder representatives given in table 9.4, and shows that it cannot be argued that bank representation on supervisory boards is more important than it appears from their numerical strength because banks have a disproportionate number of supervisory board chairmen.

The number of bank representatives on the supervisory board is not a perfect indicator of banks' ability to determine supervisory board decisions. Can it be argued that bank influence is greater than might appear simply from the number of bank supervisory board representatives because banks supply loan finance which can be withdrawn if the AG takes actions that banks do not like? Although there is some evidence that this was a possibility in the pre-1914 period,[4] it is unlikely to have applied

---

[4] Barrett Whale (1930, p. 53) gives an example of a bank exerting pressure on the behaviour of a firm's management through the power to recall loans. As quoted by Jeidels (1905), Dresdner Bank wrote to the North West German Cement Syndicate in November 1900 as follows:

> According to the notice published by your Company in the *Reichsanzeiger* of the 18th, we have to reckon with the possibility that decisions will be taken at the General Meeting to be held on the 30th which are likely to introduce changes in the scope of your business of a kind not agreeable to us. On this ground we are regretfully obliged herewith to withdraw the credit granted to you; accordingly we ask you to make no further drafts on us and at the same time politely request that you will repay the balance due to us, at the latest by the end of the month. Should, however, no decisions of this kind be taken at the General Meeting in question and safeguards be offered us in this respect for the future, we declare ourselves very ready to enter negotiations with you with a view to the granting of a new credit.

in the more recent period. Chapter 6 showed that in recent times bank loans have been a relatively minor source of finance for AGs, and that there is strong competition between banks in the market for loans to AGs. German firms are well aware of the benefits of borrowing from many banks rather than being dependent on just one. The competition among banks in the market for loans to AGs is one reason why the supposition that all bank representatives on supervisory boards act together may be rather questionable.

Bank representation on supervisory boards thus gives the banks a significant, but not a dominant, influence on the actions of the supervisory board. In order to assess whether bank influence on the supervisory board enables them to monitor and control the managers of AGs, it is necessary to analyse the degree of control exerted on the management board by the supervisory board.

As chapter 6 showed, certain major decisions of the management board may have to be approved by the supervisory board, and this is one way in which the supervisory board can control the management board. Evidence discussed in chapter 6 from the study by Gerum, Steinmann and Fees indicated that, although supervisory boards can sometimes exert control by withholding approval of specific management board decisions, the overall degree of control that the supervisory board can exercise by vetoing particular management board decisions is not great.[5] The most important way in which the supervisory board can control the management board is by dismissing the latter if its performance is not satisfactory. Unfortunately, no empirical studies exist which enable the effectiveness of this means of control by the supervisory board to be assessed. If poor performance by the management board results in its dismissal, and good performance results in reappointment, the supervisory board will create very strong incentives for managers to run AGs efficiently. But no direct evidence bearing on this means of supervisory board control is available.

However, some indirect evidence is available, in the form of studies of the information available to the supervisory board with which to evaluate managerial performance. As chapter 6 showed, supervisory boards are typically not integrated into the strategic planning process of AGs, and in such a position of limited information it is difficult to assess whether the overall performance of the management board is good or bad. Gerum, Steinmann and Fees found that in 86% of the AGs they studied, the supervisory board met only twice a year – the legal minimum number of meetings. This observation suggests that the supervisory board may not

[5] See pp. 129–130.

have the detailed understanding of the AG's operations required for effective monitoring of managerial performance. Bleicher and Paul (1986) argued that the control of management in large companies was less strong in Germany than in the USA. They found that there were many more board meetings in the USA than in Germany – 10 to 12 meetings a year in the USA compared to 2 to 4 meetings of the supervisory board a year in Germany. They also found that non-executive directors in the USA had a greater input to managerial decision-making than did supervisory board members in Germany, due to the greater importance in the USA of subcommittees of the board of directors in general, and audit committees in particular.

In the absence of direct evidence on the effectiveness of supervisory board control of the management board via the former's ability to appoint and dismiss the latter, it is not possible to reach a definitive conclusion about how much control supervisory boards have over the managers of AGs. The indirect evidence relating to the closeness of the monitoring of management by the supervisory board does, however, cast some doubt on the effectiveness of supervisory board control. This, combined with the other evidence presented in this section, which shows that banks do not have a large enough number of representatives on supervisory boards to be able to determine supervisory board decisions on their own, raises further doubts about the view that German banks act as delegated exercisers of equity control rights.

However, the evidence presented in this section is not decisive. Supervisory boards may exert a high degree of managerial control by dismissing poorly-performing managers. As noted at the end of the previous section, even though bankers do not, on average, hold a majority of shareholders' seats on the supervisory boards, it might be argued that, because in many cases banks do control a majority of the votes at shareholders' meetings, the other shareholders' representatives must, in these cases, be acceptable to banks, which will in principle enable banks to determine supervisory board decisions. The following section, therefore, continues the analysis of banks' possible corporate control role by asking what incentives exist for banks to act as delegated exercisers of equity's control rights.

Do banks have incentives to act as delegated exercisers of equity's control rights?

The analysis by Diamond (1984), which was discussed in chapter 2, emphasised that a complete account of the reasons why delegating monitoring to financial intermediaries might be an efficient means of supplying external finance to firms had to include an explanation of what incentives are present for intermediaries to use their private information in savers' interests. An argument that German banks act as delegated exercisers of equity's control rights must, therefore, explain what incentives exist for banks to use their proxy voting power and supervisory board representation in shareholders' interests.

If banks typically had shareholdings of their own in the AGs for which they also controlled a significant number of proxy votes, then it would be clear that banks had a direct financial incentive to ensure that managements acted in the interests of shareholders. As table 9.2 shows, however, this is not the case for the three big banks, which accounted for over half the bank representatives on the supervisory boards of the largest 100 AGs in 1974. As a group, the big banks had shareholdings of their own in only 13 of the 56 AGs in which banks as a whole controlled more than 5% of the votes cast at shareholders' meetings. This means that in most cases the banks which are in a position to monitor and control managers, by virtue of their supervisory board representation, do not have any direct financial interest in ensuring that managers follow profit-maximising policies.

The question thus arises whether a bank with control of equity votes derived solely from proxy votes has any incentives to use this proxy voting power to ensure that the managers of an AG act in shareholders' interests. It is possible that the role of banks, especially the big banks, as underwriters of the new share issues by AGs may provide an incentive to use proxy votes in this way. An AG typically makes an issue of new shares by means of a syndicate of banks which act as underwriters of the issue. The syndicate's leader is usually the house bank of the AG. The details of the issue are arranged by the leader of the syndicate: the other banks in the syndicate simply take some proportion of the issue. The leader typically has a relatively large share of the total issue. The leader receives an additional fee on top of the fee received by all banks for the risk they bear in underwriting the issue.[6] As we saw in chapter 5, most leaders of the syndicates which handle new share issues for large listed AGs are one of the three big banks, in particular Deutsche Bank, and the composition of these syndicates, including the leader, has been very stable over time.

The usual method by which an issue of new shares is made by an AG is that the syndicate of banks first purchases the issue from the company, in the agreed proportions, at a fixed price below the current market price of shares, and then, at a second stage, sells the new shares at this fixed price to other shareholders. The existing shareholders in the AG will typically have a preferential right to buy the new shares from the syndicate. The risk of placing the new issue of shares in the market is borne entirely by

[6] See p. 119.

the syndicate. Since new share issues usually give existing shareholders rights to purchase the new shares, a bank which has a substantial proportion of an AG's existing shares deposited with it will be particularly well placed to take up a significant fraction of a new issue, as it will have a cost advantage in arranging the sale of the new shares to existing shareholders. More generally, it is argued that a bank which has a large number of individual shareholders depositing shares with it will have access to a ready market for the profitable sale of new issues. A substantial pool of individual shareholders depositing shares with a bank may therefore give the bank a competitive advantage in the underwriting of new share issues.[7]

The leader of the syndicate for a large AG is typically one of the big banks. The leader arranges the details of a new share issue with the company, and usually takes the largest proportion of the issue. Consequently the lead bank in the syndicate has strong incentives to monitor the AG's performance around the time of the issue, since it will be bearing a significant part of the risk of placing the issue as a result of having a large proportion of it. Furthermore, the bank's position of leader is likely to be adversely affected if something occurs soon after the syndicate purchases the issue which causes the market price to fall and leave the syndicate with a loss on the new issue they have bought. The big banks' dominance of leader positions in syndicates therefore provides a reason why they might use their proxy voting power and supervisory board representation to ensure that managers of an AG were running the company in shareholders' interests, at least around the time of a new issue.

It is not obvious, however, that this link between the big banks' control of proxy votes, their supervisory board representation, and their syndicate leadership provides these banks with an incentive for continuous monitoring of AGs' managements to ensure that they are acting in shareholders' interests. Any one AG does not make new share issues sufficiently frequently that monitoring around the time of the issue will be equivalent to continuous monitoring. But the monopoly rents which appear to be available in underwriting (as evidenced by the uncompetitive nature of such business documented in the Gessler Commission report[8]) may provide an alternative explanation for why banks with proxy voting power may use it in shareholders' interests. In order to attract a large number of individual shareholders to deposit their shares with a bank,

---

[7] The Gessler Commission report gives, in paragraph 473, the size of a bank's clientele of individuals depositing shares as one of the factors influencing its ability to participate in underwriting syndicates.

[8] See pp. 118–119.

and so enable it to maintain its strong position in a highly profitable activity, it may be in a bank's interest to ensure that an individual shareholder who deposits shares with it receives a good return on the shares. Hence the bank may have incentives to use the proxy voting power that deposited shares give it to ensure profit-maximising behaviour by the AGs in question, in order to maintain its ability to earn monopoly rents in underwriting. There are, however, some problems with this argument. First, it is not obvious that individual shareholders will be able to judge whether the return on their shares is higher as a result of depositing shares with one bank rather than another unless these individual shareholders engage in costly monitoring of the performance of AGs and banks, which is precisely what the delegation of voting rights to banks is supposed to avoid. The strength of the incentives created for a bank to use proxy votes to ensure profit-maximisation as a means of attracting deposited shares is therefore questionable. Second, although the big banks are dominant as leaders of issuing syndicates, a number of other banks are also members of these syndicates. The fact that these other banks underwrite non-trivial proportions of an issue, but have relatively smaller fractions of the total number of shares deposited with banks, raises some doubts about the importance of having a large pool of individuals depositing shares with a bank for its ability to participate in underwriting business.

This discussion of the role of banks, particularly the big banks, in underwriting new share issues by AGs shows that there may be some incentive for banks which only have proxy voting power in an AG nevertheless to use it in the interests of the shareholders who have deposited shares with them, although the argument is not wholly convincing. There is, however, a more fundamental question relating to banks' incentives to act as delegated controllers of equity voting rights which must be considered. The three big banks are all large AGs with widely-dispersed share ownership. If agency problems give scope for the managements of large, widely-held AGs to pursue their own interests at the expense of shareholders, then it cannot be automatically assumed that the managements of Deutsche Bank, Dresdner Bank and Commerzbank will use their control of equity voting rights and supervisory board representation to impose profit-maximising discipline on the managements of other large AGs, even if it could be shown that so doing would increase the profits of the big banks. It certainly cannot be argued that the managements of the big banks are subject to any shareholder control at their own shareholder meetings, because the proxy vote system gives them effective control of themselves. Gottschalk (1988) found that the big banks between them controlled 60.4% of the votes cast at the shareholders' meeting of Deutsche Bank in 1986 (Deutsche Bank controlled

47.2%, Dresdner Bank 9.2% and Commerzbank 4.0%). The corresponding figures for Dresdner Bank were 64.0% (Deutsche Bank 13.4%, Dresdner Bank 47.1%, and Commerzbank 3.5%), and for Commerzbank 60.8% (Deutsche Bank 16.3%, Dresdner Bank 9.9% and Commerzbank 34.6%).

The extensive control that the three big banks have over the votes cast at their own shareholders' meetings illustrates a general weakness of the argument that German banks act as delegated exercisers of equity's control rights. The banks which are supposed to play this role are themselves large, widely-held AGs, and no explanation is given as to why the managements of these banks should wish to ensure that the managements of the relatively small number of other AGs which have a widely-dispersed share ownership should act in shareholders' interests. The study of ownership and control in large German firms by Schreyögg and Steinmann (1981), which was discussed in chapter 8, makes this point very clear. In addition to the 300 largest industrial enterprises, Schreyögg and Steinmann investigated the ownership and control of the largest 25 German banks (in terms of balance sheet assets) in 1972. The ultimate ownership pattern of these 25 banks was such that *all* of them were classified as manager-controlled.[9] In Schreyögg and Steinmann's study, banking was the only sector in which all firms were classified as manager-controlled. It is, therefore, not just the three big banks which are manager-controlled, and hence lack any clear incentives to act as discipliners of the managements of other large AGs: this is the case for all the largest German banks.

Supervisory board representation and long-term trading relationships

The evidence presented so far in this chapter casts considerable doubt on the view that German banks act as delegated exercisers of equity's control rights. The relationship between bank supervisory board representation and bank proxy voting power is weak; bank representatives on supervisory boards cannot determine supervisory board decisions by weight of numbers; and there are no obvious incentives for banks to act as delegated exercisers of equity's control rights. This suggests that bank representation on the supervisory boards of AGs may not reflect bank performance of a corporate governance function, minimising the agency costs of the separation of ownership from control in large corporations by disciplining management. An alternative hypothesis is to see bank representation on supervisory boards in terms of the general advantages resulting from links

---

[9] See pp. 188–189 for definitions of ultimate ownership and manager control.

between enterprises, both banks and non-banks, created by representation on each other's supervisory boards. According to Kester (1992, p. 25), such links between enterprises facilitate

> the building and maintenance of stable, long-term trading relationships ... [which], in turn, foster investment in efficient, relationship-specific assets, and enable companies operating within an industrial group to exploit numerous operating and transactional efficiencies not generally available to independent companies transacting on a short-term, arm's length basis

It has to be admitted that Kester advances his general argument primarily on the basis of Japanese data, and the evidence he adduces for the application of his argument to the relationships among firms in Germany that result from supervisory board links is sketchy. Nevertheless this view of supervisory board relationships between firms does appear able to explain some of the observations which create difficulties for the view that bank representation on supervisory boards is a reflection of their control of equity voting rights, particularly via proxy votes. As we saw on pp. 198–210, banks were represented on some supervisory boards among the largest 100 AGs in 1974 despite having no control of equity voting rights. Furthermore, there was only limited evidence of a relationship between bank proxy voting and bank supervisory board representation.[10] The discussion in the third section above noted that the supervisory boards of the 281 AGs in 1979 with over 2,000 employees had more representatives from domestic non-banks with no equity holding than from domestic banks. The representation of both banks and non-banks on the supervisory boards of AGs in which they have no control of the equity voting rights may reflect the existence of long-term trading relationships which need to be sustained by such representation.

In the case of non-banks, supervisory board representation may result from vertical commercial relationships between such firms, with major suppliers and customers sitting on each other's supervisory boards to ensure that important decisions are effectively coordinated and opportunistic behaviour does not restrict the benefits of long-term implicit contracting. In the case of banks, representation on supervisory boards in the

---

[10] The Gessler Commission (1979) also provides evidence consistent with these observations. A survey of 336 banks found that in 1974 these banks had been respresented on the supervisory boards of 665 AGs. A substantial proportion of bank supervisory board representatives, especially in the smaller AGs, was not associated with bank voting power. 69% of the AGs with bank representatives on the supervisory board were ones in which banks either had no shareholdings of their own, or had shareholdings of less than 10% of the total equity. More than half of the bank supervisory board representatives were in AGs in which banks either had no proxy vote rights or had proxy voting rights of less than 10% of the equity.

absence of any equity voting power may be the result of a long-term financial relationship between the bank and the firm, although in view of the evidence of highly competitive behaviour in the market for bank loans to large companies presented in earlier chapters care needs to be exercised when making this argument. Given the lack of competition in underwriting business, and the dominance of such business by the three big banks, a possible basis for supervisory board representation which reflects a long-term commercial relationship is the underwriting of new security issues by AGs. An alternative possibility would be to see banks as playing a general coordination role, concerned with economy-wide implications of a particular AG's decisions, which was complementary to the specific coordination undertaken by representatives of major customers and suppliers. This general coordination can be interpreted as the 'consultancy' function that the banks describe themselves as playing on supervisory boards. There are obvious reasons why such general coordination might best be performed by a relatively small number of banks that had extensive supervisory board representation among AGs. This would help explain the dominant position of the big banks in terms of bank supervisory board representatives.

It is, of course, perfectly possible that bank representation on the supervisory boards of German firms is due both to delegated exercise of equity control rights and to the desire to maintain efficient long-term trading relationships. Indeed, it is possible that bank supervisory board representation does not have any beneficial effects at all, whether via corporate control or via long-term trading relationships. Representation of firms on each other's supervisory boards, and in particular the extensive networks among firms which are created by common bank supervisory board representation, may allow cartel arrangements to be made, so that profitability increases for reasons unrelated to efficiency improvements. Ultimately, the questions of how to interpret bank supervisory board representation, and whether banks use their control of equity voting rights to ensure that the managers of AGs run these firms efficiently, are ones which can only be settled by empirical evidence. Unfortunately, there is hardly any such evidence available, largely because of the difficulty of finding data which would enable the various hypotheses to be tested. The only empirical study which does attempt to distinguish these various hypotheses is that by Cable (1985). As we saw in chapter 1, Cable's study is very influential, and seems to provide evidence in support of the view that German banks do play an important corporate control function. The following section discusses Cable's study in detail, and argues that it does not provide any strong evidence in favour of the hypothesis that German banks act as delegated exercisers of equity's control rights.

Cable's (1985) study of the effects of banks on the profitability of AGs

The sample of firms in Cable's study comprised 48 AGs drawn from the largest 100 AGs in 1970. The most general model estimated was:

$$Y_i = \sum_{j=1}^{18} a_j X_{ji} + \sum_{m=1}^{4} \beta_m V_{mi}^2 + \sum_{p=1}^{4} \gamma_{pi} R_{pi} + \delta\left(\frac{BL}{DT}\right)_i + u_i \qquad (1)$$

The variables in equation (1) were defined as follows. Y_i is the ratio of after-tax profits to total capital assets for firm i, averaged over the period 1968–1972. The X_j consist of various firm- and industry-specific variables such as firm size, growth rate, internal organisation, degree of public ownership, and industry dummies. These variables were intended to capture various influences on firm profitability which might otherwise bias estimates of the effects of banks. The only one of these which Cable regarded as requiring explicit attention in his study was X_{13}, a Herfindahl index of the dispersion of the largest 20 non-bank shareholdings in each firm. The four V_m variables are the proportions of equity voting rights controlled respectively by each of the three big banks, and by all other financial institutions as a group. The four R_p variables are binary variables, equal to unity if Deutsche Bank, Dresdner Bank, Commerzbank and all other financial institutions respectively were represented on the firm's supervisory board, and otherwise equal to 0. BL/DT is the ratio of bank borrowing to total debt in the firm's liabilities, and u is an error term.

Cable considered three main hypotheses linking bank involvement to firms' profitability. The internal capital markets (ICM) hypothesis sees bank supervisory board representation and control of voting rights as imposing profit-maximising discipline on managers. Bank supervisory board representation is also seen as removing informational asymmetries so that bank loans can be provided on more favourable terms. Bank involvement can increase firm profitability for either or both of these reasons under the ICM hypothesis. A second hypothesis is that bank representation on supervisory boards raises profitability because it enables banks to supply financial expertise (FE) in a way which cannot simply be purchased. This hypothesis can perhaps be thought of as reflecting the potential benefits of long-term trading relationships as suggested in the previous section. The third hypothesis is that bank representation on supervisory boards raises profitability as a result of enhanced market power (MP) due to the greater opportunities for arranging cartels provided by intercompany links through common banks. Table 9.6 shows the sign expectations for the banking variables under

Table 9.6. *Sign expectations for banking variables under Cable's alternative hypotheses*

Hypotheses	Bank voting rights	Bank supervisory board representation	Debt composition
ICM	≥ 0	≥ 0	≥ 0
FE	0	≥ 0	≥ 0
MP	0	> 0	0

Source: Cable (1985), Table 1, p. 123.

each of these three hypotheses. A positive coefficient on the bank supervisory board representation variable is consistent with all three hypotheses. A positive coefficient on the debt composition variable is seen as being consistent with either the ICM hypothesis (close bank involvement increases access to bank loans) or the FE hypothesis (lending negotiations being seen as occasions for banks to provide financial expertise), but not with the MP hypothesis. A positive coefficient on the bank voting rights variable is seen as consistent only with the ICM hypothesis.

One problem in interpreting the estimated coefficients of the BL/DT variables as tests of the three hypotheses is the possible existence of simultaneity bias. If banks are better able to screen good risks than other lenders, a positive estimated coefficient for BL/DT may reflect the greater ability of banks than other suppliers of debt finance to identify firms with greater creditworthiness and a larger volume of profitable investment projects. Cable notes the possibility of such simultaneity bias, but the results reported do not take it into account.

Unrestricted estimation of equation (1) resulted in statistically insignificant coefficients for different banks' voting rights and supervisory board representation. The models that Cable focused on embodied various restrictions on the β_m and γ_p coefficients in equation (1). Cable's model selection tests did not yield a single 'best' model: instead, three models were arrived at, and it was not possible to discriminate between them on the basis of standard model selection procedures. The estimated coefficients of these three models are shown in table 9.7. Equation (2) (in table 9.7) requires that the three big banks are alike in their effects on firm profitability while the other banks differ. Thus HB_3 is the Herfindahl index of the control of equity voting rights by the three big banks:

$$HB_3 = \sum_{i=1}^{3} V_i^2$$

and BALL is a binary variable equal to unity if any one of the three big

Table 9.7. *Estimated coefficients of key variables, selected equations*[a]

Variable	Equation number		
	(2)	(3)	(4)
X_{13}	0.375**[b]	0.0182**	0.0334**
	(3.150)	(2.071)	(2.774)
HB_3	0.0976	0.0571	–
	(1.371)	(0.822)	
HB_4	–	–	0.0952**
			(2.395)
$(V_4)^2$	0.0638	–	–
	(1.527)		
R_4	0.0142*	–	–
	(1.844)		
KALL	–	–	0.0156*
			(1.961)
BALL	0.0271**	0.0160*	–
	(2.471)	(1.863)	
BL/DT	0.0508**	0.0420**	0.0486**
	(2.841)	(2.294)	(2.760)

Notes: [a] Figures in parentheses are t-statistics.
[b] ** indicates that an estimated coefficient is significantly different from zero at the 5% level; * indicates that an estimated coefficient is significantly different from zero at the 10% level.
[c] All estimates were obtained using weighted least squares to correct for heteroscedasticity in OLS estimates.
Source: Cable (1985), Table 3, p. 124.

banks is represented on a firm's supervisory board, and zero otherwise. Equation (3) (in table 9.7) tests whether other banks apart from the big banks have any effect, by restricting the coefficients of V_4^2 (the (squared) control of equity voting rights of all other banks) and R_4 (a binary variable equal to unity if any bank other than the big banks is represented on the supervisory board, and zero otherwise) to be zero. Equation (4) (in table 9.7) requires that all banks are alike in their effects on firm profitability. Thus

$$HB_4 = \sum_{i=1}^{4} V_i^2$$

is the Herfindahl index of the control of equity voting rights by all banks, and KALL is a binary variable equal to unity if any bank is represented on the supervisory board, and zero otherwise.

The results of the model selection procedures were as follows. Equations

(2) and (4) were both preferred to equation (1) on the basis of a non-nested J-test. Equation (2) was preferred to equation (4) at the 5% level on the basis of a non-nested J-test. Equation (3) was then shown to be an acceptable restriction of (2) on the basis of a nested F-test. However, non-nested tests of (3) and (4) yielded inconclusive results: each model added something to the overall explanation which the other lacked.

Cable (p. 129) drew the following conclusions about the ICM, FE, and MP hypotheses from these estimated equations:

> The significant, overall impact of banks on profitability could not be due solely to increased product-market power, in view of the significant coefficients attracted by the voting variables and BL/DT, as well as by bank representation ... Similarly, the overall bank impact could be ascribed to inputs of financial expertise only by disregarding the significant bank voting-rights coefficient in equation (4) ... for which there is no statistical justification ... The results are wholly consistent with the internal capital markets hypothesis, which emphasises informational factors. However, the partial impact caught by the BL/DT coefficients could be a mixture of ICM and FE effects, while that caught by the representation variables could include MP effects as well, and there is no way of separating out the relative magnitudes of these influences.

Although Cable did not claim that the results support the ICM hypothesis to the exclusion of the FE or MP hypotheses, in our view these results provide less support for the ICM hypothesis than Cable claimed was the case.

As table 9.6 shows, the crucial result which is necessary to distinguish the ICM hypothesis from the other two is the existence of a positive estimated coefficient on the bank voting rights variable. But only equation (4) in table 9.7 has an estimated coefficient on a bank voting rights variable which is significantly different from zero. In both equations (2) and (3), the estimated coefficients on the bank voting rights variables are not significantly different from zero. Cable argued that there is no statistical justification for disregarding the significant bank voting rights coefficient in equation (4), but he also noted (p. 129) that 'there are some prior uncertainties surrounding model selection amongst equations (4), (2), and (3)'. As we have seen, equation (2), in which the estimated coefficients on the bank voting rights variables are not significant, is preferred by a non-nested test to equation (4), in which the estimated coefficient on the bank voting rights variable is significant. It is true that non-nested tests between equation (3), a restricted version of equation (2) in which the bank voting rights coefficient is insignificant, and equation (4) are inconclusive. This does not, however, justify Cable's interpretation of these results as providing no reason to doubt that there is a significant effect of the degree of concentration of bank control of equity voting rights on firm profitability. In our view the appropriate conclusion is that there is some weak evidence from these results in support of the hypothesis that bank control of equity voting rights affects firm profitability, but it is very limited.

The results of estimating equations (2), (3) and (4) also provide only limited support for the view that bank representation on supervisory boards increases firm profitability, whether this is due to ICM, FE or MP effects. Equation (2) contains two bank representation variables: that for representation of the three big banks is significantly different from zero at the 5% level, while that for representation of all other banks is significantly different from zero only at the 10% level. Equations (3) and (4) each contain one bank representation variable, and in both cases the estimated coefficient is significantly different from zero only at the 10% level. These results provide somewhat more support for an effect of bank supervisory board representation on firm profitability than they provide for an effect of bank control of voting rights, but it cannot be claimed that the existence of a positive impact of the former has definitely been established.

The results in table 9.7 do permit two conclusions to be drawn. One is that a greater concentration of non-bank shareholdings is associated with higher profitability. The estimated size of this effect, however, differs substantially between equation (2) and equations (3) and (4). But although the magnitude of the effect is not clear, there is unambiguous evidence that the more concentrated are non-bank shareholdings, the higher is profitability. This finding can be interpreted in terms of more concentrated non-bank shareholdings providing greater incentives for shareholders to monitor management closely and so leading to greater profitability. The other conclusion is that a higher fraction of bank borrowing in a firm's total debt is associated with higher profitability. Unfortunately, as has been noted, the precise interpretation of this association is not clear, since a positive coefficient estimate may reflect either ICM or FE effects, or be the result of simultaneity bias because more profitable firms are able to borrow more from banks.

Cable's empirical study is the only one of which we are aware that provides evidence enabling the effects of German banks on firm performance to be assessed. It shows very clearly the difficulty of distinguishing between different hypotheses, or providing strong support for any of them, on the basis of the available data. As we have seen, even if we ignore the question of whether there is significant evidence of a positive effect of bank supervisory board representation on firm profitability, the problem remains that a significant positive effect would be consistent with each of the three hypotheses Cable advances about the possible role of German banks. Our interpretation of Cable's results differs from his. In particular we regard the evidence provided by his study in support of a positive effect of bank control of equity voting rights on firm profitability as being weak. We consequently conclude that Cable's study provides only very limited support in favour of the view that banks use their control of equity voting rights to perform a corporate control function and to raise profitability by limiting management's ability to pursue objectives which are not in shareholders' interests. In our view Cable's study provides considerably more support for the view that what is distinctive about German AGs is their typically concentrated share ownership, which means that there are incentives for large shareholders to monitor managements carefully, and so improve profitability.

Conclusion

This chapter has shown that there are a number of serious problems with the view that German banks act as delegated exercisers of equity's control rights. It is certainly true that German banks, and particularly the big three banks, have a substantial degree of control of equity voting rights in AGs, and that this control is mainly due to proxy votes. But there is only weak evidence of any association between the number of bank representatives on the supervisory board and the degree of bank proxy voting power. In particular, there is no systematic tendency for the number of bank supervisory board representatives to be greater in the large widely-held AGs for which the argument that banks are delegated exercisers of equity's control rights seems most appropriate. Bank supervisory board representatives are not sufficiently numerous to be able to determine supervisory board decisions, even if all banks act in concert. The incentives for the managements of the banks which have proxy voting power to use this power to ensure that the managements of AGs act in the interests of the suppliers of equity finance are not clear. The argument that banks impose discipline on the managers of large corporations who would otherwise pursue objectives that were not in shareholders' interests is subject to a serious logical inconsistency in the absence of an explanation of why the managers of large German banks should find it in their interests to act as delegated exercisers of the control rights of the suppliers of equity finance.

These problems with the argument that German banks play a corporate control role are not sufficient on their own to result in its rejection. It is possible that the absence of a strong association between the degree of banks' proxy voting power and bank supervisory board representation is because banks use their control of equity voting rights to elect shareholder representatives to the supervisory board who are not bankers but still act in banks' interests. The same argument would be able to explain why supervisory boards acted in banks' interests despite the fact that bank representatives were not numerically dominant on them. There is, admittedly, still no obvious explanation of why the managers of large banks should use their proxy voting power in shareholders' interests, but that problem might perhaps be ignored if there was convincing evidence that banks played a corporate control role. The empirical study by Cable is widely regarded as having provided evidence that German banks do improve the performance of AGs via their control of voting rights and representation on supervisory boards. However, in our view, the results of Cable's study provide no more than weak support for the view that German banks play an important corporate control role. We interpret the results of Cable's study as providing much more support for the view that the widespread existence of large shareholders in German AGs, holding substantial fractions of the equity and hence having incentives to monitor managements, means that there is little scope for corporate control problems to arise. On this interpretation, Cable's study suggests that, if it is true that large German companies are better managed than their UK counterparts, the reason may be the greater degree of concentration of shareholdings in German corporations than in UK ones, rather than the superiority of the delegated exercise of equity's control rights by banks to the hostile takeover mechanism.

10 Conclusion

The view that German system of finance for investment has made an important contribution to German economic success is widespread, as was documented in chapter 1. Conventional wisdom emphasises the importance of a number of characteristic institutional features of the bank-based system of investment finance in Germany, which are seen as leading to greater availability of external finance at a lower cost than in the UK system. These institutional features are: the universal nature of most German banks; the house bank relationship between particular firms and particular banks; bank representation on the supervisory boards of companies; and the ability of banks to exercise proxy votes at meetings of shareholders in companies on behalf of shareholders who have deposited their shares with the banks for safekeeping. It is widely argued that the German system of finance for investment is unambiguously superior to that of the UK, and that UK investment and growth performance would improve if the UK adopted a system of investment finance more like the German one.

Although this view is widespread, it is based on very limited evidence, as chapter 1 points out. Much of this evidence takes the form of simple correlations, involving the observation that Germany's investment and growth record has been better than the UK's, and that the German system of investment finance is different from the UK system. This ignores the fact that there are many other differences between Germany and the UK which might influence economic performance. To name just two examples, Germany has a different system of education and training and, at least in the post 1948-period, a different, and more stable, macroeconomic policy. No conclusions about the contribution of the German financial system to Germany's superior investment and growth performance can be drawn on the basis of simple correlations which ignore other possible influences. To assess the contribution of the German system of investment finance to German economic growth, we would really require an empirical model of economic growth which identifies and quantifies all possible influences on growth performance. Unfortunately, such a model does not exist. In its absence, it is not possible to assess how much of the difference between German and UK economic growth performance is due to differences in the two countries' systems of finance for investment. This book, therefore, has a more modest aim: to assess whether the various components of the commonly-held view of the merits of the German system of investment finance are supported by empirical evidence from the post-war period up to 1989. The advantage of addressing this more modest question is that it is possible to answer it.

The first step in assessing the claim that the distinctive institutional features of the German system of finance for investment make it more efficient is to provide a solid analytical foundation for this claim in terms of economic theories of business finance and financial intermediation, and this is carried out in chapter 2. Economies of scale in information collection mean that external finance can be provided to firms more efficiently through financial intermediaries, which act on behalf of savers, provided that intermediaries have incentives to act in savers' interests. German banks' proxy voting rights enable them to act as delegated exercisers of the control rights of the suppliers of equity finance as well as delegated monitors of firm performance. The universal nature of German banks, and their representation on company supervisory boards, enables them to exploit not only economies of scale in information-gathering on behalf of savers, but also economies of scope between various forms of information collection and the exercise of the control rights attached to debt and equity finance.

In theory, therefore, it can be argued that the German system of finance for investment might have the following advantages. The existence of economies of scale and scope means that external finance for investment is most efficiently provided by a relatively small number of banks. These few banks can ensure that finance is provided at low cost, and that the returns on the investment for which it is provided are not dissipated by inefficient management. The banks supply loan finance at low cost for two reasons: their representation on supervisory boards gives them access to confidential information which reduces information asymmetries between borrowers and lenders; and supervisory board representation enables banks to reduce the costs of financial distress by preventing managers of near-bankrupt firms from taking actions which harm the suppliers of debt finance. Economies of scale and scope in the provision of finance may mean that house bank relationships, in which a particular firm receives all its external finance from a single bank, are efficient. It is argued that the restriction of competition implied by such exclusive relationships between particular firms and banks enables house banks to commit themselves to particular firms and provide long-term loans which would not be provided in the absence of such restrictions of competition. Banks' proxy voting power and supervisory board representation may also enable them to monitor managerial performance in companies with a widely-dispersed share ownership and replace inefficient managements. This overcomes the free-rider problems which prevent shareholders from monitoring managers directly, and avoids the need to use the imperfect hostile takeover mechanism as a managerial disciplining device. Universal banks also act as underwriters for new equity issues. The close involvement of such universal banks with firms as lenders, and their supervisory board representation, enables them to screen new equity issues on behalf of shareholders. This, it is argued, ensures that only high-quality firms approach the stock market for equity finance, and hence that shareholders are more willing to take up new issues which have been so screened by the banks. Such screening is thought to be particularly important for initial public offerings by previously unlisted companies, but it is also regarded as applying to new equity issues by already-listed companies, where banks' supervisory board representation enables them to assess how well the management will use the proceeds of a new issue.

In theory, therefore, there are a number of different mechanisms by which the distinctive institutional features of the German system of investment finance might lead to a more efficient allocation of funds for investment. But do these mechanisms operate in reality?

First, is the German banking system indeed distinguished by the restrictions on competition assumed above? The evidence in chapter 5 suggests that it is not. The market for bank loans to all firms in Germany is not dominated by a relatively small number of banks. Moreover, the majority of German banks do not have representation on firms' supervisory boards, control proxy votes, or underwrite new equity issues: these functions are exercised chiefly by the big three banks, and to a lesser extent by banks from the commercial bank sector in general. A very large part of total German bank lending to firms, therefore, is undertaken by banks which are not in a position to influence corporate governance within firms through supervisory board representation or control of proxy votes. This casts considerable doubt on the claim that significant economies of scope exist between German banks' corporate governance role and their supply of external finance in the form of loans. If such economies of scope exist anywhere, they should exist in Germany, where they would be favoured by banks' supervisory board representation; the fact that they do not seem to be important in Germany suggests that they are not important in any economy.

The supply of external finance by German banks was analysed in detail in several chapters. Finance can be provided in the form of either debt or equity. According to the theory of financial contracts, it is efficient to supply external finance entirely in the form of debt only if the supplier has no information about the returns on the investment. Thus, if German banks are better-informed about the firms to which they supply finance than UK banks, a larger proportion of bank-supplied external finance in Germany should take the form of equity. The evidence discussed in chapter 3, however, suggests that the vast majority of the finance supplied by German banks takes the form of debt. The value of the equity supplied by German banks to domestic non-banks is only about 3% of the value of bank loans made to these firms. Moreover, no evidence supports the view that German banks are sufficiently well-informed about firms in their role as underwriters of new share issues to be able to ensure an active market for such issues, and hence a significant flow of investment finance to German firms in the form of new equity. Chapter 5 shows that, until the early 1980s, German companies made very few initial public offerings of shares: this method of raising finance was completely insignificant in the German financial system. Nor was it important for already-listed AGs (public limited companies): new equity was a smaller proportion of the finance of investment by AGs than it was for GmbHs (private limited companies), and large listed German AGs financed a smaller proportion of their investment by new share issues than did comparable UK companies. Both of these observations are inconsistent with the view that German banks are better able to screen new share issues by already-listed firms, and thus enable a greater volume of new equity finance to be raised.

Does German banks' representation on the supervisory boards of firms result in the provision of a greater volume of bank loan finance? Chapter 6 suggests that empirical evidence does not support this claim about the merits of the German system. There is no evidence that bank representation on supervisory boards provides German banks with information which is used to make loan decisions. Banks with little or no supervisory board representation account for a large proportion of total bank lending to all firms. One reason for this is that most German firms do not possess supervisory boards: only AGs and large GmbHs are legally required to have them. Indeed, part of the explanation for the small number of AGs in Germany is the reluctance of German firms to adopt the legal form which requires them to have a supervisory board. This suggests that any benefits firms may derive from having greater access to external finance as a result of bank representation on their supervisory boards are not large enough to offset the costs of being required to have a supervisory board. Further doubt is cast on the theoretical benefits of bank representation on supervisory boards for firms' access to loans by the fact that AGs, the only legal form of enterprise which has to have a supervisory board, financed a smaller proportion of their investment by bank loans than did other types of firm. Furthermore, German AGs financed a smaller proportion of their investment by bank borrowing than did comparable public limited companies in the UK. In sum, bank representation on company supervisory boards is not associated with greater use of bank loans by the companies concerned. The argument that bank representation on supervisory boards increases access to bank loan finance because it enables information asymmetries to be overcome receives no support from the evidence.

The evidence reported in chapter 6 provided no empirical support for theoretical claims concerning the benefits of restricted competition among banks to supply investment finance to firms. Detailed analysis of the market for bank loans to firms in Germany confirms the impression gained in chapter 5 that it is a competitive market, especially for loans to large firms. No evidence supports the view that the house bank relationship in Germany is typically one in which a single bank provides a firm with all its loan finance, thereby (through restricting competition) promoting commitment between a bank and a firm, so that more long-term loan finance is provided. Differences between Germany and the UK in the classification of the maturity of bank lending make it impossible to say on the basis of available evidence whether more long-term bank lending takes place in Germany. Moreover, there is no clear theoretical basis for believing that it is more efficient for investment to be financed with long-term rather than short-term loans.

Nor are the procedures followed by German banks in making lending decisions discernibly different from those elsewhere, as is shown in chapter 6. There is no evidence that German banks possess special technical expertise which might enable them to make a particularly well-informed judgement of the prospects of investments, while there is evidence that collateral requirements are extensively used by banks as a condition for making loans.

German banks' special role in responding to financial distress on the part of firms receives little more support from the evidence, as is shown in chapter 7. The evidence available on German bank behaviour when firms are in financial distress is limited, so that the conclusions drawn from it must be tentative. Subject to this qualification, however, the evidence does not give much support to the theoretical arguments which suggest that the costs of financial distress are lower in Germany.

One theoretical argument is that German banks have incentives to make efficient decisions about the reorganisation or liquidation of a financially-distressed firm because they can take an equity stake in such firms as well as supplying loan finance. However, as we have seen, equity finance is a very small proportion of the loan finance supplied by banks. In most cases of financial distress, therefore, banks will only be providing loan finance, which means that, unless some loan finance is transformed into equity, they have no interest in the upside returns that would accrue to a successful reorganisation. But there are substantial costs involved in German banks' transforming loans to financially-troubled firms into equity, although this does sometimes happen.

Another theoretical argument is that German banks, by virtue of their positions on supervisory boards, are able to limit the costs of financial distress which occur as a result of managers taking inefficient decisions in an attempt to avoid bankruptcy. Furthermore, when a reorganisation of a financially-troubled firm takes place, the position of banks on supervisory boards is seen as enabling them to ensure that the reorganisation is appropriately managed. However, the evidence suggests that because German banks' loans to firms are typically secured by collateral, the losses banks suffer from a firm going bankrupt are quite small on average, and hence their incentives to reorganise rather than liquidate are limited. The evidence also shows a tremendous variation among German banks in their ability to detect problem loans at an early stage, and to reorganise firms in financial distress. Even if bank representation on supervisory boards does provide banks with advance warning of problems, and enables them to monitor and control managerial behaviour in situations of financial distress, this variation among banks is what would be expected given the large number of German banks which make loans to firms without having any supervisory board representation, and the large number of German firms which do not have supervisory boards. In this context, it is significant that AGs, all of which have supervisory boards, finance a smaller proportion of their investment with loans than do other types of firm in Germany, most of which do not have supervisory boards. Since the probability of financial distress is greater, other things equal, the higher the proportion of a firm's investment that is debt-financed, it follows that those German firms which are most likely to suffer financial distress are the ones for which bank supervisory board representation is simply not possible.

Unfortunately, available evidence does not enable any direct test of the effect of bank supervisory board representation on the likelihood that a financially-distressed firm in Germany will be reorganised rather than liquidated. However, indirect evidence reported in chapter 9 casts some doubt on the claim that supervisory board representation does increase the chance of reorganisation. Supervisory boards typically meet only twice a year, and receive relatively little detailed information about the firm's operations. Supervisory boards are not responsible for the management of the firm. If a firm has not actually defaulted on a loan then, even if a bank is represented on the firm's supervisory board, it can only influence management decisions if it carries the other supervisory board members with it. Once a firm has gone bankrupt, then lenders do have the ability to control managerial decisions, but this is independent of their representation on supervisory boards. Chapter 7 showed that German banks do not become actively involved in the management of a firm which is being reorganised: their role is limited to dealing with the financial aspects of the reorganisation, and locating a suitable new management team on the basis of their general experience and contacts. This behaviour by German banks is no different from that of UK banks. Finally, the evidence in chapter 7 suggested that it would be difficult to identify the precise relationship between bank supervisory board representation and the likelihood of reorganisation. A positive association between the two might be the result of supervisory board representation giving banks information and managerial control which permits successful reorganisation. However, an alternative explanation would be that bank supervisory board representation occurs particularly for large firms, since the firms which have supervisory boards are mostly large. For several reasons, reorganisation is more likely for large than for small firms – the effect on a bank's public image of being involved in a reorganisation is more significant if the firm is large, it may be easier to find a replacement set of managers, and the banks' loans may be less well collateralised. Even if we did find an association between bank supervisory board representation and the likelihood of reorganisation, it might simply reflect the fact that both are correlated with the size of firms.

This detailed analysis of the evidence provides no support for the claim that institutional features of the German system of finance for investment allow firms greater access to external finance at lower cost than in the UK. This conclusion is consistent with the aggregate evidence on the finance of investment by non-financial enterprises in Germany reported in chapter 3. The proportion of gross capital formation by German non-financial enterprises financed by bank loans over the period 1950–1989 was 11.7%, and varied little over the period. Every effort was made in chapter 3 to make a meaningful comparison between the finance of non-financial enterprise investment in Germany and the UK. The conclusion reached was that, over the period 1970–1989, UK non-financial enterprises had financed a higher proportion of their gross capital formation by loans from financial institutions than had German non-financial enterprises. This aggregate evidence, taken together with the evidence on individual features of bank lending in Germany, shows that it is wrong to regard German firms as depending more than UK firms on bank loans to finance investment.

The evidence analysed in this book refutes the view that the German system of finance for investment gives German firms greater access to external finance via the banking system than is the case in the UK. However, it is also argued that German banks perform another beneficial function: namely that they provide a more effective mechanism for monitoring and controlling the managements of large companies than do alternatives, in particular the hostile takeover mechanism which operates in the UK and the USA. What conclusion does our analysis yield concerning this feature of the German system of investment finance?

Evidence on the significance of different legal forms of enterprise within the German economy presented in chapter 4 already casts some doubt on this claim. The problem of dispersed share ownership leading to an absence of incentives for shareholders to monitor management is only likely to arise for listed companies. Listed AGs in Germany are, however, a much less significant form of enterprise than listed public companies in the UK. The problem of inadequately-monitored management is, therefore, likely to be less serious in Germany than in the UK. This suggestion is reinforced by the evidence in chapter 8 that only very few large listed AGs in Germany lacked a shareholder with a large enough holding both to create incentives for monitoring of management, and to give this shareholder the ability to exercise a substantial degree of control over votes at shareholders' meetings. By contrast, large listed companies in the UK do not typically have a shareholder with a comparably large holding of the equity capital. The very small number of German companies which have a widely-dispersed share ownership suggests that the failure of shareholders to monitor management is much less common in Germany than in the UK. This means that there is much less need in Germany for mechanisms to correct managerial failure, whether hostile takeover or bank control of proxy votes and supervisory board representation. However, the extensive ownership of large shareholdings in German companies by other German companies means that this suggestion cannot be accepted without qualification. As chapter 8 shows, once account is taken of the shareholdings of firms in other firms, the lack of a need for a mechanism to correct managerial failure in Germany is not so obvious. The small number of German AGs with dispersed share ownership have very substantial holdings of shares in other German companies, so that the large shareholder in a German firm is often an AG whose management is not subject to any monitoring by shareholders. German banks might then play an important corporate control role, either because the managements of AGs might fail to use their holdings of shares in other firms to ensure cost-minimisation by the managers of these other firms or, even if they do, because the managers of the AGs with dispersed share ownership might dissipate the profits from these holdings in the absence of monitoring by banks.

Chapter 9 therefore examined the available evidence on German banks' corporate control function. The argument that German banks act as delegated exercisers of equity's control rights claims that banks use their control of proxy voting rights at the general meeting of shareholders in an AG to put bank representatives on the supervisory board, the body which appoints, dismisses and monitors the management of an AG. However, the evidence for Germany shows only a weak relationship between bank proxy voting power and supervisory board representation. This casts doubt on the view that proxy votes enable banks to act as delegated exercisers of equity's control rights. The evidence on supervisory board composition shows that, even if all bank representatives acted together, they would not be able to determine supervisory board decisions on their own (although it could be argued that bank control of equity voting rights is strong enough that those shareholder representatives on supervisory boards who are not bankers must nevertheless be acceptable to banks). In any case, there are several reasons to doubt the extent of control exerted by supervisory boards over the managers of AGs. Unfortunately, no evidence is available about the influence of the threat of dismissal by the supervisory board on managerial behaviour. However, the available indirect evidence which relates to the extent of the information available to the supervisory board and the range of managerial decisions that require supervisory board approval, does not suggest that the supervisory board is in a position to subject German managers to a high degree of monitoring and control.

There are a number of problems, therefore, with the various links in the chain of argument which sees banks acting as delegated exercisers of equity's control rights by using proxy votes to put bank representatives on the supervisory boards of AGs who then monitor and control the managers of these firms. In addition to these problems, there is a further difficulty: the incentives for banks to act as delegated exercisers of equity's control rights are not clear. Typically, the three big German banks together exercise the largest proxy voting power in German AGs. However, in most cases where these banks controlled a significant propor-tion of the equity voting rights in an AG, they had no shareholding of their own in the AG, and hence no direct financial incentive to use their proxy votes in the interests of shareholders. The big banks' important position in underwriting syndicates has been proposed as a possible link between the possession of proxy voting power and financial incentives to use proxy votes in shareholders' interests, but there are reasons to doubt the existence of such a link. An even more fundamental stumbling-block is the fact that the three big banks are all AGs with a widely-dispersed share ownership. It is not clear why the managers of these banks should act to ensure that managers of other German AGs with widely-dispersed share ownership pursue the interests of shareholders. If dispersed share ownership leads to a lack of monitoring of managers by shareholders and hence the pursuit of managers' interests at shareholders' expense, this problem applies equally to the managers of the three big banks. The question of 'who monitors the monitors?' is one for which the hypothesis that German banks are delegated exercisers of equity's control rights has no answer.

Whether German banks perform a corporate control function is ultimately an empirical question, and there is only one study, that by Cable (1985), which attempts to test this view using data on individual AGs. Cable's study is often claimed to provide support for the view that banks act as delegated exercisers of equity's control rights. However, the analysis of Cable's results carried out in chapter 9 shows that they provide only very limited evidence for the view that bank control of equity voting rights has a positive effect on the profitability of AGs, since in most of the estimated equations reported by Cable the effect of bank control of voting rights on profitability was not statistically significant. The one unambiguous conclusion to be drawn from Cable's study is that the profitability of AGs is positively related to the concentration of non-bank shareholdings in them. This conclusion is consistent with our view that the scope for managers to pursue their own objectives at the expense of shareholders is very limited in Germany, because most AGs have a large shareholder with strong incentives to monitor the management. This would suggest that if it is true that large German firms suffer less from managerial failure than do large UK firms, the reason is not that banks monitor and control managers, but that the structure of share ownership in Germany means that the managers of most large companies are subject to monitoring by shareholders.

The argument that German banks perform a corporate control function is, therefore, one which lacks both a solid theoretical foundation and convincing empirical support. It is true that the quality of available evidence on this second major claim about the merits of the German system of investment finance is less good than on the first, concerning the supply of external finance via the banking system. In particular, it would be very useful to have more evidence along the lines of Cable's study, in which the relationship between the performance of German firms and the nature and extent of bank involvement with them was analysed. Unfortunately, the limited availability of data on the performance of individual firms in Germany (as noted in chapter 4) makes it very difficult to conduct such studies. The conclusions to be drawn from the analysis of the evidence on German banks' corporate control function must, therefore, be somewhat less definite than those concerning German banks' role as suppliers of external finance. Despite this qualification, the weight of the available evidence points clearly towards rejection of the claim that banks use their proxy voting power and supervisory board representation to act as delegated exercisers of equity's control rights, ensuring good performance by the managers of AGs with dispersed share ownership.

Does this mean that bank representation on the supervisory boards of German AGs is of no consequence for the performance of the German economy? The answer to this question is no, because it is possible that bank representation on supervisory boards performs a wholly different function from that of corporate control, as the fifth section of chapter 9 suggests. The argument here is that the extensive representation of the three big banks on the supervisory boards of large firms is simply the most pronounced aspect of a different German institutional feature, whereby large firms are represented on each other's supervisory boards.[1] In general, such representation might have advantages of the form suggested by transaction cost economics. Examples of these advantages include the fostering of investment in assets which are specific to a particular relationship; ensuring that opportunistic behaviour does not restrict the benefits of long-term trading relationships which are not formalised in a contract; and the coordination of major decisions between firms. Broadly speaking, the argument is that representation of independent large firms on each other's supervisory boards provides some of the benefits of hierarchical organisation of economic transactions without losing the benefits of high-powered market incentives. It therefore suggests the following reasons why the three big banks are the large firms most extensively represented on the supervisory boards of other large firms. The supply of financial services is an input required by all firms, and supervisory board representation by the banks supplying these services might be required to sustain efficient long-term trading relationships between suppliers of financial services and their customers. Furthermore, a relatively small number of banks which have extensive supervisory board representation among large firms for the reasons just mentioned might also be able to perform a function of general coordination, ensur-

[1] See Monopolkommission (1990), Table 33, for evidence on the extent of representation of the largest 100 German firms on the supervisory boards of other firms among the largest 100.

ing, say, that the implications of a particular large firm's investment decision are consistent with those of other large firms.

This claim about the benefits the German economy receives from bank supervisory board representation is different from the claims which comprise the commonly-held view of the merits of the German system of finance of investment. It focuses neither on the supply of external finance nor on corporate control. Instead it sees the system in which large firms generally have representation on the supervisory boards of other large firms as being one which has advantages in terms of efficient organisation of economic transactions. According to this claim, the extensive supervisory board representation of the big banks means that they play an especially important role, but the function performed by bank representation on the supervisory boards of large firms is not qualitatively different from the supervisory board representation of other large firms. Although the theoretical basis for this claim is relatively recent, deriving from the approach of transaction cost economics (Williamson, 1975), the argument that the benefits conferred on the German economy by bank supervisory board representation result from these considerations rather than the supply of finance or corporate control has been made before. Shonfield (1965, p.261) argues that

> The big banks have always seen it as their business to take an overall view of the long-term trend in any industry in which they were concerned and then to press individual firms to conform to certain broad lines of development. They saw themselves essentially as the grand strategists of the nation's industry.

An essential component of this system of coordination, according to Shonfield (p. 254), is bank representation on supervisory boards:

> one of the purposes served by plural membership of the [supervisory boards] of various companies is to provide a channel for the diffusion of advanced business practice. The bank's representative ... will regard it as part of his duty to bring to the attention of the management new ideas and techniques which have been developed by other companies in which he is concerned ... the banker on the [supervisory board] will also make it his business to inform himself about what is happening to other firms competing in the industry with which he is concerned.

Though he is careful not to suggest that bank representatives on supervisory boards plan the entire long-term futures of various German industries, Shonfield regards this system of 'coordination by banker' as providing a degree of planning of investment and rationalisation of production which assists the German economy to adjust efficiently to changing conditions.

Clearly, before this claim can be accepted, it must be subjected to careful analysis. Evidence is required on whether the representation of large firms on the supervisory boards of other large firms does sustain efficient long-term trading relationships. In the case of the big banks, it is necessary to establish that they have incentives to use their extensive supervisory board representation for the economy's benefit, by coordinating economic decisions, rather than for its harm, by creating cartels and monopolistic inefficiencies. An analysis of this claim would require another book, and hence will not be embarked upon here.

Although we have suggested a possible way in which bank supervisory board representation may benefit the German economy, this should not be seen as qualifying the conclusion of the book. The commonly-held view of the merits of the German system of finance for investment, in terms of the supply of external finance to firms and corporate control, receives no support from the analysis of available evidence.

Bibliography

Aghion, P. and P. Bolton (1992) 'An Incomplete Contracts Approach to Financial Contracting', *Review of Economic Studies*, **59**, 473–494.

Bank of England (1983) 'A Note on Real Short-term Interest Rates', *Bank of England Quarterly Bulletin*, **23**, 471–476.

—— (1984) 'Business Finance in the United Kingdom and Germany', *Bank of England Quarterly Bulletin*, **24**, 368–375.

—— (1986) 'New Issue Costs and Methods in the UK Equity Market', *Bank of England Quarterly Bulletin*, **26**, 532–542.

—— (1988) 'Trends in Real Interest Rates', *Bank of England Quarterly Bulletin*, **28**, 225–231.

Barrett Whale, P. (1930) *Joint Stock Banking in Germany*, London: Macmillan.

Baums, T. (1990) 'Höchststimmrechte', *Die Aktiengesellschaft*, June, 221–242.

Bayliss, B. T. and A. A. S. Butt Philip (1980) *Capital Markets and Industrial Investment in Germany and France*, Farnborough: Saxon House.

Bester, H. and M. Hellwig (1987) 'Moral Hazard and Equilibrium Credit Rationing: An Overview of the Issues', in G. Bamberg and K. Spremann (eds.), *Agency Theory, Information, and Incentives*, Berlin: Springer Verlag.

Binks, M., C. Ennew and G. Reed (1988) 'Small Businesses and Banks: An International Study', Forum of Private Business, unpublished paper.

—— (1990) 'Small Businesses and their Banks', Forum of Private Business, unpublished paper.

Bleicher, K. and H. Paul (1986) 'Das amerikanische Board-Modell im Vergleich zur deutschen Vorstands/Aufsichtsratsverfassung', *Die Betriebswirtschaft*, **1986(3)**, 263–288.

Braun, P. A. (1981) 'Das Firmenkundengeschäft der Banken im Wandel', University of Augsburg, unpublished Ph.D. thesis.

Broecker, T. (1990) 'Credit-worthiness Tests and Interbank Competition', *Econometrica*, **58**, 429–452.

Bundesministerium der Justiz (1988) 'Gesetz zur Reform des Insolvenzrechts: Diskussionsentwurf', Köln: Bundesanzeiger.

Bundesverband deutscher Banken (1989) 'Zur Diskussion um die "Macht der Banken"', unpublished paper, Köln.

Cable, J. R. (1985) 'Capital Market Information and Industrial Performance: the Role of West German Banks', *Economic Journal*, **95**, 118–132.

Cable, J. R. and P. Turner (1983) 'Asymmetric Information and Credit Rationing: Another View of Industrial Bank Lending and Britain's Economic Problem', Warwick Economic Research Paper, no. **228**.

Carrington, J. C. and G. T. Edwards (1979) *Financing Industrial Investment*, London: Macmillan.

Charkham, J. (1989) 'Corporate Governance and the Market for Control of Companies', *Bank of England Panel Paper, no. 25.*

Coase, R. H. (1937) 'The Nature of the Firm', *Economica*, 4, 386–405.

Committee on Finance and Industry (1931) *Final Report*, Cmd. 3897, London: HMSO.

Corbett, J. (1987) 'International Perspectives on Financing: Evidence from Japan', *Oxford Review of Economic Policy*, **3(4)**, 30–55.

(1993) 'An Overview of the Japanese Financial System', in N. H. Dimsdale and M. Prevezer (eds.), *Capital Markets and Corporate Governance*, Oxford: Clarendon Press.

Cosh, A. D., A. Hughes and A. Singh (1990) 'Analytical and Policy Issues in the UK Economy', in A. D. Cosh, A. Hughes, A. Singh, J. Carty and J. Plender, *Takeovers and Short-termism in the UK*, London: Institute for Public Policy Research.

Cowling, K. *et al.* (1980) *Mergers and Economic Performance*, Cambridge: Cambridge University Press.

Crafts, N. F. R. (1992) 'Productivity Growth Reconsidered', *Economic Policy*, **15**, 387–414.

Cubbin, J. and D. Leech (1983) 'The Effect of Shareholding Dispersion on the Degree of Control in British Companies: Theory and Measurement', *Economic Journal*, **93**, 351–369.

Cuny, R. H. and D. Haberstroh (1983) 'Gesetzgeberische Ursachen steigender Insolvenzzahlen', *Die Betriebsberater* **1983(1)**, 717–721.

Deutsche Bundesbank (1965) 'The Results of the Investigation into Security Deposits for the End of 1964', *Monthly Report of the Deutsche Bundesbank*, **17** (July), 3–13.

(1971) 'Trends in the Business of the Banking Groups 1960 to 1970', *Monthly Report of the Deutsche Bundesbank*, **23** (April), 29–53.

(1977) 'The Annual Accounts of Partnerships and Sole Proprietorships for 1974', *Monthly Report of the Deutsche Bundesbank*, **29** (January), 23–37.

(1984a) 'The Share Market in the Federal Republic of Germany and its Development Potential', *Monthly Report of the Deutsche Bundesbank*, **36** (April), 11–19.

(1984b) 'Company Pension Schemes in the Federal Republic of Germany', *Monthly Report of the Deutsche Bundesbank*, **36** (August), 30–37.

(1987) 'Longer-term Trends in the Banks' Investments in Securities', *Monthly Report of the Deutsche Bundesbank*, **39** (May), 24–33.

(1988) *Methodological Notes on the Capital Finance Account of the Deutsche Bundesbank 1960 to 1987: Translation*, Special Series, no. 4 (5th edn).

(1989) 'Longer-term trends in the Banking Sector and Market Position of the Individual Categories of Banks', *Monthly Report of the Deutsche Bundesbank*, **41** (April), 13–22, 52–71.

(1990) *Zahlenübersichten und methodische Erläuterungen zur gesamtwirtschaftlichen Finanzierungsrechnung der Deutschen Bundesbank 1960 bis 1989*, Special Series, no. 4 (6th ed).

Diamond, D. W. (1984) 'Financial Intermediation and Delegated Monitoring', *Review of Economic Studies*, **51**, 393–414.

Dicks, M. J. (1989) 'A Cross-Country Comparison of the Links between the Financial System and Industry', Bank of England, unpublished paper.

Dowd, K. (1992) 'Optimal Financial Contracts', *Oxford Economic Papers*, **44**, 672–693.

Drukarcyk, J. *et al.* (1985) *Mobiliarsicherheiten, Arten, Verbreitung, Wirksamkeit*, Köln: Bundesanzeiger.

Dyson, K. (1986) 'The State, Banks and Industry: The West German Case', in A. Cox (ed.), *State, Finance and Industry: A Comparative Analysis of Post-War Trends in Six Advanced Industrial Economies*, Brighton: Wheatsheaf.

Eatwell, J. L. (1982) *Whatever Happened to Britain?*, London: BBC and Duckworth.

The Economist (1990) 'Punters or Proprietors?: A Survey of Capitalism', (5–11 May), 24 pp.

(1992) 'Bankruptcy' (1–7 August), 69–71.

Edwards, J. S. S. (1987) 'Recent Developments in the Theory of Corporate Finance', *Oxford Review of Economic Policy*, **3(4)**, 1–12.

Farrar, J. H., N. E. Furey and B. M. Hannigan (1991) *Farrar's Company Law* (3rd edn), London: Butterworths.

Fischer, K. (1990) 'Hausbankbeziehungen als Instrument der Bindung zwischen Banken und Unternehmen', University of Bonn, unpublished Ph.D. thesis.

Franks, J. R. and C. P. Mayer (1990) 'Capital Markets and Corporate Control: A Study of France, Germany and the UK', *Economic Policy*, **11**, 191–231.

(1992) 'Corporate Control: A Synthesis of the International Evidence', London Business School, unpublished paper.

Fritsch, U. (1978) *Mehr Unternehmen an die Börse*, Köln: Schmidt Verlag.

Gale, D. and M. Hellwig (1985) 'Incentive-Compatible Debt Contracts: the One-period Problem', *Review of Economic Studies*, **52**, 647–663.

Geisen, B. (1979) 'Das Finanzierungsverhalten deutscher Aktiengesellschaften', Bonner Betriebswirtschaftliche Schriften, University of Bonn.

Gerschenkron, A. (1968) 'The Modernization of Entrepreneurship', in A. Gerschenkron, *Continuity in History and Other Essays*, Cambridge, MA: Harvard University Press.

Gerum, E., H. Steinmann and W. Fees (1988) *Der mitbestimmte Aufsichtsrat–eine empirische Untersuchung*, Stuttgart: Poeschel Verlag.

Gesamtverband der Versicherungswirtschaft (1988) *Zahlenspiegel der Versicherungswirtschaft 1988*, Köln: Gesamtverband der Deuschen Versicherungswirtschaft e.V.

Gessler Commission (1979) *Grundsatzfragen der Kreditwirtschaft*, Schriftenreihe des Bundesministeriums der Finanzen, **28**, Frankfurt am Main: Knapp Verlag.

Gessner, V. *et al.* (1978) *Die Praxis der Konkursabwicklung in der Bundesrepublik Deutschland*, Köln: Bundesanzeigerverlag.

Gottschalk, A. (1988) 'Der Stimmrechtseinfluss der Banken in den Aktionärsversammlungen von Grossunternehmen', *WSI Mitteilungen*, **1988(5)**, 294–304.

Gross, P. J. (1982) *Sanierung durch Fortführungsgesellschaften*, Köln: Otto Schmidt Verlag.

Grossman, S. J. and O. D. Hart (1980) 'Takeover Bids, the Free-Rider Problem, and the Theory of the Corporation', *Bell Journal of Economics*, **11**, 42–64.

(1982) 'Corporate Financial Structure and Management Incentives', in J. J. McCall (ed.), *Economics of Information and Uncertainty*, Chicago: University of Chicago Press.

Hallett, G. (1990) 'West Germany', in A. Graham with A. Seldon (eds.), *Government and Economies in the Post-War World*, London: Routledge.

Hart, O. D. and J. H. Moore (1989) 'Default and Renegotiation: A Dynamic Model of Debt', London School of Economics, STICERD Discussion Paper, no. **192**.

Hay, D. A. and D. J. Morris (1984) *Unquoted Companies*, London: Macmillan.

Hellwig, M. F. (1981) 'Bankruptcy, Limited Liability, and the Modigliani–Miller Theorem', *American Economic Review*, **71**, 155–170.

—— (1989) 'Asymmetric Information, Financial Markets, and Financial Institutions', *European Economic Review*, **33**, 277–285.

Hesselmann, S. and U. Stefan (1990) *Zerschlagung oder Sanierung von Unternehmen bei Insolvenz*, Stuttgart: Institut für Mittelstandsforschung Bonn.

Holmstrom, B. R. and J. Tirole (1989) 'The Theory of the Firm', in R. Schmalensee and R.D. Willig (eds.), *Handbook of Industrial Organisation*, Amsterdam: North-Holland.

Hughes, A. (1991) 'Mergers and Economic Performance in the UK: a Survey of the Empirical Evidence 1950–1990', in J. A. Fairburn and J. A. Kay (eds.), *Mergers and Merger Policies* (2nd edn), Oxford: Clarendon Press.

Iber, B. (1985) 'Zur Entwicklung der Aktionärsstruktur in der Bundesrepublik Deutschland 1963–1983', *Zeitschrift für Betriebswirtschaft*, **55**, 1101–1119.

Immenga, U. (1978) *Beteiligungen von Banken in anderen Wirtschaftszweigen*, Baden-Baden: Nomos Verlag.

Jeidels, O. (1905) *Das Verhältnis der deutschen Grossbanken zur Industrie mit besonderer Berücksichtigung der Eisenindustrie*, Leipzig: Duncker-Humblot.

Jensen, M. C. (1986) 'Agency Costs of Free Cash Flow, Corporate Finance and Takeovers', *American Economic Review, Papers and Proceedings*, **76**, 323–329.

Jensen, M. C. and W. H. Meckling (1976) 'Theory of the Firm: Managerial Behaviour, Agency Costs, and Ownership Structure', *Journal of Financial Economics*, **3**, 305–360.

Journal of Economic Perspectives (1988) 'Symposium on Takeovers', **2**, 3–82.

Keller-Stoltenhoff, E. (1986) 'Die rechtstatsächlichen Auswirkungen des §613a im Konkurs', *Beiträge zum Insolvenzrecht*, Köln: Kommunikationsforum.

Kennedy, W. P. (1987) *Industrial Structure, Capital Markets, and the Origin of British Economic Decline*, Cambridge: Cambridge University Press.

Kester, W. C. (1992) 'Industrial Groups as Systems of Contractual Governance', *Oxford Review of Economic Policy*, **8**(3), 24–44.

King, M. A. (1977) *Public Policy and the Corporation*, London: Chapman & Hall.

Kocka, J. (1980) 'The Rise of the Modern Industrial Enterprise in Germany', in A. D. Chandler, Jr., and H. Daems (eds.), *Managerial Hierarchies*, Cambridge, MA: Harvard University Press.

Kreps, D. M. (1990) *A Course in Microeconomic Theory*, New York: Harvester Wheatsheaf.

Krummel, H. J. (1980) 'German Universal Banking Scrutinized', *Journal of Banking and Finance*, **4**, 33–55.

Kurth, T. (1987) 'Aktionärsschutz und öffentliche Kaufangebote – Neuere Entwicklingen im Recht der USA', University of Köln, unpublished Ph.D. thesis.

Lavington, F. (1921) *The English Capital Market*, London: Methuen.

Lee, W. R. (1991) 'The Paradigm of German Industrialisation: Some Recent

Issues and Debates in the Modern Historiography of German Industrial Development', in W. R. Lee (ed.), *German Industry and German Industrialisation*, London: Routledge.

Leech, D. and J. Leahy (1991) 'Ownership Structure, Control Type Classifications and the Performance of Large British Companies', *Economic Journal*, **101**, 1418–1437.

LeRoy, S. F. (1989) 'Efficient Capital Markets and Martingales', *Journal of Economic Literature*, **27**, 1583–1621.

Macrae, N. (1966) 'The German Lesson', *The Economist*, (15 October), 17 pp.

Marsh, P. (1990) *Short-termism On Trial*, London: Institutional Fund Managers Association.

Marshall, A. (1919) *Industry and Trade*, London: Macmillan.

Mayer, C. P. (1988) 'New Issues in Corporate Finance', *European Economic Review*, **32**, 1167–1183.

(1990) 'Financial Systems, Corporate Finance, and Economic Development', in R. G. Hubbard (ed.), *Asymmetric Information, Corporate Finance, and Investment*, Chicago: University of Chicago Press.

Mayer, C. P. and I. Alexander (1990) 'Banks and Securities Markets: Corporate Financing in Germany and the United Kingdom', *Journal of the Japanese and International Economies*, **4**, 450–475.

Meeks, G. (1977) *Disappointing Marriage: A Study of the Gains from Merger*, Cambridge: Cambridge University Press.

Modigliani, F. and M. H. Miller (1958) 'The Cost of Capital, Corporation Finance and the Theory of Investment', *American Economic Review*, **48**, 261–297.

Monopolkommission (1976) *Hauptgutachten I: Mehr Wettbewerb ist möglich*, Baden-Baden: Nomos Verlag.

(1978) *Hauptgutachten II: Fortschreitende Konzentration bei Grossunternehmen*, Baden-Baden: Nomos Verlag.

(1980) *Hauptgutachten III: Fusionskontrolle bleibt vorrangig*, Baden-Baden: Nomos Verlag.

(1990) *Hauptgutachten IV: Wettbewerbspolitik vor neuen Herausforderungen*, Baden-Baden: Nomos Verlag.

Mørck, R., A. Shleifer and R. W. Vishny (1988) 'Characteristics of Targets of Hostile and Friendly Takeovers', in A. J. Auerbach (ed.), *Corporate Takeovers: Causes and Consequences*, Chicago: University of Chicago Press.

Myers, S. C. (1977) 'Determinants of Corporate Borrowing', *Journal of Financial Economics*, **5**, 147–176.

Myers, S. C. and N. S. Majluf (1984) 'Corporate Financing and Investment Decisions when Firms Have Information that Investors Do Not Have', *Journal of Financial Economics*, **13**, 187–222.

Otto, H.-J. (1991) 'Obstacles to Foreigners are Nothing but a Myth', *Financial Times* (20 February), 19.

Paish, F. W. and R. J. Briston (1982) *Business Finance* (6th edn), London: Pitman.

Perlitz, M. *et al.* (1985) 'Vergleich der Eigenkapitalausstattung deutscher, amerikanischer und britischer Unternehmen', *Zeitschrift für Unternehmens- und Gesellschaftsrecht*, **1985(1)**, 17–49.

Prais, S. J. (1981) *Productivity and Industrial Structure*, Cambridge: Cambridge University Press.

Ravenscraft, D. J. and F. M. Scherer (1987) *Mergers, Sell-offs, and Economic Efficiency*, Washington DC: Brookings Institution.

Romer, P. (1986) 'Increasing Returns and Long-run Economic Growth', *Journal of Political Economy*, **94**, 1002–1037.

Sah, R. K. and J. E. Stiglitz (1986) 'The Architecture of Economic Systems', *American Economic Review*, **76**, 716–727.

Sappington. D. E. M. (1991) 'Incentives in Principal–Agent Relationships', *Journal of Economic Perspectives*, **5**, 45–66.

Scherer, F. M. and D. Ross (1990) *Industrial Market Structure and Economic Performance* (3rd edn), Boston: Houghton Mifflin.

Schneider, H., H.-J. Hellwig and D. J. Kingsman (1978) *The German Banking System*, Frankfurt am Main: Knapp Verlag.

Schneider-Lenné, E. R. (1992) 'Corporate Control in Germany', *Oxford Review of Economic Policy*, **8(3)**, 11–23.

Schreyögg, G. and H. Steinmann (1981) 'Zur Trennung von Eigentum und Verfügungsgewalt – Eine empirische Analyse der Beteiligungsverhältnisse in deutschen Grossunternehmen', *Zeitschrift für Betriebswirtschaft*, **51**, 533–556.

Schürmann, W. (1980) *Familienunternehmen und Börse*, Wiesbaden: Gabler.

Scott, M. FG. (1989) *A New View of Economic Growth*, Oxford: Clarendon Press.

Shonfield, A. (1965) *Modern Capitalism*, Oxford: Oxford University Press.

Singh, A. (1975) 'Takeovers, Economic Natural Selection and the Theory of the Firm', *Economic Journal*, **85**, 497–515.

Smith, E. O. (1983) *The West German Economy*, London: Croom Helm.

Stiglitz, J. E. (1974) 'On the Irrelevance of Corporate Financial Policy', *American Economic Review*, **64**, 851–866.

Stiglitz, J. E. and A. Weiss (1981) 'Credit Rationing in Markets with Imperfect Information', *American Economic Review*, **71**, 393–410.

Summers, R. and A. Heston (1984) 'Improved International Comparisons of Real Product and its Composition, 1950–1980', *Review of Income and Wealth*, **30**, 207–262.

    (1988) 'A New Set of International Comparisons of Real Product and Price Levels: Estimates for 130 Countries, 1950–1985', *Review of Income and Wealth*, **34**, 1–26.

Tirole, J. (1988) *The Theory of Industrial Organisation*, Cambridge, MA: MIT Press.

Townsend, R. M. (1979) 'Optimal Contracts and Competitive Markets with Costly State Verification', *Journal of Economic Theory*, **21**, 265–293.

Vittas, D. and R. Brown (1982) 'Bank Lending and Industrial Investment: A Response to Recent Criticisms', Banking Information Service, unpublished paper.

Wiegers, A. (1987) *Kapitalmarktpolitik und Unternehmungsfinanzierung in der Bundesrepublik Deutschland*, Frankfurt am Main: Lang Verlag.

Williamson, O. E. (1975) *Markets and Hierarchies*, New York: The Free Press.

World Bank (1989) *World Development Report 1989*, New York: Oxford University Press.

Yanelle, M.-O. (1989) 'The Strategic Analysis of Intermediation', *European Economic Review*, **33**, 294–301.

Zeitschrift für Wirtschaftsrecht und Insolvenzpraxis (1985) 'BGB §§826, 830, 613a – Haftung eines Bankenpools für Lohnansprüche der Arbeitnehmer des Kreditnehmers wegen sittenwidriger Nachsicherung', **1985(1)**, 1048–1053.

Index